HAPPY
THE NEW SEXY

To Tom & Judy
To your health!

Tammi

HAPPY
THE NEW SEXY

YOU CAN UNLEASH YOUR HAPPY HORMONES AND
BE BIO-CHEMICALLY BALANCED EVERY DAY.

CAMMI BALLECK PH.D.

TATE PUBLISHING
AND ENTERPRISES, LLC

Published by Tate Publishing & Enterprises, LLC
127 E. Trade Center Terrace | Mustang, Oklahoma 73064 USA
1.888.361.9473 | www.tatepublishing.com

Tate Publishing is committed to excellence in the publishing industry. The company reflects the philosophy established by the founders, based on Psalm 68:11,
"The Lord gave the word and great was the company of those who published it."

Book design copyright © 2013 by Tate Publishing, LLC. All rights reserved.
Cover design by Allen Jomoc
Interior design by Mary Jean Archival

Published in the United States of America

ISBN: 978-1-62746-250-1
1. Self-Help / Personal Growth / Happiness
2. Health & Fitness / General
13.07.15

DEDICATION

This book is dedicated to the best groom a girl could be blessed with.

And to YOU, may you learn the truth, learn to keep educating yourself, learn to unleash your happy hormones, and may you enjoy every day.

FOREWORD

"Today, more than 95% of all chronic disease is caused by food choice, toxic food ingredients, nutritional deficiencies, and lack of physical exercise."

Mike Adams

So I've edited both editions of this book, read all the testimonials, heard friends and family tell me how Dr. Cammi fixed them, and on occasion, had complete strangers, to me, proceed to also tell me how they have been helped with their lives. As if that was not enough, I also have several things in my life drastically changed for the better since I started dating my wonderful Dr. Cammi. So in case you are wondering, my name is Kyle and I am the groom/guide/husband/partner, and whatever other term is used for me in this book, of Dr. Cammi.

When I first met Cammi I didn't have any real "health problems," in the sense of the term. "Just because you're not sick doesn't mean you're healthy," was a good way to explain my life. I was a typical late 20's male in a small Colorado town, ten feet tall and bulletproof, a hunter, fisher, hiker, off-roader, mechanic, coal miner, construction worker, farmer, rancher, truck driver, and any other job that is done outside, I've probably done it (several had graveyard or swing shift, more about that shortly). I wasn't against Western Medicine; I just didn't go to the doctor unless something was physically broken. I ate and drank whatever I wanted, including way too much processed drive-thru food and dessert, and on occasion, too much beer. So essentially the only thing keeping me from being overweight was good metabolism and lots of exercise, otherwise I would probably weigh 250 pounds.

The first thing Cammi noticed was that I didn't fall asleep until usually way past midnight, even when I woke up at 6 a.m., so I woke up for work every morning dead tired, she also noticed that I spit up lots of phlegm every morning and all through the day. Now I've had hay fever allergies my whole life so I got "used to" a plugged or runny nose and waking up with chapped lips because my nose was plugged and I breathed out of my mouth all night.

Enter stage one of Kyle getting a health lesson and partially fixed; only partially, not all the way, due to me not changing my diet correctly, whoops! I won't get into details since you will read all about it later in the book, BUT; my entire system was so messed up from shift work, the heavy metals my system had absorbed throughout the years of all my different jobs (very bad for you), and also from drinking too much beer (full of yeast), which I then fed with sugar and dairy (way too much dessert and lots of cheesy fried foods), which combined to cause the phlegm problem, which also caused the plugged nose, which caused bad sleeping due to plugged nose and breathing out my mouth, which then enhanced the sleeping problems from my nervous system being messed up from too much late night and early morning shift work and metal toxins. In about three days with Cammi's help detoxing, cutting out yeast, sugar, and dairy, and fixing my nervous system, I was falling asleep before midnight, and barely spitting any phlegm, which I had been doing for the last 15 years!

Fast forward a few years, I fall back into the old routine of too many desserts and beers, though I'm still sleeping well. Watch out, those old habits will get you right back to where you started, as I'm sure many of you know. Enter stage two of really fixing my health and lifestyle to its full potential. The first thing Cammi did was a food allergy/intolerance test, which came back showing dairy, gluten, and casein. Now we already live pretty healthy but we still needed to change my diet, I cut out all dairy, all wheat products, processed food, most sugars, and even eggs for a month. Now for those of you who think that is extreme, so did I! This change happened in early January after the holidays full of over-eating and lots of dessert, and while meals before the change were healthy I was in a bad habit of eating 2-3 servings of dessert 4-6 nights a week (well on my way to type 2 adult diabetes, which is always self-inflicted through diet and lifestyle by the way), so needless to say the first two weeks were a bit shaky, but not nearly as hard as I thought. The other piece of this puzzle was a full detox with natural supplements that would clear the inflammation caused by my food intolerances.

The results? In the first several days I almost completely quit spitting phlegm. After two weeks I noticed I hadn't had heartburn at all, which happened more nights than not; the occasional dark circles under my eyes were never there, my dessert cravings completely disappeared, the real (not processed) food we were cooking tasted better than ever, and I lost 15 pounds with very little exercise. After a month I was down 20 pounds, had more energy than I've had in the last 10 years, especially on longer hikes, and I realized that nothing stressed or bothered me, I was balanced!

Along with Cammi's help this whole process made me care a lot more about taking care of my health, especially through diet. Several things included trying to exercise a little more regularly, not just weekend warrior stuff, I now enjoy cooking and eating real food a lot more, and if you're reading this book, you might as well take the next step like I did, and read up and educate yourself on whatever is ailing you. With my test results being what they were, along with help from Cammi, I read 'The Paleo Solution' by Robb Wolf, and 'Wheat Belly' by William Davis M.D. After learning what the sugar, dairy, and wheat were doing to my body internally, it scared the crap out of me, which is a good motivator to help a person stay on a diet and change old habits into a new lifestyle.

So I'm sure a few of you may be saying I'm biased because I'm married to Dr. Cammi, well you're right and wrong. Right, because, of course I'm biased, I love and support everything she does, I would be silly not to, she's way better than any doctor I've ever been to. But you're also wrong, she has way bigger fans than me, just read some testimonials, and she has been helping people longer than I've known her. She has gone through the same medical schools and training as the doctors in hospitals who everyone trusts and listens to with their health; she just fixes problems the right way instead of throwing pharmaceuticals at them or cutting out the problem area. She cares about helping people more than anyone I've ever known, she even does it while we're on vacation. And on top of it all, she lives and emanates the concepts and lifestyles that she has wrote about, she's always happy, energetic, kind, and caring. She never fights, nags, or complains about anything I do, which makes our marriage so wonderful, and with everything she has taught me, I'm healthier and happier than I've ever been. She really is the exact type of person to be writing a book on true sustainable health and happiness because she excels at it, even when the chips are down.

SO, as stated later in this book, YOU are responsible, and accountable (meaning you can't blame anyone else, even the government), for educating yourself and taking care of your health and happiness, no one else, so you might as well start here and get the ball rolling to a healthier and more educated lifestyle.

ACKNOWLEDGEMENTS

As with anything, it takes a lot of support to make a great book. I would like to first thank God for giving me the ability, knowledge, struggles, and strength, to write this book, and also His floods of favor. I am grateful to be living an Ephesians 3:20 life. I am thankful that God knows the plans He has for me, and that He gives me the opportunities to fulfill my dreams. I am grateful for all my blessings, I am grateful to be blessed with a great groom and a great family. I am thankful for divine connections and supernatural opportunities. I am thankful that I have been given mountains to move, in which I learned most of these secrets. I want to give a personal thank you to Kyle for marrying me and for his *endless* encouragement, inspiration, support, and help on this book, and for being a great guide to me on and off the trail. I appreciate his help so much, this book would not be perfect without his genius thoughts, and the countless hours he spent editing. I am grateful to my parents and sister for being a part of shaping my life and for helping me learn these truths. I am blessed with a wonderful family. Last but not least, I would like to thank you for the privilege of sharing my happiness secrets with you.

CONTENTS

INTRODUCTION

"My goal is to encourage you."

—Cammi Balleck PH.D

Can hormones make you happy? You can learn how to unleash your happy hormones starting right now. The feelings we all experience every moment of every day are nothing more than chemical reactions taking place inside our bodies. This is the same for men and women of every age. So what can you do to be happy? I have a Ph.D as a traditional naturopathic doctor; I have over 10 years experience working with men, women, teens, and even children who had bio-chemical imbalances. I believe it is a very simple answer. You must balance the chemicals in your body, and then you will be happy. So what is naturopathic you ask? It is a system of medicine based on the healing power of nature. Naturopathy is a holistic system, meaning to strive to find the cause of dis-ease (the state of being "not at ease," as opposed to a natural state of "ease") in someone by understanding the body, mind, and spirit of the person. Most naturopathic doctors use a variety of therapies and techniques, such as nutrition, whole food supplements, herbal medicine, and homeopathy.

As a naturopath I believe that I have two jobs:

- Support the body's own healing abilities.
- Teach people to make lifestyle changes necessary for the best possible health.

- The traditional naturopath works to restore, maintain, and optimize health by providing individualized care, according to his/her ability and judgment, by following these six principles.

1. Shall endeavor to first, do no harm; to provide the most effective health care available with the least risk to his/her patients at all times.
2. Shall recognize, respect, and promote the self-healing power of nature. (I recommend whole food supplements.)
3. Shall strive to identify and remove the causes of illness, rather than to merely eliminate or suppress symptoms
4. Shall educate his/her patients, inspire rational hope, and encourage self-responsibility for health
5. Shall treat each person by considering all individual health factors and influences. (Treat the Whole Person)
6. Shall emphasize the condition of health to promote well-being and to prevent disease for the individual, each community, and our world. (Health Promotion, the Best Prevention)

Are you stressed and overwhelmed? Do you have anxiety and mood swings? This is a step by step guide to quickly bring your body's hormones back into balance. This book is my way of following my oath and teaching you to care for your body as a whole. You can have bio-chemical balance and unleash your happy hormones, and it is easy. Bio-chemical means something relating to bio-chemistry, which is the study of chemical processes in living organisms, your body is just a bunch of chemical processes and you are a living organism. It looks at the function and structure of the things that make up cells and their chemical reactions. A bio-chemical pathway is the series of chemical reactions that are connected in your body. In addition, I also recommend whole food supplements; these are supplements made from food and not synthetics made in the laboratory. Your body normally gets nutrients from food. Thus, obtaining your vitamins from whole food supplements (real food), will allow the body to actually use the nutrients in the supplement.

I believe we must look at the body as a whole, this means that in order to balance hormones you must also balance the whole body; including the nervous, hormonal, and digestive systems. These systems, when functioning normally with balanced chemicals and a balanced mental/emotional state, will promote *total health*. Hormonal health is no different from digestive health. The body is all interconnected and what is done to one system is done to all the systems. So to balance hormone levels you cannot just take a pill. *You must balance your nervous system including the neurotransmitters and brain chemicals. The hormonal system in order of priority from top to bottom, head to feet, so first the pituitary gland (master gland), then the thyroid gland, followed by the pancreas (digestion and blood sugar), next are the adrenals (stress glands), and finally the ovaries and testes. You must also have your digestion working properly so we will look at diet. Also you must have your mental /emotional state thinking correctly. We are one body and to be happy and sexy you must treat the body as a whole.*

If you find yourself exhausted, overwhelmed, up and down, and about to meltdown, it's time to stop being stressed and depressed and learn how to unleash your happiness. Now, I know you change behaviors as your level of motivation and understanding changes. So my hope is to educate you so you understand your body and your hormones, and I also hope to give you motivation to make the changes you need. I know that you can be scared of making healthy changes because it is confusing and complicated, which makes you want to stick with what you know instead of changing, but I encourage you to make the changes I suggest. In a perfect world, we wouldn't have extreme imbalances in this system of messages at all. We might experience acute bouts of an imbalance, but we'd quickly come back. In balance, we have adequate amounts of serotonin in a healthy gut to promote the production of melatonin at night – the counter regulatory hormone to cortisol that manages our sleep cycle while cortisol manages our wake cycle. In a perfect body with perfect balance (homeostasis), we would have all the energy we need, great moods, and sleep like a baby. We would be able to fall asleep at night easily, wake up in the morning easily, and feel rested and have good energy throughout the daytime, we are in good balance. I believe if you take care of your body on a physical, mental, and chemical level, you can have this "perfect world balance." When stress takes over, that's when the balance is lost. The key is to balance it all and I will teach you how.

You could be one of the 40 million Americans suffering. I know I was, and this is the story of how I helped myself and thousands of others. I went to school for 8 years to get a PH.D, want to talk about a stressful time and a stress on my own balance, cortisol, and adrenals, I got up early to exercise, stayed up late studying, and had a demanding schedule. Any of you that have been to college know what I'm talking about. On top of it all, I was hard on myself so that led to more weight on my shoulders and my midsection. After a stressful internship, I then added the stress to myself by opening and operating my own business. These first years of course were stressful; building clientele, financial stress, and of course, the stress of keeping my patients happy. I had anxiety, I was a constant worrier, and I lived in fear. Then I realized I was in adrenal fatigue; I was moody, on an up and down emotional roller coaster, irritable to my closest friends and family, gaining weight, and I couldn't sleep. I was wired and tired at the same time. I was exhausted, overwhelmed, depressed, stressed, and living in fear. By the age of 25, I had been to more funerals for suicide than I could count on two hands. I have lost close family and friends to the enemy of suicide. I am saddened by this and this is where my passion to help people comes from. Then one day I had my AH-HA moment and realized even though I was still in my 20's, I had a hormone imbalance. The truth is, anyone at any age can have a bio-chemical imbalance, and my patients are getting younger and younger because our food is undernourished and our diets are awful. Here I was, a PH.D as a naturopathic doctor and I was helping men, women, teens, and children every day with their hormones, I needed to balance myself. I started eating even better, and for the first few weeks of healing, I was exercising less, resting more and taking the supplements I will recommend to you. Now several years later, I have 10 years experience with the endocrine system. I am very happily married, I don't have mood swings, I sleep well, and I have a successful business with lots of patients who I have helped "get balanced and happy." I am thankful that I spent the years on the disposition carnival ride, with adrenal exhaustion, anxiety, and fear, because I believe that I can help you not only with the advice I have given all my patients, but the advice I used myself. This advice I am giving you I learned in many of my natural endocrine classes, but I truly learned it firsthand in the last 20 years of my life. Oh how I thank God that I am not stuck on the mood roller coaster anymore, and believe me, I am so thankful that I feel emotionally balanced and I am so thankful that I can say I am truly enjoying every day of my life. I'm writing Happy, The New Sexy because I believe joy is our best makeup, and being happy should be our growth, our form, and our best impression of ourselves. I believe that being sexy is all about being our best. We go to the mall to buy clothes and we put them on to look our best, but what we really need, I believe, is to put on joy and strength, dignity and a good mood, every day. I believe we need the inside of us working so the outside looks and feels sexy. As you read this, you will see our insides are a miracle of chemical reactions, I still don't fully understand it. I believe when these chemicals are in balance you will not only feel good but you will look good too. When we are healthy the weight will fall off without trying, the good mood will be on your brain without a reason, and the smile will be on your face. Now that is sexy! The best feeling comes when you realize that you can be happy and you can say goodbye to all the bad days, stressful days, and sleepless nights. I am now blessed to host my own radio show, and every show I say, *"make the rest of your days the best of your days"*. I believe in just that, I believe you can feel good! You can have energy! You can be happy! This book will tell you how to be balanced so you can say goodbye to bad days now and forever! Some of this may be too deep of reading for you, if it is, feel free to just skim through it, but I do want you to know what is going on in your body too.

Each and every emotion we experience is the result of the release of certain chemicals (hormones) inside our bodies. Some hormones are responsible for making us feel good; some are responsible for making us feel bad. If you want to feel good, YOU MUST get your body working properly. You cannot be happy with toxic, unhealthy, unbalanced hormones. This book is full of ground-breaking secrets to stop stress, depression, and anxiety. We try to buy happiness, marry happiness, and even think, "If only... then I would be happy." But the truth is, happiness is ephemeral, subject to the vagaries of everything from your bank balance to the weather. I have researched myself and my patients to discover the secrets to happiness. After recognizing what can take your happiness, and then taking action to not let it be taken, I believe everyone can get back on track toward joy and enjoying everyday life.

It may surprise many of you to learn that most of our "problems" are simply not just a curse. Any hormonally related health problem you have, from bloating and emotions that accompany your cycle, to more pronounced symptoms such as PCOS and endometriosis, can be traced back to some degree of hormonal imbalance, which can be set straight with the right nutrition! Being aware of how to handle factors such as stress and a deficiency in important nutrients that contribute to hormonal problems can get you on the right track and you can experience trouble-free hormonal changes.

"It's great to know I wasn't alone, and I wasn't crazy. I had crazy hormonal swings, panic attacks, and anxiety. For years I would go from angry to scared, and this made me worry. I had several health issues from the chronic stress. You need to know that this is an easy fix, Cammi will help you, it's easy, you balance your body, you eat right, and you live life. I have come such a long way."

—Debbie

People often mistake the symptoms of imbalanced hormones in women and men with just aging. The good news is that these hormone losses and imbalances are easily correctible. And through proper diet, supplements, and lifestyle changes, these symptoms will often disappear and bring about a healthier, younger you. Depression, from a naturopathic and Christian view, can be looked at in 4 levels of depth; mental, chemical, emotional, and physical. At any level, depression is an inner unbalance of an individual. Therefore, I believe that we need to have not only our hormones in balance; but our life, relationships, diet, and spirit balanced as well. I believe we are a spirit with a soul living in a flesh body. I believe that everyone is responsible for themselves, and I believe that we have to do some work to take care of ourselves. Some of what I am going to tell you, you may not like or agree with, but it's the truth. My passion of helping people would be a lot easier if I could tell you to drink pop for breakfast and eat ice cream before bed. It would be easier and I would probably sell more books, especially if I said that you could stay up late, drink beer, and not exercise, but this won't get you balanced. I also learned in naturopathic school, that there is no such thing as hereditary genes; the truth is you inherit the lifestyle that is the cause of diseases. If you are living the same way as your parents, of course you will get the same results, and the same health problems.

It is becoming clear to me that we are a "now" generation, we have become a generation based on *instant gratification*. Although it is nice, sometimes, to google an answer and know it instantly, I think that it devalues many, otherwise very valuable, experiences. This is the age of instant gratification and "I want it now." We want, and urgently feel the need, to have what we want now; in addition, we think we need to be instantly connected to our friends, family, and work. For example, a friend of mine had an iPhone but just as soon as the newest version of the phone came out, she was quick to toss aside the once greatest machine for a new one. I think this is a big problem, of course not just with phones, but we want everything now. We have become dependent on drugs (prescriptions) to make us happy, to lose weight, to quit smoking, to give us *instant gratification* without doing any of the work. When we are fixing our needs with drugs we are in a way, giving ourselves a "quick fix, instant gratification." We are not working on the actual problems but finding an easy way out of them. This is not how life is supposed to be, the Bible says reap and you will sow, that means work and you will see results.

So here I am, here to tell you the brutally honest truth, so pay very close attention. You got the way you are because of the lifestyle you have lived. You can't just take a pill as a quick fix to cover symptoms, that's like turning up the car radio so you can't hear the noises as your engine is about to blow up. Even though the western medical system will say you can, it's just killing the messenger and not the actual problem. Therefore, to get well, you must have a healthy lifestyle, which yes, is going to require a change in diet and/or lifestyle, and it may not be easy for some, but it will dramatically alter your life for the better. Got it? Reread that again if you don't.

> *"Change starts with a decision, then there is effort involved... and discomfort...and time."*
>
> —*Joyce Meyer*

Did you know the Occupational Safety and Health Administration (OSHA) declared stress a hazard of the work place. Stress costs American industry more than $300 billion annually. Take one moment and think about that. We need to change something. We need to take responsibility and stop stressing, we need to balance ourselves. Balancing your hormones is a whole-body process. There is much more to hormone balancing than estrogen or testosterone, you also have to look at adrenal hormones, insulin, thyroid hormones, and even the pituitary hormones from the brain. Are you an investor or a gambler? You make the choice. I believe many people are gambling with their health, they eat foods they know are wrong and say, "This won't hurt me." They eat sugar and feed their kids sugar and wonder why they are overweight and have cavities. They drink beer and take antacids. They are overworked and under rested and pop an anti-depressant or anti-anxiety pill to deal with life. I am saddened by the amount of people I see and know that are living a life gambling with their health. Gamblers do things they know they shouldn't, they drink and smoke and get drive-thru fast food for dinner, they feed their kids processed food and they think that they'll be the one who gets away with it. But this is gambling a high wager of your health and this is scary to me. However, gamblers don't know they are gambling because they are uneducated and stuck in the western medical system of, "I will just go get a pill to suppress my symptoms when they come." These gamblers feed their kids sugar and let them get cavities, and then let a dentist fill the cavities with dangerous mercury or some other chemical that later can cause ADD, so they gamble again and get an ADD prescription drug (methylphenidate) that causes cardiovascular problems as they get older, and they are likely to have heart conditions including coronary heart disease, heart rhythm disorders, and structural abnormalities. Cardiovascular problems reported in people who took ADD prescription drugs as a kid include stroke, high blood pressure and heart rate, all of which may cause hypertension or heart rhythm problems. Of course, this calls for more gambling as you need to get a blood pressure drug. So as you can see, our health is just like being in Vegas, once you start gambling, you have to keep gambling, it's a snowball effect. Lastly, the side effects may be just a heart attack or sudden death. So that's all, not really a big deal to many. But this to me is scary, and this is just one example.

I am an Investor and I believe in teaching you to be an Investor. Investors make decisions that are good for their body, soul, and spirit. Investors are conscious to do things like eat healthy and exercise, and are grateful and loving. They do kind things for other people and they spend some of their time with God.

But don't just take my word for it; see the testimonials in italics throughout this book from my patients.

I have been to see Cammi and she helped my depression 100%. The information she gives is so sincere and she's not trying to sell any drugs or programs or whatever. This is a great book full of helpful tips. I was so imbalanced and stressed. I was depressed, and as Cammi put it, wired and tired at the same time. In 48 hours my depression was better and in 2 weeks of doing everything Cammi told me to do I felt 99% better.

—*Mandy*

CAN YOU FEEL YOUR BEST AGAIN?

Yes, with proper care most people experiencing any of these problems can expect to feel good again. So what do you do? Surgery? Drugs? NO, NO, NO, you don't have to be on prescriptions drugs for the rest of your life, you don't have to have surgery to have your thyroid or adrenals removed, and you don't have to take antidepressants. YOU can take responsibility for your own health and YOU can balance yourself.

What would it take for you to be happy? What would it take to make you less stressed, healthy, and content? I have discovered the secrets of happy people, and I will share them with you.

Are you unhappy? I believe the numbers are even higher and the world has a disconnection between reported happiness and actual happiness. In that respect, I have researched my patients and discovered for myself the secrets of true happiness. After recognizing what can take your happiness and taking action to not let it go, I believe everyone can get back on track toward joy and enjoy every day. If you are reading this book, you are probably searching for a smile, and my goal is to encourage you to do exactly that every day, I see patients every day who are looking for happiness and health. Unlike popular beliefs happiness does not just happen, it has to be made on purpose. Nothing good happens by accident. Just like success, happiness has to be worked for. In order to be happy, you have to make happiness happen. It's a universal law that good has to be worked for but bad is contagious. You can catch a cold; you can't just catch happiness; it must be worked for every day. We all have had a happy day and wished it would last forever. But then we can have an unpleasant day, leaving us frustrated and depressed. I have found from my studies of my own patients that people are in a happy-depressed-happy cycle. We are always looking for the next big thing to make us happy, only to be disappointed when the cycle continues. This cycle of ups and downs continue as we create our circumstances to be in our own bliss. It's okay to have bad days for sure; the difference is, after reading this book, you will have the knowledge you need to pull yourself back to being stable and happy every day.

Despite what some people think, happiness doesn't depend on your genetics or on your circumstances, it depends on your chemical balance. You can make happiness happen by creating it from the inside out. You can unleash your happy hormones. In this case, even if you are not with your dream guy or gal, or at your dream job, happiness will happen automatically even if none of your dreams have come true yet. When I ask patients what it would take to make them happy, some answer with the same response: "If only I had…," "When I have…," "Someday…"

Usually, the response is something like winning the lottery, not having to work, or finding a new mate. Maybe you would answer, "Health," "A new job," "A marriage," "A divorce," "A larger bank account," or maybe "A new car." Did ever you ever think that wherever you go, there you are? If you are not happy, you won't be healthy. Unhappiness causes stress on the body, and stress on the body causes disease. Science proves that 80 percent of all illness comes from worry, stress, and unhappiness. We are making ourselves sick. For years, it has been common knowledge that people who are under a lot of stress have an increased risk of heart disease. Disease in the body comes from not just physical stress, but emotional stress as well. If you are under stress, you have probably noticed some areas that aren't healthy in your body. Maybe you have noticed digestive issues, headaches, dizziness, or muscle aches. If you are not happy, you probably have noticed that you don't have any energy. If you are not healthy, you are probably not happy.

"Toes," a popular song by Zac Brown Band, tells it all: "Life is good today." We need to have a "life is good today, every day" kind of life. If you are not living life every day as a "life is good today" life, this book is for you. Have you ever gone into the hair salon, hoping that the change in hair color will give you a life change? Have you ever gone for a manicure, hoping to leave the shop in bliss? Maybe went golfing and shot your best game to date? Or finally bought that new truck you've been eyeballing? I agree that a good haircut might help the day or a manicure might help the hour, and a good golf game or new vehicle can always brighten up your day. But did it change your week, your year, your life? If you're like me, you've probably gotten a great new haircut, hoping it would change every circumstance in your life, and then you wake up the next morning, wash your hair, and find everything to be the same and you are still the one under the towel. Did you ever realize that even if you have a new car, you are still the one driving it? Did you ever comprehend that if you have a new mate, you are still the one there with them? Did you ever grasp that no matter if you had all of the, "if-only's," "when's," and "someday's," that the same old "YOU" is still there too? You must understand this important lesson before you change where you live or buy anything expecting it to make you happy, healthy, and content in the future. You must be happy with yourself, right now, today, for no good reason. I am here to help you do just that. If you are the baggage that is cheating you out of happiness, the raiding must stop. The truth is, no matter where you go, you are still carrying the suitcase with you. I am here to help you get rid of the baggage that you carry that is depriving you of your happiness. We have to be determined to be happy every day. This book is your curriculum to teach you how to be on cloud nine every day. Every day, we get dressed and stress over if we are putting on the right clothes or shoes. More importantly, we need to be worried if we are putting on the right attitude. Every day, life brings new opportunities and thousands of new choices. One of the first choices you get to make each day is about your attitude. When you wake up with enthusiasm and choose to be grateful, happy, and stress free, you are getting dressed with the right attitude to match your shoes. Stress is a killer, but death does not come from stress itself. What really happens is, death comes when the body is so tired of fighting and fleeing all the time, it loses all its resistance to keep away the negative effects of stress.

Are you as happy as you can be? How do you know if you aren't as happy as you could be? I have developed a quiz for you to take. If you answer yes to more than one of the following, this book can help you find more bliss.

- You feel tired for no reason. After sleeping all night you wake up tired.
- You have trouble getting up in the morning, even when you go to bed at a reasonable hour.
- You are feeling rundown or overwhelmed.

- You have depression or anxiety.
- You feel tired and wired.
- You are sick of being sick.
- You can't lose weight.
- You get headaches often.
- Your digestion is a wreck.
- You have difficulty bouncing back from stress or illness.
- You watch a lot of TV or play too many video games.
- You say, "If only," "When," or "Someday".
- You're waiting for the day you know you will be happy.
- Are you wanting a new house, car, mate?
- Do you wish others would change?
- Do you think others could make you happy if they…?
- Do you watch TV and play video games to avoid what you have to do?
- Do you have broken relationships?
- Do you fight with others?
- Do you have trouble saying no?
- Do you find things to do to keep you busy?
- Are you constantly seeking pleasure?
- Do you spend money to bring you temporary happiness?
- Do you feel stressed or add stress to yourself?
- Are you searching for bigger and better?
- Do you lie awake at night?
- Is your energy shot?
- Are you tired and fatigued?
- Have you gained weight recently?
- Is your libido gone or slowed down recently?
- Do you smile and look pretty on the outside while crying on the inside?
- Do you go days without laughing?
- Do you have digestive problems?
- Do you suffer from a health condition?
- Do you have headaches or other pain?

- Do you depend on your children to make you happy?
- Can one circumstance take away your happiness?

This book does not...

- This book does not contain traditional advice like, "be a positive thinker", "learn to love life," or "be optimistic," but instead it contains direct and practical advice that is based on your hormone and bio-chemical balance.
- This book doesn't offer quick fixes that last for a few days and then lose their effect later, but instead, it provides permanent healthy solutions to depression, mood swings, and sadness that are based on hormone balancing.
- The book will not only tell you how to get over depression like every other book, but it will also tell you how to get rid of mood swings, being emotional, how to control your emotions, how to prevent bad moods, how to become bio-chemically balanced, how to eliminate stress from your life, how to help your endocrine system heal, and how to live a happier life

I believe that one should not depend on jobs, achievements, goals, money, babies, or relationships to be happy. Most books teach you to find out who you are and what makes you happy and then do that. However, if you are like me, you probably are really horrible at speculating what will make you happy. It's like going to Vegas and betting at the craps table. You can estimate what will make you content about as well as you can estimate the next number to be rolled. If you are like most of the patients I see, you've gotten married, you have gotten the new job, you both have moved to a new town, you are in a new house, and you are still not content. Maybe you have had babies, you bought the car you wanted, you have reached most of the goals you set along the way, and you find yourself still not pleased. Maybe you don't have any of what you are still searching for, and you think that if only you did this you would be cheery. I am not here to tell you to stop dreaming in the least. I just want to lift your spirits so you can be happy today and not wait.

If you are not balanced, know right now that you don't need anything else to be happy. You just need a few tools and some knowledge. If that doesn't sound easy, if you want to be happy but you can't find a reason to smile, then this book is for you. I wrote this book so you can be ecstatic today, so you can find a happiness that is concrete, true, and secure every day. I have discovered for myself how to be blissful every day just because, and it is wonderful. I am delighted every day to wake up me, and I am content just the way things are today. I am blissful not because things are perfect but because I have an authentic and rock-hard happiness that is safe and sound on the inside. It is easy, and you can have it too. This book is to help you be happy so that no matter what your external circumstances are, you still have a feeling of joy and inner peace. No matter if you drive a convertible or ride a bike, you can be self-assured that nothing and no one can steal your joy. If you look around you, you will see that there are happy people in this world who aren't the most successful, rich, or famous. I have observed this. I am one of them, and you can be one of them too.

In my experience, we let circumstances steal our joy. We can be having a great day, and then we weigh ourselves and the day goes to hell. Or we can wake up happy, and the dog walks in with muddy feet and we exchange our smile for an angry face. If you want to have unbroken bliss every day, you must learn how to not let little circumstances steal your joy. I have found that, as humans, we are no different than a horse in forty acres of belly-deep grass; we reach over the fence and look for something better to eat. I look at this as more of a symbol that we can choose to be happy, or we can stretch our necks out a little for more. So I am asking you to stretch your neck out a little and use this book as a guideline to get happy and enjoy the life you have right now today. Be happy with no motive. Be happy today with no explanation. If you are saying, "If I only…then I would be happy," *stop today*. Stop waiting. Stop searching for materialistic things to bring you happiness. Stop charging shoes to your credit card or drinking every night just to cope.

I believe that all you need to do is work on a few areas and you can have happiness today. I know that in us all is a fire of happiness, the kind you cannot lose no matter what has happened in your life or around you. If you look at any kid, you will see that every kid is born happy. You were, and it's still in you. However, you might have to dig a little to find it. I have developed a few steps for you to be happy right now, today. I want to teach you happiness is a way of life. This book will show you the routine I use to be happy every day. You say, "Yes, Cammi, of course you are happy. You have a great life. You are beautiful. You spend every day doing exactly what you want. You only work three days a week, and you have a great home life." Yes, what is going on around me and in my life does make me happy. I have a great man, Kyle, who does make me super happy. My family, friends, and pets make me happy. Having a job I love does make me happy. Helping others does make me happy. Nevertheless, I am not free from obstacles. I have bad days just like anybody. I have testing hurdles. I have my own mountains to climb every day. I have hindrances just like anybody. But even on the bad days, I have chosen to be happy. I choose to stay stable and in bliss every day.

In my training to become a traditional naturopath, I took many chemistry and biology classes. Quantum physics teaches us that everything in the universe is a whirling mass of molecules vibrating at certain frequencies or energy. Trees, plants, animals, rocks, voices—everything has a frequency. Each cell of our body is vibrating at a certain frequency or rate. Everything is energy, and when every tiny cell is doing its job and vibrating in harmony, we have optimum health. Likewise, imagine that a belief, a fear, an accident, improper nutrition, or any other form of stress lowers our vibratory rate. Since everything is vibration and energy, this decrease in the vibratory rate causes a part of our body to alter its vibration and stop functioning properly. What this means, if you don't have a white lab coat on, is that everything affects everything. Some things are positive and cause positive energy in you. Likewise, some things are negative and cause harm or disease in your body. Every cell in your body changes with your nutrition, thoughts, and actions. The more we become aware of this, the more we can take on the responsibility for our own lives, instead of handing it over to the pharmaceutical companies. We can consciously choose to resonate at higher levels. You must choose to live at a higher level physically, chemically, spiritually, and emotionally to be totally anti-depressed and anti-stressed.

The testing I do in my office is based on this science. I test the human body and see where it is and what whole food supplements it needs to live at a higher, healthier, harmonious level. When a patient comes in, I first see if they need to detoxify or just enhance. This book is based on the same belief that everything has energy. Some of the negative in your life you might need to detoxify, and some of the positive might need enhanced.

As a traditional naturopath, I see patients every day, and I treat them on a mind and body level. I look at the body *physically, chemically, spiritually,* and *emotionally.* I believe that in order for you to be happy, you have to work on and keep in balance the physical, chemical, spiritual, and emotional components of the body you have. This book is broken down into four components designed to teach you just how to do that so you can be happy no matter what, *right now and every day.*

My intention is to tell everyone who reads this book about the power of choosing happiness in their life rather than taking life as it comes. Making the lifestyle changes and choices to be happy are the most important things you can do for yourself and others around you. Not so you can be just like me, but so you make the choices that happy people make, choices that are precise for your own life.

I encourage you to read this book twice through so you complete the circle of all four components. You can't do one without the other. Obviously, not every chapter is for everyone. This book is full of tools to help you be anti-stressed and live the happy life you were intended to live. Take what tools and implications you can and apply it to your life every day.

As a Naturopath, my job is to encourage and educate you to make a good healthy lifestyle a habit. Of course, there is going to be some hard work and will power involved. Remember to ask for help, we can try to change ourselves but we accomplish much more when we add the God factor. I've heard it takes 30 days of change to make a good habit, but really, all the advice in this book is to help you make good lifestyle habits so you can be happy and healthy forever. I encourage you to take each day one at a time and make good choices every time you can.

F.Y.I.

This book has two main sections, in Part One I will teach you about your body, how it works, and all the problems we can have and how and why they happen. Part Two teaches you how to fix these problems; from a cellular level from the inside out, a personal level, and also an entire lifestyle change; and how to be your own best doctor.

Whether you are male or female reading this book, don't skip the sections that pertain to the opposite sex, especially if you are married, living with someone, or think someday you might do either one. In my ten years of experience, I've found that some of my best insight to a patient comes from their mate; they see things from an outside point of view and notice things the patient doesn't. Also, these things are always easier to deal with and help if you have someone who understands not only what's going on but why it's going on and how to help, so you're not fighting the battle on your own.

"*Cammi is the personification of her work, In addition to being an expert in helping the body make endorphins, she effectively teaches others how to be healthy and take control of their own happiness and unlimited potential. She is someone who is a picture of happiness, positivity, enthusiasm, and self-confidence on a daily basis. There is no doubt she practices what she preaches. She is truly gifted.*"

—JoAnne

PART ONE

WHAT YOU SHOULD KNOW

" What you don't know can hurt you."

- T.D. Jakes

WHAT ARE HORMONES ANYWAY?

"Life is a cause of stress and anxiety. Some situations are unavoidable and uncontrollable, you have to control what you can, and help out what you can't."

—Cammi Balleck PH.D

In most cases, depression is involved with glandular/hormone imbalance, usually between the pancreas and adrenal gland. These glands can stimulate emotions as a physical and behavioral pattern. The brain can also secrete hormones to govern the emotions. What brain hormones try to make one feel, and what stress allows, determines the final outcome of emotional behavior.

What is Depression? Depression, one of the leading reasons for missed work in America, it is a sickness that one out of five people experiences during their lifetime. It is a chemical dis-order in the body that affects one's wellbeing on a physical, mental, spiritual, or emotional level. It is commonly described as sadness, the blues, or down in the dumps. I see many patients that suffer from depression, and although I see more women than men it affects everyone, and is sadly growing among teens. It can affect anyone of any race and age. Depression is also the main cause of alcoholism, substance abuse, and other dependencies. To me it is a symptom of other dis-eases in the body.

Did you know that Americans are popping anti-depressants like candy, and now more than ever before to deal with everyday stress. Did you know that non-psychiatrists are increasingly willing to prescribe the drugs to patients with no mental health diagnosis, a new study finds. Anti-depressants and anti-anxiety pills are now the *third* most widely prescribed group of drugs in the United States, filling the pockets of the pharmaceutical companies at a current rate of $6.1 billion a year, following number one, a cholesterol-lowering drug at $7.2 billion, and at number two, a heartburn antacid drug at $6.3 billion. Oh, and you know the drug you have seen commercials for that you need to add to your anti-depressant, an antipsychotic drug, is fourth at $4.6 billion. That is a total of $24.2 billlllllllllion dollars that is spent each year on medications that have side effects such as: lightheadedness, drowsiness, nausea, vomiting, tiredness, excess saliva/drooling, blurred vision, weight gain, constipation, and trouble sleeping. And don't forget fast/pounding heartbeat, fainting, increased anxiety, depression, **suicidal thoughts**, trouble swallowing, restlessness, shaking (tremor), muscle spasm/stiffness, mask-like expression of the face, seizures, signs of infection (such as fever, persistent sore throat), high blood sugar, allergic reactions and a minor little thing called **death**. So you didn't ask for it, really, and everyone has an opinion, but mine is, if these people had a healthy diet and lifestyle, they wouldn't need any of these top 3 money making products or the wonderful array of side-effects that go with them.

In addition to the drug companies, doctors are making money, a lot of money, at your expense. The doctors that prescribe these drugs get kick backs for every one they write. Learn the facts at: http://projects.propublica.org/docdollars/. You can even click on your state to see how much they are paying your doctors.

I have a friend who was happy at the fact that he hadn't had a prescription in over a year and wasn't in the pharmacy system. But as a fact, my husband and I haven't had a prescription in over 12 years. It's ok to go without them.

Depression is real, I don't doubt that, but I believe it is a biochemical imbalance in our chemistry and spirit. I agree it is bad and it causes many hard relationships, alcoholism, social isolation, and decreased work productivity. It crashes not only the person suffering from it but those close to them, especially their family, relatives, and close friends. Sadly, untreated depression may lead to suicide, *but don't forget the main side effect of anti-depressants is suicide.* Suicide is one of the leading causes of death worldwide as reported by The World Health Organization. In my belief, most of my patients and people do not recognize the symptoms of depression, and most don't know it's even happening to them. Symptoms of depression could include not sleeping, or sleeping too much, unhappiness, trouble concentrating, anxiousness, loss of appetite, loss of interest in usual hobbies and activities, and mood swings such as angry to sad. The most frequent type is reactive depression, which is a depression that is induced by a painful or stressful event. I believe that when your body is balanced chemically your depression will go away. I recommend you see a Christian counselor, someone trained in psychotherapy, they are excellent alternatives for mild depression and are highly effective. Psychotherapy provides people the opportunity to understand the factors that lead to their depression and to cope effectively with the mental, behavioral, social, and situational triggers. There is always a cause, and yes, even though it is a chemical imbalance, we have to look at the body as a whole. There is always a leading factor to depression that needs to be forgiven and dealt with.

Yes, I know you have stress, everyone has stress, I have stress, I live in the real world. I have a family and a job and people that rely on me every day. However, it is how we "react" to this stress that makes the difference. Why do some people handle stress so much better than others? Well, it is due to the condition of one's hormone balance. When you follow this program, you will feel better balanced and be healthier, guaranteed. This book will without doubt help you feel much better, get rid of your depression, have a more stable mood, and live a much happier life. If you do what I tell you to do, YOU can say goodbye to bad days forever.

There's a lot to appreciate about our hormones. They play a huge role in everything we do and feel. They help with our digestion; they are our energy and our falling asleep. Let's start with the hormones I am going to talk about a lot in this book, because it's first important to understand how your body and the hormones work. I will try to keep it simple, but bear with me for a minute here, it's important you understand this. But think of it like this – the stress is like a hole in a bucket, causing neurotransmitter levels to decline (or become imbalanced). In order to fill the bucket back up over time, you have to first fix the hole.

The word hormone comes from the Greek word "impetus," meaning in motion. A hormone is a chemical released by a cell or a gland in one part of the body that sends out messages that affect cells in other parts of the organism. Only a little amount of hormone is required to alter cell metabolism. In essence, it is a chemical messenger that transports a signal from one cell to another. Hormones are produced by the endocrine system in the body. These glands are also called "ductless glands," meaning that the glands directly empty the hormones into the bloodstream. There are four types of hormones; steroid, lipid, protein, and amino acid hormones. Hormones are chemical substances produced within us that are called "neurotransmitters," they act as "chemical messengers," as a means of communication among various parts of an organism. They help these parts function in a coordinated way. Hormones control such body activities as growth, development, digestion, and reproduction. These chemicals also control the various metabolic activities of the body. And without our hormones we wouldn't know love, how awful would that be. They help to provide the proper amount of energy and nutrition your body needs to function. The first definitive evidence of the existence of hormones was found in 1902, when British researchers discovered that a chemical substance controlled certain activities involved in digestion. Since then more than 30 hormones produced by the human body have been identified.

Hormones have the following effects on the body:

- growth
- mood swings
- induction or suppression of apoptosis (programmed cell death)
- activation or inhibition of the immune system
- regulation of cellular metabolism
- preparation of the body for reproduction, fighting, fleeing, and other activities
- preparation of the body for a new phase of life, such as puberty, parenting, and menopause
- control of the reproductive cycle
- hunger cravings
- sexual arousal
- energy
- sleep

Most hormones in the human body are produced by organs called glands, which are primarily endocrine glands. All these endocrine glands secrete hormones into the blood, which carries them throughout the body. When a hormone arrives at its target organ or tissue it causes certain actions to take place. Hormones may be grouped according to the functions they control. These functions include the way the body uses food; our growth; sex and reproduction; the regulation of the composition of the blood; the reaction of the body to emergencies (flight or fight), and the control of hormones themselves.

I will talk more about these glands, since this is where all the work for our body is done. However, right now I will try to keep it simple so you understand, bear with me here, I know it's a lot of information, but it's the only part in the book I get scientific. I just want you to understand your body. These glands include the master glands in the brain, the pituitary gland and the hypothalamus. The glands in our neck area are the thyroid and parathyroid glands. The glands that sit on our kidneys are the size of grapes and are called the adrenal glands. The pancreas, which is a fish shape, is in our left front, and last, the sex glands, the ovaries and testes. A few hormones are also produced by endocrine tissue present in organs. The make-up of the hormone enables it to combine with a receptor in the cells of its target. The union of the hormone with the receptor triggers a change in the chemical processes of the cell. This change, in turn, modifies many of the hundreds of chemical activities of the cell, causing the target to behave in a certain way. BEHAVE is the key word here. If one of these hormones are out of balance, it will cause you to behave, or mis-behave, a certain way.

TO BE HAPPY YOU MUST HAVE YOUR HORMONES BALANCED. (And yes, there are a lot of them to keep in balance, but don't fear, it's easy when you know how.)

The Hormones I'm talking about are also called neurotransmitters, found in the 1920's to be the messengers of the body. There are hundreds of chemicals in the brain, called neurotransmitters, but first, here are the main starters of the game.

Serotonin is the "happy" and calming brain chemical that can improve your mood and help you to sleep well. Serotonin is a monoamine neurotransmitter. Most is produced by and found in the intestine (approximately 90%), and the remainder is in central nervous system neurons. It functions to regulate appetite, sleep, memory and learning, temperature, mood, behavior, muscle contraction, and function of the cardiovascular system and endocrine system. It is speculated to have a role in depression, as some depressed patients are seen to have lower concentrations of metabolites of serotonin in their cerebrospinal fluid and brain tissue.

Dopamine and noradrenalin are the "feel-good" neurotransmitters, helping you feel energized, focused, motivated, and in control. Dopamine has a number of important functions in the brain; this includes regulation of motor behavior, pleasures related to motivation, and also emotional arousal. It plays a critical role in the reward system; people with Parkinson's disease have been linked to low levels of dopamine, and people with schizophrenia have been linked to high levels of dopamine.

GABA (gamma-amino butyric acid) is the "cool" neurotransmitter, calming you down during periods of stress.

Adrenaline, made in the adrenal glands, is the "motivator," stimulating you and helping you respond to stress.

Endorphins promote that blissful feeling, a sense of euphoria often found in runners' high, or even, paradoxically, in emergencies and after an injury.

Acetylcholine enhances memory, cognition, alertness, and concentration.

Melatonin (actually a hormone, not an herb) affects your ability to sleep soundly and to dream. It helps you to keep in tune with the cycles of nature by responding to seasonal shifts and regulating your inner clock for day and night, known as your circadian rhythm.

Opioid peptides are neurotransmitters that act within pain pathways and the emotional centers of the brain; some of them are analgesics and elicit pleasure or euphoria.

Glutamate is capable of increasing or decreasing in strength, such as when a mom can pick up a car, however, excess glutamate can over stimulate the brain and keep you awake when you are trying to sleep. Excessive glutamate release can lead to toxicity causing cell death and this causes aging. So this is why stressed people look older than they should.

Epinephrine (also known as adrenaline or adrenalin) is a hormone and a neurotransmitter. Epinephrine has many functions in the body, regulating heart rate, blood vessel and air passage diameters, and metabolic shifts; epinephrine release is a crucial component of the fight-or-flight response.

The fight-or-flight response (also called the fight-or-flight-or-freeze response, hyper-arousal, or the acute stress response). This is how we react to concern, unease, apprehension, fear, threats, pressure, intimidation, harassment, stress, constant worry, nervous tension, hassles, trauma, anxiety, and worry, we feel on the inside that we either need to fight back or run away. For example, say you are running down the street and a dog comes out of the neighbors yard barking at you, you are either going to grab a stick and hit it or run faster. Therefore, you are fighting or fleeing. This response is the first stage of our stress responses. The bad thing is we are in this stress response all the time now. Our bodies are in fight or flight mode and making epinephrine or adrenaline when we drive home in traffic, have a long to do list, get a bad phone call, aren't getting along with someone, or have a deadline, or just any of life's stresses. Again, this is how we react to concern, unease, apprehension, fear, threats, pressure, intimidation, harassment, stress, constant worry, nervous tension, hassles, trauma, anxiety, and worry, we feel on the inside that we either need to fight back or run away. And I know that if you are human like me and you live in the real world, you have some concern, fear, and pressure on you coming from somewhere every day.

Substance P is responsible for transmission of pain from certain sensory neurons to the central nervous system.

Cortisol is a steroid hormone produced by the adrenal cortex. It is released in response to stress and a low level of blood sugar. Its primary functions are to increase blood sugar through the body and suppress the immune system. It also aids in fat, protein, and carbohydrate metabolism. It also decreases bone formation. This stress hormone can cause depression if levels rise too high or fall too far below average. High levels of cortisol can create irritability, increased belly fat, insomnia, and sugar cravings. Low levels can be associated with inability to handle stress, extreme fatigue, low libido, and mood instability. The effects of having too much cortisol develop over time, and can vary according to the individual. It is common for the limbs to remain thin while fat collects around the torso and face, and the ankles may become swollen due to water retention. The face may take on a flushed appearance and, in women, facial hair may begin to grow. What is described as a buffalo hump is sometimes seen, with fat building up behind the neck and over the shoulders. The skin becomes easily bruised and stretch marks may develop. Too much cortisol can lead to fatigue, aching, and muscle weakness, with the shoulders, upper arm, and upper leg muscles being most affected. The immune response becomes less efficient, with infections more likely to occur, and spots and cuts taking longer to heal. In women, menstrual irregularities may develop or menstruation may stop completely. High blood pressure, osteoporosis, and diabetes are all associated with having too much cortisol. In addition to memory problems, loss of libido may occur, with anxiety, depression, and sleep problems developing or becoming worse.

Insulin is a peptide hormone, produced by pancreas, and is in us to regulate carbohydrate and fat metabolism in the body. Insulin causes cells in the liver, skeletal muscles, and fat tissue, to take up glucose from the blood. In the liver and skeletal muscles, glucose is stored as glycogen, and in fat cells it is stored as what you know as triglycerides.

And a few more, but not all of the hormones include the ones you have heard about:

Estrogen is responsible for the healthy development of your female sexual characteristics. Particularly for women, this hormone is necessary in the proper development of the bone and the metabolic processes. It boosts serotonin, which helps fight depression and promotes sleep. It also increases GABA, the calming neurotransmitter, and raises endorphins, which help you feel good. Low estrogen levels often found in menopause can cause feelings of sadness and hopelessness.

The common causes of high estrogens are:

1. Weight gain. Fat cells have an enzyme called aromatase. Aromatase converts testosterone into estrogen. Therefore,

obesity can contribute to high estrogen, low thyroid hormone, and low testosterone.

2. Poor liver function. If the liver is sluggish, and unable to detoxify estrogens out of the body, estrogens will accumulate.

3. It's in our food.

Progesterone, on the other hand, is the other hormone that regulates your menstruation. It supports pregnancy and tempers the highly stimulatory effects of estrogen. Progesterone improves your bone density and has beneficial influence on your cardiovascular system and cholesterol. Progesterone also increases the metabolic rate of your digestive system. It has anti-inflammatory actions and regulates the body's immune response. This hormone helps to balance estrogens, helps promote sleep, and has a natural calming effect. Crap you say, you mean to tell me progesterone balances estrogens and estrogens make serotonin? Yes, now you see why we have to balance everything. It also normalizes libido, is a natural diuretic, and a natural anti-depressant. Abnormal levels of progesterone cause insomnia and contribute to bad moods.

DHEA (Dehydroepiandrosterone) is an important steroid hormone. It is the most abundant circulating steroid in humans, in whom it is produced in the adrenal glands and the brain, where it functions mostly as a metabolic intermediate. And, DHEA also has many potential bio-chemical effects on its own.

Testosterone is a steroid hormone, it is primarily secreted in the testicles of males and the ovaries of females, although small amounts are also secreted by the adrenal glands. It is the main male sex hormone and a steroid. In men, testosterone plays a key role in the development of male reproductive tissues such as the testes and prostate, as well as promoting helping sexual characteristics such as increased muscle, bone mass, and the growth of body hair. In addition, testosterone is essential for health, thinking, memory and well-being, as well as the prevention of osteoporosis.

FSH (Follicle-stimulating hormone) is a hormone that is made and secreted by the pituitary gland. FSH regulates the development, growth, pubertal maturation, and reproductive processes of the body. FSH and luteinizing hormone (LH) act synergistically in reproduction. Specifically, an increase in FSH hormones from the pituitary is the cause of ovulation in women.

AND (Androstenedione) is the common precursor of male and female sex hormones. Some AND may be converted to testosterone and estrogens. However, two key parts of the brain (the hypothalamus and pituitary gland) are known to be important in the control of androstenedione secretion from the testes, ovaries, and adrenal cortex. The release of androstenedione by the adrenal cortex is thought to be related to the pituitary gland's secretion of a specialized hormone. The effects of too much androstenedione are likely to result from its conversion in the body to estrogen or testosterone. In men, too much androstenedione may lead to an imbalance in estrogen and testosterone production, leading to changes such as breast development. In women, too much leads to excess body and facial hair growth, irregular periods, and acne. Not enough AND, and you don't have enough testosterone or estrogen.

Hormones as you can see are NOT JUST for women, this imbalance can affect teens, growing kids, and men too. YES, I SAID MEN TOO. Did you know, after age 20, a man's hormone levels fall about 14% for every 10 years. By the time he reaches 40, he's lost almost half the growth hormones he had at 20 years old, and by the time he reaches 80, men are left with just 5% of their original hormones. But you don't have to be middle-aged or older to experience an imbalance, I see teen boys that experience the same numbers now.

Some of the most common hormonal imbalances in men include:

- Andropause–Also known as male menopause, andropause occurs as men grow older and their testosterone levels decline.
- Adrenal fatigue–If your stress levels remain high for a prolonged period of time, your adrenal glands can't produce enough of the stress hormone cortisol.
- Hypothyroidism–When your thyroid gland is underactive, it's not producing enough thyroid hormones.
- Hyperthyroidism–An overactive thyroid gland results in high levels of thyroid hormones and an increased metabolism.

Men experience a more gradual loss of hormones, mainly testosterone. The result is andropause, known as "male menopause." Andropause can make daily life feel like an uphill battle, and because men are living longer, more active lives, they are seeking and finding relief from the serious symptoms of hormone imbalance. And men can experience the same adrenal fatigue, thyroid symptoms, and diabetic problems. How do we help men? With the information that is in this book.

The signs of a bio-chemical imbalance in MEN include:

Muscle Loss
Weight Gain
Fatigue
Sleep Problems
Night Sweats
Lower Sex Drive
Irritability
Depression
Hair Loss
Erectile Dysfunction
Urinary Problems

Memory Loss
Feeling stressed

I have gained muscle and much more vitality... My libido has increased which is pleasant at my age. I'm taking on projects that I had thought were things of the past, like skiing again. I'm looking forward to many years of health and happiness with my wife (who is happy now too.)

—*Jeff a 60 year old male*

So now you can see that when any of our neurotransmitters are out of balance, we may feel depressed, anxious, stressed, and unmotivated. You may be wired and tired but unable to fall asleep or stay asleep. You could have anxiety, be irritable, have PMS, bad digestion, headaches, or you may feel depressed. Maybe even a combination of any or all of the above.

Earlier I gave you one hormone at a time, but in our bodies, each of these four systems affects the other three in a complex balance game. Basically, when one hormone goes up, another goes down to compensate. This continues until a patient becomes so sick, that almost all of these hormones go down.

My passion is helping YOU feel balanced and better.

OK TAKE A BREAK, if you need one, we don't want you fighting or fleeing from this book.

NEUROTRANSMITTER QUIZ

"Don't be afraid to take a big step if one is indicated. You can't cross a chasm in two small jumps"

—David Lloyd George

Neurotransmitters are our messengers. There are over 50 known neurotransmitters and each is made from a specific combination of amino acids and co-factors (vitamins, minerals, and other chemicals). To keep it simple, each neuron receives an impulse and must pass it on to the next neuron and make sure the correct impulse continues on its path, just like your mail comes to you. Through a chain of complicated chemical reactions in the body we either function like we were meant to or we don't. If you are not feeling good it's because your neurotransmitters are getting lost in the mail so to speak. Take this quiz to see how your neurotransmitters are working.

ADD UP THE NUMBER TO THE LEFT IF YOU CAN ANSWER "YES".

PART 1–Are You Under a Dark Cloud?

3   Do you have a tendency to be negative, to see the glass as half-empty rather than half-full? Do you have dark, pessimistic thoughts?

5   Are you exhausted and feel tired every day? Are you not sleeping well?

3   Are you often worried and anxious?

3   Do you have feelings of low self-esteem and lack confidence? Do you easily feel self-critical self-critical and guilty?

3   Does your behavior often get a bit, or a lot, obsessive? Is it hard for you to make transitions, to be flexible? Are you a perfectionist, or a control freak? A computer, TV, or work addict?

3   Do you really dislike the dark weather or have a clear-cut fall/winter depression (Seasonal Affective Disorder)?

2   Are you apt to be irritable, impatient, edgy, or angry?

3   Do you tend to be shy or fearful? Do you get nervous or panicky about heights, flying, enclosed spaces, public performance, spiders, snakes, bridges, crowds, leaving the house, or anything else?

2   Have you had anxiety attacks or panic attacks (your heart races, it's hard to breathe)?

2   Do you get PMS or menopausal moodiness (tears, anger, depression)?

3   Do you hate hot weather?

2   Are you a night owl, or do you often find it hard to get to sleep, even though you want to?

2   Do you wake up in the night, have restless or light sleep, or wake up too early in the morning?

3   Do you routinely like to have sweet or starchy snacks, booze, or marijuana in the afternoons, evenings, or in the middle of the night (but not earlier in the day)?

2   Do you find relief from any of the above symptoms through exercise?

3   Have you had fibromyalgia (unexplained muscle pain) or TMJ (pain, tension, and grinding associated with your jaw)?

2   Have you had suicidal thoughts or plans?

Total Score _____ If your score is more than 12 then you are probably experiencing symptoms of low serotonin. Serotonin is our "Happy Hormone", DEPLETION of the inhibitory neurotransmitters are the most common cause of depression and anxiety.

PART 2–Are You Suffering from the Blahs?

3   Do you often feel depressed–the flat, bored, apathetic kind?

2   Are you low on physical or mental energy? Do you feel tired a lot; have to push yourself to exercise? Inability to feel pleasure?

2   Is your drive, enthusiasm, and motivation quota on the low side?

2   Do you have difficulty focusing or concentrating, been diagnosed with ADD?

3   Are you a thrill seeker or risk-taker?

3   Are you easily chilled? Do you have cold hands or feet?

2   Do you tend to put on weight too easily?

3   Do you feel the need to get more alert and motivated by consuming a lot of coffee or other "uppers" like sugar, diet soda, ephedra, or cocaine?

Total Score _____ If your score is more than 6 points then you are probably experiencing symptoms of low dopamine, epinephrine, and norepinephrine. These are excitatory neurotransmitters.

PART 3–Is Stress Your Problem?

4   Do you stay in bed until noon or later on days off, even when you go to bed at a normal time?

3   Do you often feel overworked, pressured, or deadlined?

1   Do you have trouble relaxing or loosening up?

1   Does your body tend to be stiff, uptight, tense?

2   Are you easily upset, frustrated, or snappy under stress?

3   Are you easily chilled? Do you have cold hands or feet?

2   Do you tend to put on weight too easily?

3   Do you often feel overwhelmed or as though you just can't get it all done?

2   Do you feel weak or shaky at times?

3   Have a history of panic attacks or severe anxiety?

3   Are you sensitive to bright light, noise, or chemical fumes?

2   Do you need to wear dark glasses a lot?

3   Do you feel significantly worse if you skip meals or go too long without eating?

2   Do you use tobacco, alcohol, food, or drugs to relax and calm down?

Total Score _____ If your score is more than 8 then you are probably experiencing symptoms of GABA depletion and possibly adrenal fatigue.

PART 4–Are You Too Sensitive to Life's Pain?

3   Do you consider yourself or do others consider you to be very sensitive?

3   Does emotional pain, or perhaps physical pain, really get to you?

2   Do you tear up or cry easily–for instance, even during TV commercials?

2   Do you tend to avoid dealing with painful issues?

3   Do you find it hard to get over losses or get through grieving?

3   Do you use drugs such as methadone, oxycontin, codeine, or other opiates?

2   Have you been through a great deal of physical or emotional pain? Suffer from chronic back pain or headaches?

3   Do you crave pleasure, comfort, reward, enjoyment, or numbing, from treats like chocolate, bread, alcohol, romance novels, marijuana, tobacco, or lattes?

Total Score _____ If your score is more than 6 then you are probably experiencing symptoms of low endorphins.

You may want to mark this section so you can reference back to it when we go over all the supplements in the "You Can Have Bio-Chemical Balance" chapter.

WHAT IS DIS-EASE

"Be not astonished at new ideas; for it is well known to you that a thing does not therefore cease to be true because it is accepted in many ways"

—Spinoza (1632-1677)

Diseases ARE CAUSED by the way we live, eat, and handle stress. In order to get well, we must CHANGE the way we live, eat, and handle stress. We must follow GOD'S way, and NOT the ways of "man" – the ways of doctors! For those of you who aren't religious, just substitute nature in this next section, and think to yourself how good all of nature works; particularly the self-healing abilities of plants and animals; without a drop of human intervention, then think how bad humans have screwed up nature, then realize that we are a part of nature. I am not against medical doctors, and I love our emergency system, however, I believe way too many drugs are prescribed to only treat symptoms and not the underlining problem.

Western Medical Doctors learn only TWO methods of treatment:

1. Give DRUGS, to cover up the symptoms and in the long run, poisoning the patient.
2. Whack it out if it isn't working -Take out–or cut off–the "problem" organ with mutilating surgery.

Drugs never solve the underlying problem. They only "treat" symptoms, and they ALL have side effects. Drugs only change the form or location of the disease, they NEVER cure the disease. That is why, in many instances, the doctor will tell you that you have to be ON the drugs for the rest of your life.

The World Health Organization (WHO) estimates that 4 billion people, 80% of the world population, presently use herbal medicine for some aspect of primary health care. Herbal medicine is a major component in all indigenous peoples' traditional medicine and a common element in Ayurvedic, homeopathic, naturopathic, traditional oriental, and Native American Indian medicine. The WHO notes that of 119 plant-derived pharmaceutical medicines, about 74% are used in modern medicine in ways that correlate directly with their traditional uses as plant medicines by native cultures. Major pharmaceutical companies are currently conducting extensive research on plant materials gathered from the rain forests and other places for their potential medicinal value.

The Bible says in Revelation "ALL will be tricked." I believe this is where we are heading, if not already close to it. Look at the world, most of it is being deceived by the DRUG medications prescribed by doctors. God defines them as Witchcraft. Think about it, most Drug medications are essentially the same as street drugs. They are given to make a patient FEEL better, or to make the lab test numbers LOOK better, but they are only a temporary "Quick Fix." They NEVER solve the underlying problem,–the actual CAUSE of the disease, which always begins in the "heart" because we want to live, eat, and handle stress OUR way, rather than GOD'S way.

Drugs NEVER Cure Disease and Diseases DON'T Just Happen. We GIVE them to ourselves by the way we live, eat, and handle stress. This is Satan's way to take us down. God says to us, "Turn to Me. I want to CHANGE your life in every way."

But Satan whispers in our ear, "You don't need to change anything. You can keep living, eating, acting, thinking, and handling stress the way you always have. Here, take a PILL. It will make you FEEL better." And that it will, but your disease will continue to progress, and will eventually kill you.

That is why doctors Never Have, and Never Will, find a Cure for ANY disease, because they only "treat" symptoms – with innately harmful and poisonous drugs, or by burning radiation, or by cutting out organs, none of which can CURE anything.

How long have DRUGS been around?

The origin of modern Drug medicine ("Quick Fix" medicine) in "treating" disease is considered to have begun in the 1930's and 1940's with the discovery of the first antibiotic, Penicillin, by Sir Alexander Fleming in 1928. Subsequently, the Drug industry exploded, and today there are more drugs (ALL of which are harmful and have side effects, some of which we don't even know about) than one can count. Chemical patents came into use in the USA in 1925. As I write this it is 2013... that means chemicals have been used for less than 100 years. The first U.S. Pharmacopeia was published in 1820. This volume's listings of "prescriptions" included only herbal drugs, with descriptions of their properties, uses, dosages, and tests of purity. I don't have to tell you, just watch a commercial for the latest drug; they do terrible harm to the body. They are excruciatingly painful in most instances, and they can be expensive. They will NEVER make you well; they will never help you to make good healthy cells. They will only make you worse – much worse – in the long term, and NO doctor will ever guarantee that their "therapies" will make you well. Today, the Pharmacopoeia, with its reliance on herbal compounds, has been all but forgotten. Most modern physicians rely on the Physician's Desk Reference, an extensive listing of chemically manufactured drugs. It is important to note that each entry in this enormous volume, in addition to specifying the chemical compound and actions of a particular drug, also includes an extensive list of contraindications, which is defined as; a reason that makes it inadvisable to prescribe a particular drug or employ a particular procedure or treatment; and of course, that giant laundry list has possible side effects.

How long has Natural medicine been around?

Ayurvedic principles and practices were written sometime between 1500 and 500 Bc. Based on these texts, Ayurveda was widely adopted throughout India and Southeast Asia.

Massage dates back to *approximately 3000 B.C* in China, *possibly earlier.*

In 2735 B.C., the Chinese emperor Shen Nong wrote an authoritative treatise on herbs that is still in use today.

Many herbs and vegetables and perennials are mentioned in the Bible. So they're about as old as the earth, 6600 years or so. Today we still study a few in detail and look up where they are found in the Bible. People who lived in Jesus' time were wonderful herbalists! They used the herbs not only for food, but to flavor food, and also for medicinal purposes. Genesis 1 says God created the herbs, seeds and trees.

We know that biblical people set aside plots specifically for herbs: read 1 KINGS 21:2.

Mint was well known as being used for flavoring food as it still is today. Some Bible experts say mint was among the "bitter herbs" mentioned in Exodus 12:8 and Numbers 9:11, along with leaves of endive, chicory, lettuce, watercress, sorrel, and dandelions. All of these were eaten as a salad. Mint was also eaten after eating as a form of digestive aiding.

Parsley, although not mentioned in the Bible, was abundant and was used at the Passover as a symbol of a new beginning because it was one of the first herbs to pop up in the spring. The Romans served it at banquets as a breath freshener. Another passage reflecting the bitter herbs is EXODUS 12:8 and also NUMBERS 9:11.

Present-day doctors say their medicine is advanced and laugh about these supposedly "unintelligent" treatments used by doctors hundreds of years ago. They think that today's science has advanced remarkably. I don't think that medical doctors are bad people; I believe that they are just taught to believe the wrong information. I believe the pharmaceutical companies are the bad people and they make billions of dollars off what doctors prescribe each year. I blame these people who are driven by the love of money (the root of all evil) and not by a real concern for the well-being of patients. And again, I am not against western medicine, several years ago I was burned very badly with 3rd degree burns, the first place I went was to the ER and I was thankful for the pain medication. I am not saying our advances aren't useful, I just believe that if we can fix our symptoms by fixing the cause we should. I am thankful that pain drugs and such are available for people who need them in an immediate, right-now situation. However, I believe we should take care of our body as chemically free as we can. When I was burned, I thanked God for chemical pain medication. There is a place for it, just not in long term everyday circumstances and certainly not in your hormone balancing. They may not be bleeding people as they did to George Washington (almost killing him), but they are doing the same stupid things today. They give numerous mercury-containing vaccinations to tiny babies and young children and claim that they are good for them, even though they cause autism and other types of brain damage. Dentists put mercury-containing amalgam fillings in everyone's teeth and claim they are harmless in one's mouth, even though the government demands that the material must be treated as highly toxic "hazardous waste" when the filling is removed from the patient's mouth, and is in the dentist's hand.

So it's your choice, I'm just the messenger here. Are you going to do something that is less than 100 years old or something that is as old as the earth? Are you going to put something in your body we don't know the long term side effects of, or are you going to nurture your body with nutrition that we know heals the cells? God's way to physical and spiritual health has been around for 6,600 years. It is available to everyone on the face of the earth, rich or poor, educated or uneducated.

So is a natural doctor the answer? Well, Yes, I am one so I am going to recommend a natural approach, but only to an extent, however, you need to be careful who you trust here as well. Some believe that the way a person eats is important – and they are right, but the "diet" they promote is not an Ideal Diet. And, the sad fact is, that the vast majority of this alternative, "holistic" practitioners, don't even believe in God as our creator. The majority of them don't believe in God at all, and if they do, it's a New Age god of Eastern Medicine – a combination of Hinduism/Buddhism/New Ageism. They promote the universe will take care of you, eastern meditation – a dangerous emptying of the mind, a "spirit force" that is not Bible based.

DO YOU KNOW YOUR ENDOCRINE SYSTEM?

Do You know your endocrine system? If you are like most people you may know your body is always working, but you may not know how. I want to tell you how so you get a better understanding about what I am taking about. I will try to keep it as simple as I can. Let me introduce you to your glands.

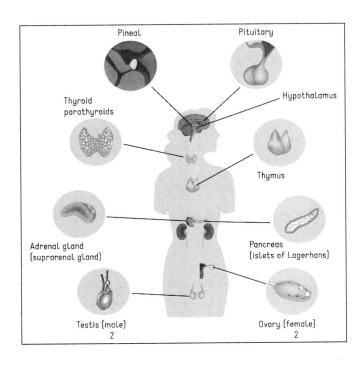

STRESS AND ADRENAL FATIGUE

I myself write this from experience, I have suffered from a bio-chemical imbalance, times of fatigue. When I was in college and during my internships, I had papers to write, class to go to. The whole time I went to school I lived off of caffeine because I needed it to function. Yes, caffeine was my endorphin. In addition, I wasn't sleeping, wasn't eating fats, and I was over exercising trying to stay the size I thought that I should be. To say the least, I had 10 years of stress on myself, causing adrenal fatigue, and I wondered why I was exhausted, sick all the time, couldn't lose weight, and had bad skin and dry hair. And this still happens to me to this day if I overdo it. Watching your balance is a life time of work but it's so worth it to yourself and the ones that live with you and around you.

Ok, so you are stressed, so is everyone, so let's talk about some of the effects of stress on your body, your thoughts and feelings, and on your behavior. I'm sure you know what your stress is, but some examples of stressors include poor physical health, financial strain, and trying to manage a household.

What I finally learned in naturopathic school that saved me from the insanity was:

- People who exercise hard are not always healthy.
- Eating fat will not make us fat.
- Eating protein and animals will not make you fat.
- Sleep is the foundation of being able to function.
- We must eat well.
- We should take supplements every day.
- We must chill out and allow the body to re-set.
- We must detoxify.

WHAT IS ADRENAL FATIGUE?

If you have been stressed too long you may have adrenal fatigue. Adrenal fatigue is a collection of signs and symptoms known as a syndrome, which results when the adrenal glands function below the necessary level. This means you have used your adrenals too much and they can't work like they should because they are tired. Most commonly associated with lingering, long-drawn-out stress, it can also arise during or after acute or chronic infections, especially respiratory infections such as stomach flu, influenza, bronchitis or pneumonia, in addition to heavy metal or chemical toxins. As the name suggests, its top symptom is "fatigue" that is not relieved by sleep. This is why you are tired all the time, even if you sleep 12 hours a night. This is however hard to see like a wart on your foot. You may look and act relatively normal with adrenal fatigue and may not have any obvious signs of physical illness, yet you live with a general sense of being "off", un-well, tired, or you may have a "gray" feeling. People experiencing adrenal fatigue often have to use coffee, colas, and other stimulants to get going in the morning, and burst their energy at 2 pm with another cup.

This syndrome has been known by many other names throughout the past century, such as non-Addison's hypo-adrenia, subclinical hyper-adrenia, neurasthenia, adrenal neurasthenia, adrenal apathy, and of course adrenal fatigue. Although it affects millions of people in the U.S. and around the world, conventional western medicine does not yet recognize it as a distinct syndrome; therefore your MD will treat the symptoms such as depression with an anti-depressant instead of treating the cause and fixing the adrenals.

I have had adrenal fatigue several times in my life, and every time it is no one's fault but my own. I have a tendency to let myself take on too much and in the past I had a major problem saying "No". I used to be bad about letting myself get into a downward spiral of being exhausted and pushing more, being exhausted and pushing more, until I was sick, and even when I was sick I would keep pushing. I lived with stress headaches and tension in my shoulders for years.

I have a Type A personality, and this fights against me sometimes I know. Type A people are more prone to stress. Type A's climb the mountains because they are there, Type B's sit at the bottom of the mountain and read a book by the lake. Type B personalities can still experience hormone imbalances, but they usually don't have the stress related problems that Type A's do. Type A's are the multi-taskers that get themselves wound up, Type B's are the ones that can procrastinate and take things one at a time. I can quickly become impatient with delays and unproductive time, I am known to schedule commitments too tightly, and try to do more than one thing at a time, such as talking on the phone while placing an order on the computer. I have a tendency to get excited and want things done right now and done perfect. I also have to watch myself about being overwhelmed and then letting the stress, stress me. I admit, I still have all these issues, it's who I am, but now I have learned to watch for them and not let them get too far into the out of control spiral before I do something about it. I have learned to change my ways and correct myself when I fall toward my old ways.

What I have learned over the past five years from my husband is that it is ok to be what I call a Type A/B personality. It has taken me years, but I have learned it's ok to be driven and successful as long as you relax and enjoy life and live in the moment too. Lifestyles are inherited, I inherited my drive from my dad who worked full time and also ran a ranch full time as I was growing up. My dad has many accomplishments and has been able to afford to buy a lot of great property that is priceless because of his hard work. I inherited his lifestyle of never taking a day off from work, I was taught from my dad who is also a Type A that we need to work hard, and I am a very driven hard worker.

However, I have learned from my husband who is an A/B personality how to be driven but how to slow down and enjoy my life too. I have learned to work hard and to play hard, I have learned to climb the mountain because "it's there" and then relax by the camp fire with the radio playing Pink Floyd because "it's there." I have taught myself not to feel guilty about a day off and not to feel bad if I put something off for tomorrow so I can sit on the couch and hold my husband's hand while we watch our favorite shows. And I have learned to control my balance better. This is all I want to teach you, the problems we can have when we cause our hormones to be imbalanced and what you can do to catch it before it's too bad. I have taught myself to recognize when I am using coffee to keep going, when I am too tired, when I need a day off, when I exercise too much, when I'm feeling overwhelmed and up and down. Now, I can happily say, instead of feeling guilty about a day off hiking and fishing in the high desert with my husband and no cell service, I welcome it full hearted and know it's the best thing for me.

Adrenal fatigue can wreak havoc with your life. In the more serious cases, the activity of the adrenal glands is so diminished that you may have difficulty getting out of bed for more than a few hours per day. With a continuous downward spiral of reduction in adrenal function, every organ and system in your body is more profoundly affected. Meaning, when you are stressed, you keep adding energy stimulants (coffee, energy drinks, etc.) to your day to keep going. Changes occur in your carbohydrate, protein, and fat metabolism, fluid and electrolyte balance, heart and cardiovascular system, and even sex drive. Many other alterations take place at the bio-chemical and cellular levels in response to, and to compensate for, the decrease in adrenal hormones that occurs with adrenal fatigue. Your body does its best to keep homeostasis and balance to make up for under-functioning adrenal glands, but it does so at the price of your health.

Effects on your body:

- A tendency to sweat
- Back pain

- Chest pain
- Headaches
- Muscle tension
- Digestive issues
- Cramps or muscle spasms
- Erectile dysfunction
- Fainting or dizzy spells
- Heart disease
- Hypertension (high blood pressure)
- Loss of libido
- Lower immunity against diseases
- Muscular aches
- Nail biting
- Nervous twitches
- Pins and needles
- Sleeping difficulties
- Stomach upset
- PMS
- Constipation
- Acid reflux

Effects on your thoughts and feelings:

- Anger
- Anxiety
- Burnout
- Depression
- Feeling of insecurity
- Forgetfulness
- Irritability
- Problem concentrating
- Restlessness
- Sadness
- Fatigue

Effects on your behavior:

- Eating too much
- Eating too little
- Food cravings
- Sudden angry outbursts
- Anxiety
- Drug abuse
- Alcohol abuse
- Higher tobacco consumption
- Social withdrawal
- Frequent crying
- Relationship problems
- Fighting with others

If you have stress and any of these you probably have "Adrenal fatigue" or "hypo-adrenals", hypo meaning not working as well as it should. These are terms used in alternative medicine to describe the belief that the adrenal glands are exhausted and unable to produce adequate quantities of hormones, primarily cortisol. Adrenal fatigue is the number one cause of hormonal imbalance that I see in my office; however, remember that our body is a whole system so it's never just one gland not working like it should.

Sharon's Story—

Sharon came into my office after being referred by a friend to see me for her headaches. She was working long hours and was a single mom raising two boys. As I talked with Sharon, I learned she didn't just have headaches. Sharon had anxiety, she wasn't sleeping, she was exhausted all day, she drank coffee in the morning, and always went for a latte in the afternoon. Sharon was sick all the time but thought it was because she was taking night classes at the local community college; in addition, she had been dealing with an alcoholic ex for years. Adrenal fatigue? Yes, that is what she had. Sharon had been digging herself into a hole for years, her body was in a downward spiral and she came in for headaches. Sharon felt the headache pain, therefore she wanted it gone so she could think, however, she didn't feel the other pain all the stress had caused her. I got Sharon on a good program of B vitamins, glandulars, and whole food minerals, within 60 hours her headaches, head cold, and anxiety were gone. I taught her how to eat healthy and what she needs daily in supplements and she is living a healthy lifestyle with energy now. She has finished school, got a new job, is in a good relationship, and of course, doesn't suffer from headaches anymore.

We generally use the word "stress" when we feel that everything seems to have become too much—we are overloaded and wonder whether we really can cope with the pressures placed upon us.

Anything that poses a challenge or a threat to our well-being is a stress. Some stresses get you going and they are good for you—without any stress at all many say our lives would be boring and would probably feel pointless. You are supposed to have stress, that's how your bills get paid and the kids have dinner cooked for them. However, when the stresses undermine both our mental and physical health they are bad. So, we shall be focusing on stress that is bad for you, the stress that causes your hormones to lose homeostasis, otherwise known as "out-of-whack."

Stress brings us out of "homeostasis". This means stress causes you to be unbalanced in many areas of your body; this includes muscles, kidneys, digestion, and the immune system. This is why when you are run down you get sick, or why women who are getting married and stressing about the wedding get cold sores. In biology, most bio-chemical processes strive to maintain balance or equilibrium, a steady state that exists more as an ideal and somewhat achievable condition. For example, your body keeps its temperature at 98.6%. Homeostasis is a key concept in biology. The concept of homeostasis is the description for when the internal conditions of living organisms remain stable (within a normal range), regardless of what is going on in the external environment. These internal conditions include your body temperature, pH level, and glucose level. Homeostasis attempts to maintain your system in a normal range; if toxins build up in your system, homeostasis will be disrupted, and this is when you become sick.

Environmental factors, internal stimuli, or external stimuli, continually disrupt homeostasis; an organism's present condition is a state in constant flux moving about a homeostatic point that is that organism's optimal condition for living. Factors causing an organism's condition to diverge too far from homeostasis can be interpreted as stress. A life-threatening situation such as a physical insult or prolonged starvation can greatly disrupt homeostasis. On the other hand, an organism's effortful attempt at restoring conditions back to or near homeostasis, oftentimes consuming energy and natural resources, can also be interpreted as stress.

Samantha's Story—

Samantha is in college and taking demanding classes, in addition she is an avid bike rider. Samantha came to me with anxiety and mood swings; we did a saliva test on her and found her cortisol level was through the roof. After doing a detox and starting whole food supplements, she noticed right away it helped her feel calmer, and less restless. Samantha is a great patient because she doesn't just want to take a pill to feel better she works hard at a healthy lifestyle. She didn't question me when I wanted to change her diet and she did other reading to learn as much as she could about a healthy lifestyle. Samantha wanted to get better and she wanted to be balanced, and within 3 months she was able to come off the herbs I had given her and just maintain her health with a daily vitamin and mineral and is now just on a whole food maintenance program.

"I think more clearly, without my hormones controlling my moods quite as much, and generally feel calmer. I am now eating well, (other than my cookies the other day) and taking the pro cortisol balance; I am at ease and have a better sense of inner peace. When I would eat processed foods, and have wheat be the majority of my daily consumption, my social anxiety and depression would spike. I would feel extreme hormonal imbalances. What a difference supplements and fresh foods can make. I also sleep better at night, and feel rested. The supplements helped balance me and that helped calm me down, de-stressed me, and helped me control my hormonal mood swings. It truly is amazing how what you consume affects your overall wellness."

—*Samantha*

WHAT CAUSES ADRENAL FATIGUE?

Adrenal fatigue is produced when your adrenal glands cannot adequately meet the demands of stress. The adrenal glands mobilize your body's responses to every kind of stress (whether it's physical, emotional, or psychological) through hormones that regulate energy production and storage, immune function, heart rate, muscle tone, and other processes that enable you to cope with the stress. Whether you have an emotional crisis such as the death of a loved one, a physical crisis such as major surgery, or any type of severe repeated or constant stress in your life, your adrenals have to respond to the stress and maintain homeostasis. If their response is inadequate, you are likely to experience some degree of adrenal fatigue.

During adrenal fatigue your adrenal glands function, but not well enough to maintain optimal homeostasis because their output of regulatory hormones has been diminished–usually by over-stimulation. Over-stimulation of your adrenals can be caused either by a very intense single stress, or by chronic or repeated stresses that have a cumulative effect.

We all act in response differently to a given circumstances for three reasons:

- We do not all interpret each situation in the same way.
- Because of this, we do not all call on the same resources for each situation.
- We do not all have the same resources and skills.

Some situations which are not negative ones may still be perceived as stressful. This is because we think we are not completely prepared to cope with them effectively. Examples being: having a baby, moving to a nicer house, and being promoted; all good things that add stress to our lives.

When we are stressed the following happens:

- Blood pressure rises
- Breathing becomes more rapid
- Digestive system slows down
- Heart rate (pulse) rises
- Immune system goes down
- Muscles become tense
- We are wired and tired and we do not sleep (heightened state of alertness)

Yea, I know that's about how you feel every day or you wouldn't be reading this book. Or maybe you don't realize it, but if you are stressed this is what is going on inside of your body. For example, a fever is a natural, healthy response to an immune challenge. If you develop a fever, let it do its job of making your body inhospitable to a virus or bacteria. Don't hide the fever with aspirin, ibuprofen, or acetaminophen right away. Oh so you have been sick a lot this year? Immune system maybe? Or do you get headaches and tight shoulders and you need a massage? Muscles tense maybe? Or do you have IBS, heart burn, constipation, diarrhea, indigestion? Hmmm… digestive system slowed down? Ok, you get the picture; you have some of the symptoms of stress. But because I am a naturopath, let's not look at the symptoms, but talk about the causes.

WHO IS SUSCEPTIBLE TO ADRENAL FATIGUE?

YOU, and ANYONE who experiences stress. This means your spouse, kids, and grandma. Anyone who is living a life can experience adrenal fatigue at some time in his or her life. This is because adrenal fatigue can be brought on by daily stress, an illness, a life crisis, or a continuing difficult situation such as custody battles and difficult people in your life. Any stress can drain the adrenal resources of even the healthiest person.

However, there are factors that can make you more susceptible to adrenal fatigue. These include:

- Certain lifestyles
- Poor diet
- Substance abuse
- Too little sleep and rest
- Too many pressures
- Chronic illness
- Repeated infections such as bronchitis or pneumonia
- Prolonged situations that you feel trapped or helpless in
- Bad relationships
- Stressful jobs
- Poverty
- Pregnancy, called maternal adrenal fatigue during gestation
- Shift work and pulling all nighters
- Pushing through
- Not taking a nap when you need it
- Financial stress

- Fast food
- Drive through coffee after lunch

HOW COMMON IS ADRENAL FATIGUE?

Although there are no recent statistics available, it is estimated by one naturopath that 91% of Americans suffer from adrenal fatigue. In 1969, a medical doctor who specialized in low adrenal function, said that he estimated that approximately 16% of the public could be classified as severe, but that if all indications of low cortisol were included, the percentage would be more like 66%. That was over 44 years ago, think how much more pressure we have on us now. That was before the extreme stress of 21st century living, and the severe economic recession, fast paced world we are living in. So yes, it's very common, that is why I want to help you know how to recover from it.

HOW CAN YOU TELL IF YOUR ADRENALS ARE FATIGUED?

You may be experiencing adrenal fatigue if you regularly notice one or more of the following:

- You feel tired for no reason. After sleeping all night you wake up tired.
- You have trouble getting up in the morning, even when you go to bed at a reasonable hour.
- You are feeling rundown or overwhelmed.
- You have depression or anxiety.
- You feel tired and wired.
- You are sick of being sick.
- You can't lose weight.
- You get headaches often.
- Your digestion is a wreck.
- You have difficulty bouncing back from stress or illness.

- You crave salty and sweet snacks.
- You feel more awake, alert, and energetic at 6-8 p.m. than you do all day.

You can also do a saliva lab test to help you determine if you are experiencing adrenal fatigue. See my website www. happythenewsexy.com or see your nearest natural doctor.

ARE THERE HEALTH CONDITIONS RELATED TO ADRENAL FATIGUE?

Yes, because it is stress to every cell in your body, and a hormone imbalance affects every organ in your body, you may suffer from chronic diseases, from arthritis to cancer, in addition to autoimmune diseases, diabetes, and other endocrine problems. So, if you are suffering from a chronic disease and morning fatigue is one of your symptoms, your adrenals may be fatigued to some degree. Also, any time a medical treatment includes the use of cortico-steroids, diminished adrenal function is probably present. All cortico-steroids are designed to imitate the actions of the adrenal hormone, cortisol, and so the need for them arises primarily when the adrenals are not providing the required amounts of cortisol.

ADRENAL FUNCTION IN ALCOHOLISM

A very common, but often ignored, component of alcoholism and some other addictions is fatigued adrenal glands. Adrenal fatigue may often precede substance abuse, and create physiological and bio-chemical conditions that can be conducive to addiction— whether the addictive substance is alcohol, carbohydrates, or stimulants.

For many alcoholics (and food and drug addicts) these conditions also tend to intensify their craving for the abused substance. Conversely, the adrenal glands can become fatigued by the continual overuse of alcohol or stimulants. In either case, adrenal fatigue may be an intimate component of addiction. Adrenal support can greatly enhance the treatment protocol for alcoholism and many other types of addiction. Alcohol and stimulant cravings are often driven by the body's desperate need for quick energy that may result partly from weak or fatigued adrenal function. For example, alcohol is sugar in an extremely refined form. This sugar quickly finds its way into the cells, forcing them to generate energy at a rapid rate. However, this sets off a blood sugar roller coaster and uses up nutrients that are not replaced by the alcoholic beverage, or the diet of the alcoholic. Although the alcohol consumption may temporarily compensate for some of the effects of low adrenal function, it also requires the adrenals to respond by manufacturing and secreting hormones to regulate the energy production, help balance blood sugar, and maintain homeostasis (balance in the body). As a result, the extra demands placed on the adrenals may further fatigue them, exacerbating the craving for alcohol. In a similar way, carbohydrate binging and the use of stimulants can temporarily mask, but ultimately exacerbate low adrenal function. I recommend that people experiencing adrenal fatigue DO NOT consume alcohol or stimulants, and AVOID SUGAR and refined carbohydrates as much as possible. The adrenals being fatigued leads to a depressed feeling causing the alcoholic to want to depress the feelings they are experiencing with alcohol. This is a downward spiral that no one should have to experience. If you are recovering from alcoholism make sure that you are replacing what was stolen from your body. There are many, many ways for you to be happy without alcohol.

Now that you know all about adrenal fatigue, let's move on to the glands and organs involved.

PANCREAS

The pancreas is a gland organ that is located in the abdomen, behind the stomach, and below the ribcage. It is part of the digestive system and produces important enzymes and hormones that help break down foods. It has an endocrine function because it releases juices directly into the bloodstream, and it has an exocrine function because it releases juices into ducts. Enzymes are produced by the pancreas for digestion and blood sugar. When these functions are disrupted and you're not healthy you can end up with chronic pancreatitis.

What are the symptoms of chronic pancreatitis? (Inflammation is always a sign the body is working harder than it should be to do its job.)

- Pain—the patient may feel pain in the upper abdomen. The pain may sometimes be severe and can travel along the back. It is usually more intense after eating. Some pain relief may be gained by leaning forward or curling into a ball.
- Nausea and vomiting—more commonly experienced during episodes of pain.
- Constant pain—As the disease progresses the episodes of pain become more frequent and severe. Some patients eventually suffer constant abdominal pain.
- As chronic pancreatitis progresses and the pancreas' ability to produce digestive juices deteriorates, the following symptoms will appear:
- Smelly and greasy feces (stools)
- Bloating
- Abdominal cramps
- Flatulence (breaking wind, farting)
- Eventually the pancreas may not be able to produce insulin, leading to diabetes type 1, with the following symptoms:
- Thirst

- Frequent urination
- Intense hunger
- Weight loss
- Tiredness (fatigue)
- Blurred vision
- Stress, anxiety, depression

The disease may have an effect on the patient's psychological and emotional well being. Constant blood sugar imbalance or recurring pain, which is often severe, may cause distress, anxiety, irritability, stress, and depression.

OVARIES

The ovaries are a key part of the normal development and reproductive function of women. They are a pair of glands (approximately the size and shape of an almond) in the female reproductive system where eggs are stored and estrogen is manufactured. They are held in place by several ligaments on either side of the uterus.

Many women are not aware of how important the ovaries are and how diverse their role actually is. This is one reason why PCOS can be so challenging: The hormones they respond to as well as produce have an impact on so many systems. The ovaries are sensitive to the effects and changes of the endocrine or hormonal system. They respond to and produce their own hormones as needed by the body. In fact, the second major role of the ovary is to secrete the sex hormones, like estrogen, progesterone, and very small amounts of androgens, which cause the typical female sex characteristics to develop and be maintained. In addition, the ovaries also respond to FSH and LH which are produced by a small gland in the brain called the pituitary gland. FSH, or Follicle Stimulating Hormone, causes the estrogen level to rise and a group of egg follicles to grow each month.

PCOS is the most common problem of the ovaries, this is where the ovaries, and in some cases the adrenal glands, produce more androgens (a type of hormone, similar to testosterone) than normal. While all women produce some androgens, women with Polycystic Ovarian Syndrome have higher levels of these hormones, leading to increased hair growth, acne, and irregular periods. This is also easily treated by hormone balance!

Ovarian cysts can be another problem in the ovaries, speaking from experience, they are very painful but usually go away without treatment. They happen during ovulation and if everything isn't just right a cyst will form. They are fluid-filled sacs, and are common among women during their reproductive years. They form on the ovaries, the almond-sized organs on each side of the uterus. Abnormal ovarian cysts may occur as the result of an imbalance of female hormones (estrogen and progesterone).

THYROID PROBLEMS

It's estimated that as many as 59 million Americans have a thyroid problem, but the majority don't know it yet. The thyroid, a butterfly-shaped gland located in the neck, is the master gland of metabolism. When your thyroid doesn't function, it can affect every aspect of your health, and in particular, weight, depression, and energy levels. Many thyroid problems are misdiagnosed because western medicine does a blood test, and if you are "in range" they say your thyroid is fine. I look at the inflammation of the thyroid gland, this means I ask, "how hard is it working to keep you in this range?" And since undiagnosed thyroid problems can dramatically increase your risk of obesity, heart disease, depression, anxiety, hair loss, sexual dysfunction, infertility, and a host of other symptoms and health problems, it's important that you don't go undiagnosed.

The most common problems that develop in the thyroid include:

- Hypothyroidism—An underactive thyroid.

- Hyperthyroidism—An overactive thyroid.
- Goiter—An enlarged thyroid.
- Thyroid Nodules—Lumps in the thyroid gland.
- Thyroid Cancer—Malignant thyroid nodules or tissue.
- Thyroiditis—Inflammation of the thyroid.
- Autoimmune Thyroid Disease.

Most thyroid dysfunction such as hypothyroidism or hyperthyroidism is due to autoimmune thyroid disease. Autoimmune disease refers to a condition where the body's natural ability to differentiate between its own good tissues, organs, and glands; versus outside bacteria, viruses, or pathogens; becomes disrupted. This causes the immune system to attack on the affected area, by producing antibodies. In the case of autoimmune thyroid disease, antibodies either gradually destroy the thyroid, or make it overactive.

You don't need to have all of these symptoms in order to have a thyroid problem, but here are some of the most common signs that you may have a hypo or hyper thyroid condition:

You get cold easy.

The thyroid gland regulates your body temperature, when the thyroid hormones are low your body gets cold. When your body temperature is low, many of the body's energy producing enzymes don't work well, and when they don't work well, every organ in your body lacks energy, and therefore doesn't work well.

Muscle and Joint Pains, Carpal Tunnel/Tendonitis Problems.

Aches and pains in your muscles and joints, weakness in the arms, and a tendency to develop carpal tunnel in the arms/hands, tarsal tunnel in the legs, and plantar fasciitis in the feet, can all be symptoms of undiagnosed thyroid problems.

Neck Discomfort/Enlargement.

A feeling of swelling in the neck, discomfort with turtlenecks or neckties, a hoarse voice, or a visibly enlarged thyroid can all be signs of a "goiter"—an enlarged thyroid gland that is a symptom of thyroid disease.

Hair/Skin Changes.

Hair and skin are particularly vulnerable to thyroid conditions, and in particular, hair loss is frequently associated with thyroid problems. With hypo-thyroid (under working), hair frequently becomes brittle, coarse, and dry, while breaking off and falling out easily. Skin can become coarse, thick, dry, and scaly. In hypothyroidism, there is often an unusual loss of hair in the outer edge of the eyebrow. With hyperthyroidism (over working), severe hair loss can also occur, and skin can become fragile and thin.

Bowel Problems.

Severe or long-term constipation is frequently associated with hypothyroidism, while diarrhea or irritable bowel syndrome (IBS) is associated with hyperthyroidism.

Menstrual Irregularities and Fertility Problems.

Heavier, more frequent, and more painful periods, are frequently associated with hypothyroidism, and shorter, lighter, or infrequent menstruation, can be associated with hyperthyroidism. Infertility can also be associated with undiagnosed thyroid conditions.

Cholesterol Issues.

High cholesterol, especially when it is not responsive to diet, exercise, or cholesterol-lowering medication, can be a sign of undiagnosed hypothyroidism. Unusually low cholesterol levels may be a sign of hyperthyroidism.

Depression and Anxiety.

Depression or anxiety–including sudden onset of panic disorder–can be symptoms of thyroid disease. Hypothyroidism is most typically associated with depression, while hyperthyroidism is more commonly associated with anxiety or panic attacks. Depression that does not respond to anti-depressants (which are bad for you anyway) may also be a sign of an undiagnosed thyroid disorder.

Weight Changes.
You may be on a low-fat, low-calorie diet with a rigorous exercise program, but are failing to lose or gain any weight. Or you may have joined a diet program or support group, such as Weight Watchers, and you are the only one who isn't losing any weight. Difficulty losing weight can be a sign of hypothyroidism. You may be losing weight while eating the same amount of food as usual–or even losing while eating more than normal. Unexplained weight changes and issues can be signs of either hypothyroidism or hyperthyroidism.

Fatigue.
Feeling exhausted when you wake up, feeling as if 8 or 10 hours of sleep a night is insufficient, or being unable to function all day without a nap, can all be signs of thyroid problems. (With hyperthyroidism, you may also have nighttime insomnia that leaves you exhausted during the day.)

Oh no, did you realize that these are about the same symptoms for adrenal fatigue. Don't worry; we will take care of it the same way.
Alternative doctors have a few natural treatments that can help reduce thyroid problems. The first treatment you can do to help reduce thyroid problems naturally is to exercise the thyroid gland. To help balance the energy in the throat, where the thyroid gland is located, perform this simple exercise. Lie on your back,

relax, and warm your diaphragm. Gently massage your abdominal area for about a minute. Put one hand on your throat and exhale and start making a sound with every exhalation. Imagine that the sound is coming out of your thyroid; do this exercise for 5 to 10 minutes a day to help reduce thyroid problems.

Another natural treatment is to get some sunshine. Try going outside within the first hours of dawn, if it's not too early for you, and look to the sun for ten minutes, of course, don't look directly at the sun. You have to go outside to get enough direct sunlight, looking through the window won't work because glass blocks direct sunlight. Like many health conditions, a change of diet helps to reduce the symptoms of many conditions or the condition altogether. Be sure you read the nutrition chapters in this book.

Kim's Story—

Kim came to me at 30, saying "my life is out of balance." She had her own successful real estate career and had been working long hours. She was on the run all the time and ate whatever was convenient. Add to that the stress of being a mom and wife. She was physically fit; she went to the gym several times a week and ran three to five miles every day. The first time she noticed something was wrong with her was when she was running. Instead of getting stronger each day, she was progressively getting more and more tired and each day running a shorter distance. Her heart also would just keep on pounding. It would even start racing while sitting in bed. She told me she finally had to stop running, not exercising, she had dropped from a size 9 to a size 5, was eating three large meals a day and a pint of *ice cream*, but kept losing weight. She told me she knew she was too thin. After about a month of tiredness and, now, full blown exhaustion, she decided to seek a western medical doctor, but they said all her blood tests "were in range." She was given an anti-anxiety medication that she told me she quit taking because it made her feel crazy, she even spent a night in the hospital because of the bad side effects and reactions to the pharmaceutical drugs. Over time she became sensitive to heat, and her skin became clammy. In addition, she was losing her hair and had lost the hair on her arms and legs. Six months after dropping to a size 5, suddenly, everything reversed and she started gaining weight. She went from that size 5 to size 13, her menstrual cycle stopped, and her pubic hair turned grey. In addition, months later, she realized her eyesight had changed. She had even been in a small car wreck because she didn't see a car coming and turned in front of it. She noticed her throat hurt, was fatter, and she was even choking. Kim came to me frightened. She not only had all these "symptoms," she was now in panic and had trouble sleeping at night because her heart was pounding so hard. Kim was a mess, she had a thyroid issue. I tested her on my bio-meridian (an FDA approved meridian machine) and found she was in need of help; she was in the chronic stage. I put Kim on whole food supplements of iodine, minerals, and glandular thyroid. Within a few days she called me crying, overwhelmed because she felt better. Why didn't the western medical doctors see what was going on? Kim had symptoms present, but her tests of thyroid function were only slightly abnormal; for example, her thyroid stimulating hormone was only slightly elevated, with normal levels of T3 and T4. Some argue that the "normal" range for TSH in most labs (0.5–5.0 mU/L) is too broad, I agree. In addition, the western medicine wanted to treat her anxiety and racing heart, her "symptoms", instead of fixing her problem, they just tried to cover up the signs of a deeper problem, so they didn't see the deficiency problem or how hard her endocrine system was working to keep her in the "normal range". Does this sound familiar? It happens all the time, symptoms are just the messengers to a deeper problem that needs fixed. Would you pay your mechanic if he cut the wires to the chime and put a piece of black tape over the "service engine soon" light?

"Let food be your medicine."

—Hippocrates

A few whole food supplements you might need are vitamins B2, B6, and B12, needed for all gland health, also, vitamins A, C, E, niacin, and folic acid. And the two really important nutrients most people are lacking are iodine and calcium. Iodine from kelp is necessary for the synthesis of thyroid hormones, and 2/3rds of the body's iodine is stored in the thyroid. Also, calcium is very important because as a chelate it promotes energy production and helps structure our protein in the RNA and DNA. It is important to break down fats for utilization by the thyroid, and a deficiency can lead to depression, hyperactivity, nervousness, cramps, and insomnia. Also, some women need a natural progesterone cream, lack of progesterone can affect the thyroid glands function. Follow the directions on the label and start using the cream about two weeks before your menstrual period. L-Tyrosine helps balance the thyroid gland so take 500 to 1000 mgs of L-tyrosine for 3 to 6 months. Fatty acids help the production and balance of hormones, which in turn will help reduce thyroid problems. You can take either flaxseed and/or fish oil, or you can eat nuts, certain fish, and seeds, to get fatty acids. As a supplement, you can take 3,000-6,000 mgs a day of fatty acids. In cold weather, take a higher dosage. It's okay to take oils at the same time to increase the effectiveness of reducing thyroid problems. Also you may need to help the pituitary gland heal.

> *I had hyperthyroidism; I want to share this with you in case you feel this way. I went to see Dr. Cammi last April and felt terrible when I first started her treatment. I had no energy and all I wanted to do was sleep all of the time. After beginning supplements I feel great and have more energy, and I feel better than I felt since my early 20s. And I'm sleeping again throughout the night. I was very skeptical about natural treatment methods at first. But I'm almost back to normal*

again and I feel great, and I'm glad I made the decision to try the natural protocol. I couldn't have made a better decision. I'm so thankful for Dr. Cammi because she really changed my life. Natural is the way to go. I'm off all my prescriptions and my moods are better than ever.

—*Norma Lee*

Okay, okay, we're over halfway through your anatomy lesson, go take a short break if needed, I know it's a lot but hang in there; we're almost done.

PITUITARY GLAND

Hypo-pituitary Overview

Hypopituitarism is a condition in which the pituitary gland (a small gland at the base of the brain) does not produce one or more of its hormones, or not enough of them. This condition may occur because of disease in the pituitary or hypothalamus (a part of the brain that contains hormones that control the pituitary gland), when there is low or no production of all the pituitary hormones. This condition may affect men or women, children or adults.

The pituitary gland sends signals to other glands (e.g., thyroid gland) to produce hormones (e.g., thyroid hormone). The hormones produced by the pituitary gland and other glands have a significant impact on the body's functions, such as growth, reproduction, blood pressure, and metabolism (the physical and chemical processes of the body). When one or more of these hormones is not produced properly, the body's normal functions can be affected.

The pituitary gland produces several hormones. Some of the important hormones are as follows:

- ACTH is a hormone that stimulates the adrenal glands (glands on the kidneys that produce hormones). ACTH triggers the adrenal glands to release a hormone called cortisol, which regulates metabolism and blood pressure.

- Thyroid-stimulating hormone (TSH) is a hormone that stimulates production and secretion of thyroid hormones from the thyroid gland (a gland in the hormone system). Thyroid hormone regulates the body's metabolism and is important in growth and development.
- Follicle-stimulating hormone (FSH) and luteinizing hormone (LH) are hormones that control sexual function in males and females. They are also known as sex hormones (e.g., estrogen, testosterone).
- Growth hormone (GH) is a hormone that stimulates normal growth of bones and tissues.
- Prolactin is a hormone that stimulates milk production and female breast growth.
- ADH is a hormone that controls water loss by the kidneys.

In hypopituitarism, one or more of these pituitary hormones is missing. The lack of hormone results in a loss of function of the gland or organ that it controls.

HYPO-PITUITARY CAUSES

A loss of function of the pituitary gland or hypothalamus which results in low or absent hormones. Tumors can cause damage to the pituitary gland or hypothalamus and can therefore result in a loss of function. Damage to the pituitary gland can also be caused by radiation, surgery, infections (e.g., meningitis), or various other conditions. In some cases, the cause is unknown.

HYPO-PITUITARY SYMPTOMS

Some people may have no symptoms or a gradual onset of symptoms. In other people, the symptoms may be sudden and dramatic. The symptoms depend on the cause, rapidity of onset, and the hormone that is involved.

ACTH deficiency: Symptoms include fatigue, low blood pressure, weight loss, weakness, depression, nausea, or vomiting.

TSH deficiency: Symptoms include constipation, weight gain, sensitivity to cold, decreased energy, and muscle weakness or aching.

FSH and LH deficiency: In women, symptoms include irregular or stopped menstrual periods and infertility. In men, symptoms include loss of body and facial hair, weakness, lack of interest in sexual activity, erectile dysfunction, and infertility.

GH deficiency: In children, symptoms include short height, fat around the waist and in the face, and poor overall growth. In adults, symptoms include low energy, decreased strength and exercise tolerance, weight gain, decreased muscle mass, and feelings of anxiety or depression.

Prolactin deficiency: In women, symptoms include lack of milk production, fatigue, and loss of underarm and pubic hair.

Sarah's Story—

Sarah came to me so frustrated with western medicine that she was unsure that I could help her. Sarah was referred to me by a friend of hers that bought her a gift certificate to see me. When I first heard Sarah and Jorins stories I honestly prayed for the wisdom to do the right thing as they were both very serious cases. Sarah had a brain tumor near her pituitary, and her daughter Jorin had an autoimmune disease, they both had the best attitudes of any of my patients. I was overcome how happy they both were and how they both lived in the moment. I had to be very careful what I gave them and every visit I had to change what the Biomeridian suggested they needed due to the ingredients of some of the supplements. I instantly had a connection to Sarah and her daughter and I wanted to help them back to health so bad. Sara's daughter Jorin hugs me every time I see them and loved the fact that I was a doctor without needles and shots. When Sarah called to tell me her MRI was clean, and Jorin's urine tests were good every day, it brought tears to my eyes. Here is Sarah's story in her own words:

"When I first went to see Cammi I was suffering from almost daily debilitating migraines. I had a benign mass (non-cancerous tumor) which generated pressure in my brain and created problems with my normal pituitary functions. At her office we did a bio-meridian feedback test and Cammi started me on a regimen of whole food supplements. In less than a week I was experiencing days with NO headache at all, which was something I had not been able to enjoy in years. As my pituitary functions began to normalize I found that I had renewed energy, increased ability to concentrate, better memory, and an overall healthy glow. When I went to see Cammi I had been battling migraines for over seven years, had brain surgery, and was showing signs of re-growth of the benign mass. Prior to seeing Cammi I had tried countless medications to decrease the pressure in my brain and relieve my migraines, but none had been successful and my neurosurgeon was suggesting another surgery and chemotherapy injections. I continued to work with Cammi for 6 months taking the supplements suggested with my bio-meridian feedback. In January of 2013 I returned to my neurosurgeon's office to complete my annual brain MRI and found that the mass was reducing in size. My doctor told me that the MRI was "clean" and that it looked good enough that I would not need to return for another MRI for two years. I feel healthier than I ever have and I continue to be migraine free! I continue to see Cammi to maintain my health!

I experienced so much success with Cammi that I decided to take my 8 year old daughter, Jorin, to see her. Jorin has an auto-immune disorder known as nephritic syndrome where her body attacks her kidneys. She had been on daily oral steroids for two years to suppress the syndrome but then became steroid resistant. Following the steroids she endured a year of immune system suppression medications that completely took away her immune system and brought with them a variety of side effects. My daughter's kidney specialist was not confident that Jorin could remain in remission if we took her off the immune-suppression therapy. I worked with Cammi to come up with a plan to support my daughter's system and we transitioned off of immune-suppression therapy and onto Cammi's supplement program. I am thrilled to say that Jorin has been in remission for seven months now!! During this time Jorin has grown and flourished. We have not needed steroids or immune-suppression drugs to keep her kidneys functioning properly, we simply follow Cammi's supplement plan that is specifically designed to address Jorin's needs. Prior to meeting Cammi our lives consisted of doctors visits, tests, surgeries and medications. I cannot say enough about Cammi's program and the happiness and health it has brought to our family!

Thank you Cammi for giving us our lives back!!!"

—*Sarah*

HYPOTHALAMUS

The brain is a major part of the body, as you know. The hypothalamus is known to control the neurotransmitters. Remember, neurotransmitters are the chemical substances which take the messages across the body. The body is known to have different reactions for different situations. If the hypothalamus is not working efficiently then there is an imbalance of neurotransmitters. The effects of imbalance of neurotransmitters are depression and other mental disorders. The hypothalamus forms the most important part of the brain. There will be a lot of communication gaps between the organs and the brain if the hypothalamus is not working properly. This may cause physical illness, and sometimes this may also result in seizures. Remember, one of the biological causes of depression is imbalance of neurotransmitters. In simple words, this means your hypothalamus is not working up to the requirement of your body. When the hypothalamus is not working properly, then wrong signals are generated and this will lead to misinterpretation between the organs and the perception of the person. This means "your mail is lost." This will lead to you becoming lethargic and slowly becoming depressed. This kind of depression is termed to be hypothalamus depression. This kind of depression becomes very difficult to diagnose because there is no external stress or pressure the person is facing and this makes it all the more confusing for doctors.

CAUSES OF DYSFUNCTION OF THE HYPOTHALAMUS

Just like the other glands, some of the causes are improper diet, substance abuse, alcohol, stress, vitamin and mineral deficiencies, and toxins. These things will lead to not letting the hypothalamus function properly.

CURE FOR HYPOTHALAMUS DEPRESSION

As mentioned before, the main workers of the hypothalamus are neurotransmitters. Neurotransmitters are chemicals which carry the message to different parts of the body. There are about 30 different types of neurotransmitters. Some of the most common chemicals which participate in the functioning of the hypothalamus are serotonin, norepinephrine, and dopamine. When these chemicals are imbalanced then the person is prone to get into depression. To treat this ailment, the body should be supplied with sufficient amounts of nutrients. Western medicine will prescribe anti-depressants which make the brain think it's working, but it's really not. They can't supply these chemicals to the brain; they are only a smoke screen so you don't notice it not working. You need whole food nutrition so every physical aspect of the hypothalamus becomes normal and works like it should. By doing this the functioning of the hypothalamus becomes normal.

TESTES

I was concerned about an ongoing "mental fog" and forgetfulness I had – which is one of the symptoms of Hashimoto's disease. I was having trouble losing weight and also felt very low in energy. Since following Dr. Cammi's recommendations I have found that I have a greater sense of calm – something I didn't expect from the treatment and changes in diet and lifestyle. In addition to getting my Hashimoto's under control, I have enjoyed other health benefits as well. I no longer suffer from anemia, my Vitamin D levels are normal and my immune system is strong. My thyroid blood tests also improved. Although it's a commitment and initial expense, it is completely worth it in the long run. Given the alternative (taking thyroid medication for the rest of your life), in my opinion it's a no brainer. If you give a natural treatment protocol a fair chance you'd be surprised at how much more empowered you'll feel about your illness and treating it. A natural treatment protocol is an effective solution that puts you in the driver's seat when it comes to your health. Traditional methods do the exact opposite.

—Marie

Men have testes, also known as testicles. The testes have two functions–to produce sperm and to produce hormones, particularly testosterone. They sit behind the penis in a pouch of skin called the scrotum. They are attached by the spermatic cord which passes through a cavity in the pelvis and into the abdomen. The cord contains the nerves and blood vessels for the testes as well as the vas deferens, which carries the sperm from the testes into the urethra; the urethra is the passageway for sperm to the outside of the body. The most common problem to the testes is physical injury. However, male infertility is a rising problem due to hormonal imbalances and due to reduced sperm production, or the production of sperm that do not function normally. There can be many causes including lifestyle factors, age, certain prescription drugs, and disorders of the pituitary gland can cause low testosterone.

So your hormones and systems look something like this, yes, it looks very complex and it really is, but it really is very simple and easy to balance. And we're also now done with anatomy section, good job, now take a breath and let's learn some more, just not so scientifically.

INSIDE SECRETS OF YOUR BRAIN

"The way to get started is to quit talking and begin doing."
—The Walt Disney Company

I am going to tell you the inside secrets of your brain. To have a healthy, balanced body in homeostasis your nervous system/ brain is the MOST important. We were designed by an all wise creator; we are not a random collection of chemicals formed by chance. Every anatomy class I have ever taken overwhelms me with how awesome our bodies work together in order for us to live. Life really is a miracle in itself. Our bodies are so complex and they are run by a very complex brain (the boss). Our ANS is the boss of all the functions in our body, it is very important you understand what your brain does and how to help it do its best job for you.

The Autonomic Nervous System (ANS) is the control center and "boss" for every organ and part of your body. When I see a patient, I know that if I don't get their ANS balanced, they will *never* get better, no matter what else I do. No matter what else they do, no amount of supplements, exercise, or diet will help if the boss of their brain is off. If the boss isn't at work, you know how much usually gets done.

There are two parts to the autonomic nervous system (ANS):

- Parasympathetic – You have the parasympathetic part, it's what you go into when you sleep or get a massage, for example. It's like the clutch and brakes of your body. This is the part of your brain that slows you down and relaxes you; it also controls all your body functions that work in a relaxed state. For example, you don't say, "Hey stomach, digest that hamburger I just ate," or "Hey lungs, breathe in, breathe out, pancreas balance my blood sugar, heart beat, liver detox, lungs breathe." Thank God we don't have to think like that, the autonomic nervous system is doing the bossing for you so you can think about other things.

- Sympathetic – You also have the sympathetic part, it is what you go into when you are in flight or fight. It's like the gas pedal of your body. It speeds you up; it controls everything to do with the fast-paced world. It is your energy and where Type "A" personalities tend to hang out. You don't say, "Hey heart, beat faster, and blood, flow faster," the autonomic nervous system is doing the bossing for you here too.

For health and balance, your body needs to normally function more in the parasympathetic state because that's when your body rests, and repairs. Your body is what we call in "anabolic" when the nervous system is in a parasympathetic dominant state (clutch and brake), and "catabolic" when the nervous system is in a sympathetic dominant state (pressing the gas pedal).

Anabolic is where I want you to be, because this is where your body is able to repair itself, you will have good absorption and elimination (digestion, bowels, and toxins are removed), you are sleeping well and wake with energy, you will feel relaxed but energetic, your muscles, bones, joints, hair, and nails will be healthy and look healthy. If you get an injury you will heal quickly. In addition, you will look sexy. In anabolic (parasympathetic) you will be able and want to train hard and recover quickly.

Catabolic is where most stressed people are, and this is bad because this is where dis-ease comes from. Your body is not able to heal itself, you can have digestive problems (IBS, acid reflux, heartburn, and indigestion) and poor elimination (constipation), you could have insomnia and you are always tired, you could have joint and muscle aches and pains, and you could have dry skin and hair. This is exactly why you get sick, and then get sick of being sick every time you are stressed.

ARE YOU IN SYMPATHETIC OVERLOAD? DO YOU:

- Have prolonged stress?
- Get angry easy?
- Feel prone to anxiety?
- Have sweaty hands?
- Have a fast heart beat?
- Feel weak and lethargic?
- Have a type A personality?
- Have mental fuzziness?
- Find everyday tasks hard to do?
- Feel overwhelmed with the plans you have for next Saturday?
- Feel fatigued?
- Feel wired and tired?

If you answered yes to more than one of the above, you are probably in overdrive in the wrong part of your nervous system. You can not heal or balance your hormones until you fix the boss part of the brain. This is very, very important; for you to heal the workers, you must heal the boss first. I know about this first hand, remember, I am more type A, I have a tendency to drive with my foot on the gas all the time. I have been known to be in a hurry to get things done and I rush and rush until life is no fun. The sad thing is, even when I know what I know, I sometimes let myself get into the sympathetic too much. The key is balance of course. If you are known to be a rusher, remember, even the army gives R and R days (rest and relaxation). Your brain and body need R and R too. We must be in the parasympathetic part of the nervous system MORE than the sympathetic to heal, make new cells, be happy, and look sexy.

Don't forget you cannot be balanced, feel good and energetic, or be happy unless you are in the anabolic state.

So how do you balance your body, so you function more in the safe, healthy, healing, parasympathetic state? You do everything in this book, honestly, you must do it all. You need to eat healthy, take whole food supplements, have safe sex, watch your stress level, exercise, do yoga, go for walks, get sunshine, breathe, and relax. People that have been in sympathetic for too long will need a strong adrenal gland support such as a glandular. Acupuncture massage, reiki, and chiropractic body work are also helpful in balancing the ANS.

A yoga breathing technique that is good for the ANS is Alternate Nostril Breathing. You block one nostril by pushing from the side with your thumb or fingers. Breathe slowly and deeply into the open nostril, pause, and breathe out through the opposite nostril and pause again. Repeat this pattern, breathing in through the other nostril and out. Do this several times, and last, exhale out through both nostrils, focus on your breathing, coming back to that focus each time your mind wanders. This will balance both parts of the brain.

If you are in sympathetic overload it's very important that you take vitamins and minerals daily to heal your body, I can't stress that enough. You also need to slow down, push in the clutch and/or brake, and take your foot off the gas.

WHAT ARE ANXIETY AND PANIC ATTACKS?

"You can be pitiful, or you can be powerful, but you can't be both"

—Joyce Meyer

WHAT IS ANXIETY?

Anxiety is a general term for several disorders that cause us to feel nervousness, fear, apprehension, and to worry. These disorders affect how we feel and behave, they affect our emotions and our actions, and they can manifest real physical symptoms. Mild anxiety is vague like the butterfly feeling in your stomach before public speaking. Severe anxiety can be extremely unbearable, having a serious impact on daily life. If you suffer from any stage of anxiety it is not fun. How would you like to wake up every morning feeling completely calm, relaxed, and confident? Would you like to cure your anxiety and panic once and for all without it ever coming back? Would you like to spend more quality time with your family, friends, and loved ones, without your anxiety affecting your happiness? Well it's easy; you just have to balance your hormones.

People often experience a general state of nerves or fear before doing something new, such as how I felt before my first live TV interview, these feelings are considered normal. Real anxiety is considered a problem when symptoms interfere with a person's ability to sleep or otherwise function. Generally speaking, anxiety occurs when the reaction we have is out of proportion with what might be normally expected in a situation. For instance, when you are scared to go to the grocery store alone or you are afraid to drive so much you stay home.

Generalized Anxiety Disorder (GAD) is a disorder characterized by long-lasting anxiety and worry about nonspecific life events, objects, and situations. GAD sufferers often feel afraid and worry about everything like health, money, family, work, or school, but they have trouble both identifying the specific fear and controlling the worries. With this your fear is usually unrealistic, but you don't realize that it is out of proportion with what may be expected in your situation. Usually these sufferers expect to fail, the why did I get my hopes up attitude is always there, and they expect disaster so much that it gets in the way of their daily life. These people are failing at work and school and have disturbed relationships.

WHAT ARE PANIC ATTACKS?

Panic is a type of anxiety characterized by brief or sudden attacks of intense terror and apprehension that leads to shaking, confusion, dizziness, nausea, sweating and difficulty breathing. Panic attacks tend to arise abruptly and peak after 10 minutes, but then they may last for hours. In addition, panic attacks lead a sufferer to expect future attacks, which may cause drastic behavioral changes in order to avoid these attacks. For example, staying home and missing out on things because they are afraid they may have an attack.

When there is an imbalance in one's thyroid, panic attacks and anxiety become a part of life. Thyroid glands are responsible for the production of hormones. Under or over production of hormones may trigger some physical symptoms of panic attacks like accelerated heart rate, nausea, stomach pains, chills or hot flashes, or shortness of breath. Also due to an imbalanced thyroid, panic attacks are also common among menopausal women. No one says that changes in hormones and panic attacks are easy to deal with, but they should also not be a complicated process. Proper understanding and the correct therapies can make a difference so people can lead a normal, stress-free life. Most people look for ways to just manage their anxiety – to get through each day with anxiety affecting them as little as possible. But why just manage it when you can fix the problem causing it? Do everything I tell you in this book and you will fix the hormonal imbalance causing these symptoms.

In addition, know that Philippians 4:6-7 says, "Do not be anxious about anything but let the peace of God guard your hearts and your minds in Christ Jesus." This is very good advice for anxiety in the Bible. The practice of believers is to take our worries to Jesus in prayer and leave everything to Him. Life today is full of many worries, fears, and apprehension, concerns stemming from making the mortgage to the weather, and we have a lack of anything certain anymore, in addition we have a lack of control over everything, our future, our money, our taxes, even our own family we can't control. However, the good news is you can have joy every day and we are supposed to be anxious about nothing. Through reading the Bible, prayers, and our constant faith in God, we can minimize worry and anxiety in our lives.

Stacy's Story—

Stacy came to me with anxiety, she said it had started when she was 18, she had just started college and was at a new school. She had her first panic attack in class. "It was terrible, my heart was racing and I felt like I was going to pass out or throw up!" she said. And after that she noticed it happening more frequently, but not only at school, at her friend's house, parties, the mall, crowded places, even at home alone. She described to me how she remembered a panic attack experience at the mall with her friends when all of a sudden she felt such fear and panic, everyone around her was blurry and time was speeding up, her heart was racing. "It was insane!" she told me. She had been to a therapist several times but was still experiencing the attacks several times a week. I tested Stacy and found her to have food allergies and a cortisol imbalance. She had a deficiency in minerals and vitamins; she needed endocrine cellular health and balance. I gave her supplements and minerals to balance her autonomatic nervous system. I also taught her what not to eat from her food allergy test, we eliminated dairy, gluten, and also sugar because of how it was affecting her. Within 48 hours she told me she felt calmer. At her re-check she hadn't had any attacks in 6 weeks and she is still on a good diet, supplement, and lifestyle program, anxiety attack free.

What is it that you worry about? What is it that you want? Do you worry about your kids? Your job? Your money? Your future dreams? I have learned that God will do as he promises; He will grant the desires of hearts only if we learn to trust in him and should not only lean to our own understanding. It was the understanding part that was so hard for me to learn, I know we say "but I don't understand why...." But we are not meant to understand, we are meant to trust. We are meant to have faith. And if we have just a tiny bit of faith, the size of a mustard seed, we can move mountains, and believe me this works. It has worked for me and every other believer. If we pray with thanks and remember everything is God's will we can relax in peace. The Bible promises that we will experience God's peace and we will have everything he wants us to have. So what if you are not married yet, you don't have the job you want yet, and you don't have the car or health you want yet. You will have it in the time you should. When you live in faith, it's not easy, but eventually your anxiety and depression will be cured. Believers are commanded to pray about life's worries and fears. When we pray we are reminded of the many blessings He continually gives us and His great love for us.

Pats story—

A few years ago Pat was so stricken with panic attacks he was literally a prisoner in his own home. He came to me because his wife made him; he even had an attack in my office. He became fearful of doing even simple tasks such as driving, shopping, or eating out at a restaurant. As his symptoms got worse and his panic attacks more frequent, he became frustrated, withdrawn, and depressed. Before it was all over it nearly cost him his job, his friends, and his sanity. Prior to this nightmare he was a regular, normal, happy guy. Then one day this life-altering problem literally came out of nowhere like a bolt of lightning to disrupt his life. He became fearful of many places and situations that had 'freaked him out' so he would avoid them altogether. What was his problem? Pat had been driving himself into mineral deficiency. Pat was a real-estate agent; he ate fast food all day long and drank coffee all day, he would go home stressed and have a martini and then wake up and do it all over again, for years. I helped Pat very quickly become balanced by changing his eating habits and adding whole food minerals to his diet. Pat was about to blow his stack every few minutes and he was on his way to hypertension.

"My condition became so debilitating that I actually thought I was going crazy. All of this created an enormous strain on the relationships with my family and finances. I couldn't hold down a normal job anymore due to my constant panic attacks. I soon sank into a depression-like state of self-condemnation, failure, and misery. In short, I was desperate. My wife, who has been incredibly supportive, eventually talked me into seeing Cammi. Wouldn't you know it—I actually suffered a panic attack while there too! However, that turned out to be a blessing in disguise since she was able to see what I was going through. Soon, with Cammi's advice and a bottle of mineral supplements, I was able to get my life back under control. My panic attacks decreased to the point where I was confident enough to 're-enter' society, I now hold a job and I lead a normal life again."

—*Pat*

WHEN IT COMES TO WEIGHT AND WRINKLES

"You can suffer the pain of change or suffer remaining the way you are."

—Joyce Meyer

Ok, so I believe that Happy IS The New Sexy. I do believe that your joy comes from the inside and your happiness comes from hormonal balance, and that when I say "sexy", I want it to be more about what and who you are, than about your appearance. I want to discuss the positive "side effects" to having your hormones balanced. Looking young and strong and sexy are the positive side effects to being balanced. We all want to be sexy, we all want to look young and be strong. We all want to keep the wrinkles away as long as we can.

Did you know reports show Americans spent **$61 billion** on weight loss last year, that's a lot! If you consider that reports say only 75 million Americans are trying to lose weight, that's $800 per person per year. Did you know that Americans spent only $3 billion on diet pills? That means $58 billion was spent on fad diet programs and schemes, most of which don't work, and most of the ones that do help you lose weight, don't teach you anything and you gain the weight back as soon as you're off them. The delicate hormone balance really affects everything from how fast we lose weight to how fast our skin wrinkles. The hidden key to shedding pounds has got little to do with calories or willpower.

Well, you have met your hormones, and now I'm going to tell you the surprising affect they have on weight. Remember that nasty cortisol I was talking about? You guessed it; cortisol is the devil here too. You have probably heard your weight loss is affected by the thyroid gland, and that the thyroid regulates metabolism and insulin, which allocates sugar in the bloodstream. But cortisol could be causing your weight gain and wrinkles too, as it does to me too if I'm stressing too much. And for men, low testosterone has been associated with a worsening of memory and mood, and more fat on your belly.

Our bodies, male or female, should produce more cortisol in the morning than in the evening, giving us the energy we need all day. In the evening, as we unwind and leave the stress behind, cortisol levels should drop by 90 percent. However, most people don't do this. We don't sleep and we don't leave our stress behind and unwind. I don't know about you, but I'm just being honest with you here, I have to "make" myself leave work behind, or my husband reminds me to. According to studies, excess cortisol leads to a heightened appetite and cravings for sugar and simple carbs, as well as increased belly fat. Too much belly fat is linked to cardiovascular disease, diabetes, and other health problems. We know cortisol results in greater food intake, what we think of as comfort food, which is usually high in sugar, or spikes your blood sugar. Also, serotonin, the happy neurotransmitter, which affects mood and appetite, needs proper blood sugar levels to be right.

Did you know there are at least 40 chemicals in our bodies that influence our appetite and what we eat? I know it sounds contradictory to what you have been taught to believe, but calorie counting really is not everything. The truth is, when insulin is high, your body will feel hungry causing you to eat more. Willpower is hard to have when your insulin and cortisol are high. This is why I stress a diet to keep your insulin low and balanced. It is very important you do everything I tell you to improve your hormone levels throughout the day, and don't forget to sleep well, and lower your stress.

As for the wrinkles, we live in an aging planet, with all the pollution, chemicals, sun exposure, loneliness, the economy, and much more. As you should know by now, when stressors hit us they disrupt our delicate hormone balance and this affects everything including how old we look. The effects of stress are often plainly seen and obvious. It is indeed possible to "age overnight." When we have too much cortisol, what is happening on a cellular level can change a person with a healthy glowing complexion, energetic body, and a great attitude into someone with dry, wrinkled, aging skin, dull gray eyes, weight gain, mood swings, and of course a frowned face. If you don't want to be healthy for your health, will you do it for your looks?

On top of it all, when our blood sugar goes up, we look old and saggy because cortisol, the "devil hormone," actually attaches to the collagen in our skin, making it loose and saggy. Cortisol also breaks down tissue all over our body. For example, it can break down muscle tissue, thins our skin, make our bones weak, and it elevates our blood sugar and makes us depressed. Of course, when blood sugar is elevated, we are in an inflammatory state, and this means every cell is inflamed causing dis-ease and any diagnosis that ends in the letters -itis, for example arthritis, dermatitis, etc.

When your skin is saggy it causes wrinkles. Extra weight and wrinkles begin with lack of sleep and too much stress. Remember, when we do not get enough sleep, it results in elevation of a hormone called cortisol, that is why people who are not sleeping look older.

Stress = saggy skin

DO YOU HAVE TOO MUCH CORTISOL?

You can do a quick check to see, all you need is your body and a tape measure.

We have two kinds of fat; visceral fat is the fat around and between your organs. Sub-cutaneous fat is the fat layer beneath your skin.

Excess fat leads to the "beer belly," "love handles," "apple and pear shape," and "muffin top" look, but it's not just a look problem, it's a health problem. Visceral fat is connected to insulin resistance, heart disease, and glucose intolerance. Abdominal fat, around the heart, liver, and kidneys, has been found to be worse than anywhere else in the body, in terms of heart disease and diabetes.

Are you at risk?

Get naked and get out that tape measure. Wrap the tape measure around your abdomen at the level of your belly button. Make sure the tape measure is level all the way around.

Men–A waist measurement of 40 inches or greater equal's abdominal obesity.

Women–A waist measurement of 35 inches or greater equal's abdominal obesity.

You can also do a ratio test, measure your waist at the smallest point, just above the belly button, and your hips at the largest point, then simply divide the waist measurement by the hip measurement. The total you get is the cortisol ratio.

Waist measurement ÷ Hip measurement = Cortisol ratio

Men–should have a measurement of less than 0.9.

Women–should have a measurement of less than .085.

If you are more than either of these you have too much of the dangerous belly cortisol fat and you are at risk for heart disease and other health problems, and this is a sign you have too much stress and too much cortisol.

Kids–You can also test your kids this way as well, measure their waist and their height in inches, the waist should be ½ or less of their height. This test can be done with any person at any age. This I believe is better than the BMI (Body Mass Index) test that doesn't take into consideration where the fat is located, but just looks at the % of fat and mass overall. If your waist is more than ½ of your height you have too much cortisol and you have too much of the fat that's bad for your health.

Stress = cortisol

Cortisol = old and fat

OVERWHELMED, ANGRY, AND CRANKY?

"Anger is one letter away from being danger."

—Joyce Meyer

Adrenaline and testosterone are a big part of an anger reaction. Adrenaline is a hormone produced by the adrenal glands during high stress or exhilarating situations. Again, this hormone is part of the human body's stress response system, and as I mentioned earlier, the "fight or flight" response. Adrenaline is what gives us a rush of energy when the heart rate goes up, it also gives us more blood flow to muscles by contracting blood vessels. In addition, it gives us more oxygen by opening the air passages. In a flight or fight time, we don't have good reactions and this can lead to anger. Anger can lead to dangerous situations because we can't and don't think straight when we have too much adrenaline. Excessive anger and stress increases adrenaline and cortisol. This increases blood sugar and risk of insulin resistance and can lead to diabetes and other heart disease. In addition, with too much anger every day, the good white blood cells of your immune system become depleted, leaving you more prone to a host of illnesses. As if disease isn't bad enough, anger leads to shrinkage of the brain, hurting your memory.

Now, I love adrenaline, and I am an adrenaline junkie a little bit, in that I love to climb mountains and be adventurous, but with too much adrenaline, we may have additional strength, but we also have "tunnel vision," meaning we can only see things one way. This is scary, because sometimes when we are angry, the way we see things is the wrong way. This is how anger and adrenaline can lead a person to do stupid things such as drive dangerous or even suicide. Hormone imbalance can truly cause you to feel angry or to throw your own temper tantrum. I know patients who come in very angry when they have an adrenal or thyroid problem too.

Here's the scoop, when estrogen levels drop, or fluctuate, blood vessels can change and that can result in the feeling of anxiety. When experiencing decreased levels of progesterone, irritability and anger often arises (usually with menopause). When a woman has high testosterone, anxiety is often the result. On the other side, too much testosterone may result in intolerance to stress and a tendency to jump to anger.

So, whether you are a Woman experiencing issues with irritability and anger, or a Man who is dealing with anger, doing everything I say in the 'What You Can Do' section will help! Some clients have told me I saved their marriages, when I got them both balanced. Dealing with anger will drastically improve your relationships with everyone. For many men and women anger is straining to their relationships. Hormone imbalance will interrupt your day to day life until you don't know who you are anymore. Many western medical doctors are very quick to prescribe medications for anxiety and anger and other mood altering medications such as tranquilizers; however, this does not get to the root of the problem, and usually causes the mood swings to get worse. It is important that you balance your cortisol and testosterone to avoid feeling angry.

In addition, anger can also be coming from the inside of our soul. Most of us get angry at something from time to time, but it's how we deal with it that is really important. Anger is an emotion often characterized by our dissatisfaction in life. It's defined in Greek as the strongest of all passions. Sometimes angry people come from angry families, they never learned boundaries or how to control themselves, and getting mad was what they were taught was the answer to get what they wanted. To get rid of anger it helps so much to be balanced bio-chemically, but it is also important to deal with anger God's way. Anger is not a sin but what we do in anger can be; anger does come from the enemy and when we get angry we need to remember it's just the enemy trying to keep us from our dreams. When I get angry my husband always tells me to simmer down, and in Timothy, Paul told Timothy to be calm and to keep performing his duties. We all need to remember this advice. When we get angry, we should all simmer down and keep ourselves calm, cool, and collected.

Being overwhelmed is usually our own fault, we create our own schedules and when we are overwhelmed it's usually because we didn't use our boundaries. I have a problem with this, and often I have to take some off my plate so I don't get overwhelmed. When we are overwhelmed, we also make more adrenaline because our adrenals are stressed, therefore being overwhelmed is usually the cause of anger. We get upset when we can't handle all we have to do and all that is coming at us. The truth is, we can do something about it all, we can practice boundaries.

Disappointment = adrenaline and testosterone

Adrenaline and testosterone = anger

Anger = danger

PMS, PREGNANCY, AND POSTPARTUM

"You cannot expect victory and plan for defeat."

—Joel Osteen

PMS (PRE-MENSTRUAL SYMPTOMS)

You know, referred to as that time of the month. You may be one of the 35 million women that suffer from PMS symptoms. However, I don't agree that this is an excuse to have mood swings either. I know you may feel emotional, and the menstrual cycle is not a steady straight line where your mood and personality stays the same. I believe that PMS is the result of a nutritional imbalance, and that if you make the changes in your diet and lifestyle I suggest, you can reduce, if not eliminate, those pesky PMS symptoms. Even birth control pills are sometimes used as a PMS medication, because they contain synthetic hormones that prevent ovulation and keep hormonal levels relatively stable throughout the month. The thought process being that no change in hormonal levels could mean no PMS symptoms. Also, lower levels of estrogen may play a role in the lower levels of serotonin. This is not the case with many women. I can honestly say, and you can ask my husband, I don't have PMS and I'm happy about this.

Though turning to an over-the-counter or prescription drug may seem to be an easy solution, it only masks the root of your PMS symptoms and does little to solve your monthly suffering for good. Many researchers believe that mood swings and other symptoms of PMS are caused by low levels of serotonin circulating in the blood stream. Serotonin transmits signals between nerves in the brain and body helping to regulate mood, sleep cycles, and appetite. Low levels of serotonin are found in people who suffer from depression, anxiety, sleep disorders, and eating disorders. In order to help women avoid PMS symptoms, doctors prescribe certain anti-depressants that are supposed to prevent serotonin from breaking down so quickly. My question is, why not just take whole food supplements to help with the low serotonin and balance, remember, anti-depressants are the enemy. I recommend 5-htp all month long if your moods are severe, or take it a week before you are to start your cycle if you know you have PMS symptoms.

5-htp is manufactured differently and believed to be a safe alternative to tryptophan and a safe alternative to PMS medications such as anti-depressants. It has been shown in clinical studies to be a promising anti-depressant, since continued use increases levels of serotonin. And there are NO side effects associated with it like there is from a prescription anti-depressant. I also recommend you take a multi-vitamin, vitamin D, magnesium, and calcium, these are great to take to help relax muscles and help cramps. You can also have a warm glass of herbal tea (caution, don't take if you are on prescriptions). Try a nice cup of red raspberry, chamomile, catnip, and partridge berry teas for PMS. You can also take valerian, for its relaxing properties, and dandelion leaf tea, because it acts as a diuretic (do not drink if you are taking prescription diuretics). See my answers chapter for other supplements you should take.

PCOS–If you have PCOS please read my kindle edition book *Beat PCOS and Boost Fertility* (Fit Expert Series–Book 8)

BIRTH CONTROL

Another thing that we throw at and into our bodies is birth control. We have many options from pills, to shots, to IUD's. Some options are better than others; all of them will affect a woman's hormones in some way. All medications can have side effects for some of the people using them. The most common birth control pill side effects are breakthrough bleeding, breast tenderness, nausea, mood swings, and headaches. And for a few women, the pill may cause some weight gain, often due to fluid retention.

The Pill–Like many other things in our society, the contraceptive pill is a quick-fix. And it's not even really a fix. It's meant to help you enjoy sex without getting pregnant, but with the side effects to a woman's hormonal imbalance, and also the fact that it can kill a woman's libido, it actually works against its own claims, it does no good helping you not get pregnant if you have no libido and don't want to have sex anyway.

Turns out, the Pill can affect everything from your bones, your brain, and your moods. The Pill works by tricking your body (by adding artificial estrogen and progesterone hormones) into thinking it has already ovulated. In other words, your ovaries don't release a monthly egg. The process sounds simple, and it's great that it works, but years of extra hormones floating through your bloodstream can do much more than just turn off reproduction. This extra amount of estrogen has been linked to certain estrogen cancers. In my opinion you shouldn't be adding artificial chemical hormones to your blood. I don't advocate the use of birth control pills. Yes, they are effective at preventing unwanted pregnancies, but the risks far outweigh those benefits. There are numerous safe and effective ways to prevent pregnancy. In addition to your health, your hormonal imbalance can cause a low sex drive low, or even worse, no sex drive, and cause your hormones to go out-of-whack, making your relationship suffer, not to mention a waste of money. Oral contraceptives also increase cortisol levels.

Estrogen in the pill side effects are:

- Weight gain
- Mood swings
- Breast tenderness
- Increased risk of breast and cervical cancers
- Increased risk of blood clotting, heart attack, and stroke
- Migraines
- Gall bladder disease
- Increased blood pressure
- Breast cancer

The Depo Shot–Also an option, but because of the side effects, I don't recommend it either. In addition to all the birth control pill negatives, it also increases the risk of osteoporosis.

IUD's–In my opinion, birth control is a necessity for some of us and we all live in the real world, there is a need for it for sure. None of our choices, except a vasectomy for your mate, are healthy and great, but some are better than others. IUD's are good for long term and better than releasing your hormones into the blood daily. For many, and maybe most women, IUD's create stress on the body. It is a foreign object in the uterus. All stressors, and I'm speaking in the physiological sense, have the same reaction in the body. The HPA axis or (hypothalamic pituitary adrenal) is responsible for cortisol production and release from the adrenal cortex. This in turn causes immune suppression, muscle breakdown, and weight gain. However, excess cortisol may occur when the stressor is continuous, such as an IUD, this causes excess fat stores, particularly in the abdomen/trunk and face.

There are two types of intrauterine devices (IUDs) available:

Progestin-Releasing (Mirena)–This type of IUD can remain in the uterus for up to 5 years. As soon as it is in place, it starts releasing small amounts of the hormone levonorgestrel into your uterus. It is estrogen-free, but not hormone free. It releases small amounts of a progestin hormone found in many birth control pills into your uterus at a slow and steady rate (up to 5 years). Only very small amounts of hormone enter your blood, but this can still cause a hormonal imbalance. On the other side, many women find this helpful when they are low in progestins.

Copper-Releasing (ParaGard)–This type of IUD can remain in the uterus for up to 10 years. Copper ions released by the IUD are toxic to sperm, thus preventing fertilization. I recommend this as the safest, because the copper doesn't contain hormones. However, there are still side effects to it. First, you can be allergic to copper, and second, you can get metal toxins from it. Some people also experience other side effects too.

It's a fact: happy, healthy mothers produce happy, healthy babies!

Of course you know there are many hormonal changes with pregnancy.

Please see my article on pregnancy hormones at http://www.foxnews.com/health/2012/05/30/your-pregnancy-hormones-explained/.

POSTPARTUM

Pregnant women experience many adjustments in their endocrine system. With these changes can come a negative bio-chemical imbalance and cause Postpartum Depression. According to the National Institutes of Health (NIH), postpartum depression affects around 10 to 15% of women a few weeks to a year after they give birth. Symptoms include feeling restless, anxious, sad, having a sense of worthlessness, and sometimes worrying about hurting themselves or their babies. Women in depression are unable to take care of themselves and function as a mother due to negative thoughts about their child and themselves too. Of course with what you now know, you know that this is caused by a hormonal imbalance. Whole food supplements work as an anti-depressant, therapy is also used to remove anxiety, agitation, sleeplessness, sadness, and nervousness. Whole foods are the perfect help for postpartum women to remove their depression completely in a natural way and in very short time. Proper care, healthy diet, regular exercise, and positive thinking can keep new mothers away from all type of depression.

Baby blues:
Occurrence: 80% of new mothers
Onset: Up until third week postpartum.
Signs: moodiness, weepiness, nervousness, sleeplessness.
Treatment: Resolves on its own, though increased communication with caring people and catching up on lost sleep helps.

Postpartum Stress Syndrome:
Occurrence: One in five new mothers
Onset: From birth until about 3 months postpartum.
Signs: anxiety, self-doubt, helplessness, frequent crying, frustration, irritability, negative feelings.
Treatment: I recommend whole food supplements of vitamins and minerals to help the body balance. The body becomes deficient during pregnancy and this will give the body what it is lacking to be balanced. Recovery is hastened when a woman nurtures herself and reduces her standards of performance and demands on herself during this time.

Postpartum Depression:
Occurrence: 15 -20% of new moms
Onset: from 3 weeks postpartum to one year; average 3-6 months.
Signs: depression, frequent crying, difficulty concentrating, difficulty sleeping, lack of energy, reduced interest in marital relations, reduced appetite or binge eating (carbohydrate cravings), irritability, anger, yelling, feelings of lack of control, and hopelessness.

Treatment: Treatments such as talk therapy, good diet, and vitamins and minerals are a MUST!

Implications for future: May recur with succeeding childbirths. Women should be aware that preventive therapies are needed.

Postpartum Psychosis:

Incidence: 1 in 1,000 new mothers

Occurrence: within the first 2 weeks postpartum

Signs: hearing voices or sounds no one else hears, thoughts of hurting oneself or baby, no sleep in 48 hours, cannot care for baby or self, rapid weight loss without trying; can't control thoughts, as if someone else were controlling her thoughts and actions.

Treatment: Same as postpartum depression with more emphasis on mental care and watch over the children.

Implications for future: Should be under joint psychiatric/obstetric care during next pregnancy and postpartum.

High levels of cortisol (the stress hormone responsible for the body's fight-or-flight response) in pregnancy are associated with babies who cry more and sleep less after birth. Chronic stress in pregnancy has also been linked with low birth weight in babies. It's therefore in everyone's interests for Mom to pay extra attention to her emotional state, making relaxation and stress reduction two of her top priorities. Sometimes, despite our best efforts, life is stressful during pregnancy. If this is the case for you, then be sure to take time out regularly to do something that soothes you—be it yoga, meditation, listening to your favorite music, watching your favorite TV show, or taking a warm bubble bath. It is important for Mom to keep her own gas tank full. The simple act of relaxing will alter the chemical composition of your blood, reducing cortisol levels and improving immune function. Not only is this good for your baby's developing nervous and immune systems, but you will feel stronger and less frazzled, particularly as you contend with the dramatic physical changes of the third trimester. Mom will of course also want to keep her energy levels up in preparation for the birth and to care for a new baby. Now is the time for the whole family to pull together and help Mom and the baby be as healthy and happy as possible. Mom needs to eat well and get plenty of rest, and everyone in the family help by reminding her to take her pregnancy supplements, and by helping her to remain as calm and relaxed as possible. If you are pregnant or know someone who is, make sure that they start eating and taking supplements as I recommend, and make sure they have this book and do everything in it too.

Another problem of imbalance is infertility, which is when a woman cannot get pregnant after one year of trying. I have helped many women get pregnant when they couldn't, including my own sister in law. Infertility is also just a bio-chemical imbalance; the body just needs nutrients and a healthy lifestyle to have a healthy pregnancy. Usually the common cause of infertility is an irregular cycle, PCOS, problems with the pituitary gland, and ovary deficiency. It can also be a symptom of a hypo or hyper thyroid gland, blood sugar issues, obesity, and, occasionally, just stress of the adrenal glands. If you are struggling and infertility is heavy on your heart, I really advise that you eat the diet I recommend and you take the supplements listed in this book to balance yourself, you can help your body to get balanced for a healthy pregnancy.

LAUGH, CRY, OR BOTH?

"Male menopause is a lot more fun than female menopause. With female menopause you gain weight and get hot flashes. Male menopause–you get to date young girls and drive motorcycles."

—Rita Rudner

For women it's menopause, for men its andropause, and it occurs naturally at the end of everyone's reproductive life. For women it's easy to admit the change, for a guy, it is always hard to admit weakness, and even more so when that weakness affects sexual activity. *It's natural*, why not treat it in a natural way? Menopause and andropouse can happen at any age these days with all the medical procedures causing medical menopause. However, it is most often something that happens between the ages of 42 and 55. Many factors play into when you will experience it. Western medicine doesn't look at this change as natural; they see it as a disease that needs a drug. Therefore, the most often treatment prescribed is hormone replacement therapy (HRT), however, since we now know that HRT is synthetic (chemical made) estrogen and progestin, and we know it increases the risk of breast cancer and heart disease, many women want another answer. In the 60's, women were thought to be "crazy," and in the 80's, HRT became popular with a Big drug push, HRT was called the magical "fountain of youth," women were told it would prevent memory loss and bone deterioration. The truth came in 2002 when the HRT drug did not prevent aging, but in fact, caused cancer. A federal study done in 2002 revealed HRT increased the risk of breast cancer, and many women got breast or ovarian cancer because of HRT prescriptions. In fact, I am passionate about this because my own grandma lost her life to ovarian cancer after taking HRT. With HRT, women's heart attacks increased 30%, and the risk of blood clots was found doubled. But this didn't stop HRT from being popular; many women still get prescriptions from their OBGYN every day. The pharmaceutical business is a business; a smart business, they are making a lot of money, and if you get cancer they will make more money off of you. In health pamphlets the pharmaceutical companies try to scare you into thinking you need estrogen so you don't get cancer; the truth is they are lying.

Bio-identical hormones have become the newest best way, and women are told they are safer hormones because they are made naturally, they are more identical to a woman's natural hormones. This is true, but I recommend that the best method is to balance the women's endocrine (hormonal) system and look at the other systems of the body first, and then if hormone replacement is really needed, it will be a very small amount that hopefully will not trigger cancer cells to develop. Although they are natural, bio-identical hormones are still hormones, and if taken in too large a quantity, or for too long, they can still stimulate cancer cells to develop. I look at the body as a whole, this means that in order to balance hormones you must also balance the nervous, hormonal, and digestive systems. These systems, when functioning normally with balanced bio-chemistry and balanced mental/emotional states, promote *total health*. Hormonal health is no different from neurological health or digestive health. They are all interconnected and what is done to one is done to them all. So balancing estrogen and progesterone levels does not lie in just taking potentially safer "bio-identical hormones," *but in balancing your nervous system, including the neurotransmitters. The hormonal system in order of priority: first the pituitary gland (master hormone regulator), then the thyroid gland (metabolism), followed by the pancreas (digestion and blood sugar), next are the adrenals (stress response), and finally the ovaries which produce estrogen and progesterone.* Women need to understand that ovaries are last in order of importance in the hormonal system. The first priority is the brain and then it works its way down to the ovaries. So I think it's much more than taking a hormone to feel better, but *balancing all systems and states in order of priority.* When this is accomplished, if a woman still needs to take a hormone, they will be a safer dose and less likely to produce cancer. Then, and only then, can the body be in balance.

"The change" is the result of our body changing back to lower hormones, specifically estrogen and progesterone in women. Andropause is the changing to lower testosterone in men. Many men and women experience symptoms with this natural change. As a women's body re-balances itself, it can have symptoms such as night sweats and hot flashes, vaginal dryness, bleeding, irritability, moodiness, and depression. Men can experience fatigue, forgetfulness, depression, and sexual dysfunctions. In addition, vigorous exercise such as running or lifting heavy objects becomes harder; in addition, men also have trouble kneeling or bending.

Natural treatment with herbs, whole food supplements, and diet changes, can offer relief in place of the dangerous HRT.

For Women–you will want to do the diet I recommend and you want to take whole food vitamins and minerals, iodine, and also you might want to add the following.

Black Cohosh–contains a plant-based estrogen that helps regulate hormones, offering relief to a wide range of women with menopause symptoms such as vaginal dryness, itching, moodiness, depression, and hot flashes.

Wild Yam Complex–is an excellent female hormone balancer and it works great as a natural menopause treatment for regulating hormones, especially progesterone. This hormone plays a role in controlling moods, and is used to help with depression, moodiness, irritability, and anger.

Phytoestrogen Foods contain plant-based estrogens can provide natural relief for women with menopause symptoms. Phytoestrogens are found in a variety of foods such as sesame and flax seeds, red clover tea, and fermented soy (avoid unfermented soy products); such as tempeh, and miso, help balance hormones during and after menopause. Be sure to only consume organic products that contain no GMO soy. Other foods with positive estrogenic effects are alfalfa sprouts, apples, cherries, beets, garlic, olive oil, and sunflower seeds.

Iodine and Calcium Lactate–taken together are very helpful for hot flashes and night sweats.

Tribulus–an herb cattle ranchers don't like, is very good for menopause symptoms and helps hot flashes and night sweats.

Both men and women want to use their diet and lifestyle as an important tool to help control symptoms. Avoid high amounts of caffeine. Also watch your sugar and alcohol intake as this limits your liver's ability to metabolize estrogen and weakens the immune system.

MALE VITALITY

"Growing old is mandatory; growing up is optional."

—Chili Davis

I see males of all ages, from teens to grumpy old men, and most of them have many hormonal issues that they don't like to admit to. They come into my office and whisper to me that their energy is gone, they are angry, they have panic, they have ED, they don't have the energy and stamina they once did, they are depressed, or they aren't sleeping. Men have a lot of pride with their manliness, most ignore for as long as they can the fact that there are even any issues or imbalances. It is finally getting easier for men to recognize symptoms of hormonal imbalances, I think, because of radio and TV commercials. Men are bombarded by media, by advertising campaigns, "Don't feel well? Ask your doctor about viagra." They come in saying they feel excessively fatigued, weaker in strength, depressed, have joint pain, and/or that they have lost their sex drive. These are all common symptoms of a drop in testosterone and hormonal imbalances. Testosterone, prolactin, and estrogen are some of the many hormones produced in the male body. Of all of these hormones, testosterone is responsible for maintaining and expressing male features such as facial hair, body hair, and maintenance of muscles and bones. Symptoms of hormonal imbalance in men are often easy to identify, but often ignored.

Testosterone is a hormone. It's what puts hair on a man's chest. It's what makes a man's muscles, deep voice, and boost his size; it's what makes a man a man, at least physically, that is. At the age of 40, most men have a gradual decline in testosterone. A decrease in sex drive, increase in ED, or change in mood, is usually a symptom. Some say it's just a part of aging, but that's not always the case.

Most men are overworked and stressed more than women, they just deal with it on the inside rather than letting everyone know what is going on with them. I think that most men work hard, and worry about the future and finances probably more than women do. The men I see are always in adrenal fatigue and are always overworked and undernourished. It is just as important for men to follow the diet, and lifestyle, I recommend in this book for vitality, as it is for women. It is also important for men to add supplements to their day. Not all men, but most, are hard for me to get to take their supplements; *they are too big to hold down, but we could always wrap them in bacon like I do for the dog*! I have found it easier to get a man to take their supplements if they have someone or something to remind them.

Stress can have the same effect as a cold shower. ED is a common whispered symptom in my office, but it is often misunderstood. It happens when the body has higher levels of prolactin, lower levels of testosterone, and an imbalance in thyroid hormone levels; a chemical imbalance of hormones that determine how fast metabolic processes occur in the body may lead to erectile dysfunction. In addition, because ED is a cardiovascular circulation problem, it is good for men to be checked or watched for other cardio issues.

Prostrate problems are common in men 50 years old and older. The prostate is a small organ about the size of a walnut, it is found below the bladder. The prostate makes a fluid that becomes part of semen. Sometimes men feel symptoms themselves, or sometimes their doctors find prostate problems during routine exams. There are many different kinds of prostate problems. Many don't involve cancer, but some do. Treatments vary but prostate problems can often be treated without affecting sexual function.

Signs of Prostate Problems include: frequent urge to urinate, blood in urine, painful or burning urination, and/or difficulty in urinating. If you have any of these it's a good idea to be checked out.

For Men–You want to do the diet I recommend and you should take a multi vitamin and mineral, and possibly add the following.

Rhodiola and Ginseng herbs – are great for men with any of the above issues, they are very good for chronic mental and physical fatigue and will increase libido and impotence, and it enhances strength and is good for performance.

Ashwanganda and MACA–are good for men that are wound up and run down, that wired tired feeling. Good for men that are exhausted because they "keep going". This is good for elderly men but **cautioned** if they have high blood pressure.

Hawthorn – is a good herb for circulation and cardiovascular issues. It is really good for men with high blood pressure.

Tribulus – yes, was for women, but it is very good to boost male libido, endurance, and stamina. Tribulus helps andropause symptoms by enhancing hormonal release from the pituitary gland, thus raising testosterone levels. This is also good for ED.

Zinc–a mineral, is a micronutrient necessary for maintaining the normal functions of the pituitary gland.

Saw palmetto–is a great herb to help the prostate, and will help problems that accompany male menopause and any of the prostate issues above.

Cranberry juice – is a great way to clear out kidneys and it's also good for the prostate problems that accompany male menopause.

HerbaVital–from Standard Process is a 5 herb combination that is helpful in supporting men with the aging process. It can help vitality and stamina and health issues that come with aging.

PART TWO

WHAT YOU CAN DO

"Happiness in not a matter of intensity, but of balance, order, rhythm, and harmony."

—Thomas Merton

YOU CAN HAVE BIO-CHEMICAL BALANCE

"My main goal is to guide you in developing the skills and tools you need to become your own best doctor, and therefore to make conscious healthy choices in your mind for your body."

—Cammi Balleck

- SLEEP! Make sure you get at least 8-9 hours of sleep a night.
- Learn to say "NO" to things!
- Do not over exercise.
- Do restorative exercises such as Qigong, prayer, restorative breathing, walking, very light/restorative yoga/ stretching.

Whenever you are not enjoying your life and it is draining you, remember you are in control of your own health:

1. Change the situation
2. Change yourself to fit the situation
3. Leave the situation

This is the chapter you have been waiting for I know. Or maybe some of you skipped the boring scientific, how it all works together section, and just wanted the answers so you turned forward to this page. Either way, this is the part of the book that is going to give you all the answers you need to be bio-chemically balanced regardless of your age or sex.

SLEEP! I'm saying it again, make sure you get at least 8-9 hours (or more if you need it) of sleep a night.

Have a well-balanced diet – focus on quality proteins, vegetables, fruits, and fats. Eat a variety of organic vegetables and fruit.

EAT GOOD FATS–EFAs (omega 3 fatty acids) to slow down the process that feeds into higher cortisol production.

Add mineral sea salt to your foods.

TAKE Whole Food Supplements every day and add herbs if you are chronic or at stressful times in your life where your body needs an extra boost. I really recommend Standard Process and Nutri-West brand supplements. These supplements are sold only by a licensed health care provider. You can find them all over the world.

Why do you need whole food supplements? First and most important, we need supplements because our food is 60% more nutritionally deficient than it was just 20 years ago. Standard Process, my favorite whole food supplement company, tells us that, "as a nation we are over fed and under nourished." As a nation, we eat poor-quality foods that have been stripped of nutrients. We do not consume enough fresh fruits and vegetables. We eat a tremendous amount of processed, pre-packaged, and pre-made meals. One-quarter of Americans eat at fast food restaurants each day. They are absolutely right; Americans are definitely overfed and undernourished.

> There is good news in that given proper nutrition, the human body has an amazing ability to heal itself.

That statement is 100% true, but to do so, we need to eat a healthier diet, exercise, and take high-quality supplements made from whole foods. Whole food supplements supply our bodies with nutrients we are not getting from our diet, all the vitamins, minerals, trace minerals, and phyto-nutrients that foods possess in a way that nature intended, in a whole food form.

Whole food supplements are made by concentrating foods for use in supplements. Whole foods are clinically designed pills, liquids, or powders that supply you with the nutrients your body craves. When processed correctly, they supply a multitude of the plant's components. Foods provide nutrients that work synergistically. They work together to provide you with optimal nutrition for good health. Remember, this information is just generic for everyone, your needs may be different. You should talk to a licensed health care provider that sells Nutri-West or Standard Process for an evaluation or contact myself.

There are many different kinds of supplements on the market, and it can be very confusing to determine the true value of a supplement. This is why I trust Standard Process and Nutri-West. Contact me at my website if you need help with your supplements. Understanding the label will help you know if you are taking a quality supplement. We often think that more is better when choosing supplements, wrong, quality is far more important than quantity. A small amount of a vitamin in whole food form is far more effective in the human body than a large dose of an isolated vitamin that is just a fraction of the whole.

You want to look for a manufacturer who grows many of their ingredients and has the unique ability to control the quality of the ingredient from seed to supplement. Certified organic farms further enhance the quality of these ingredients. Also, different foods reach their peak nutrient value during different times within the growing season. Pea vine, for example, is at its peak during the flowering stage. Once harvested, food begins to lose its value. If there is a delay of hours, days, or months from when an ingredient is harvested to when it's processed, many of its very delicate phyto-nutrients are lost. In addition, each ingredient has its own set of rules in relation to how to best extract and package its vital life. The manufacturing process needs to retain the vital nutrients within the ingredients. Too much heat will destroy enzymes and phyto-nutrients.

"Unless man duplicates a blade of grass, nature can laugh at his so-called scientific knowledge. Remedies from chemicals will never stand in favor compared with the products of nature, the living cell of the plant, made from the rays of the sun."

—Thomas A. Edison

I take a lot of Standard Process and Nutri-West whole food supplements daily and I recommend them daily, so of course, I agree with this statement. Did you know that natural whole food and herbal supplements can help to restore the body to a place of balance? This is the truth; however, it's probably going to take more than one thing, or even two. In fact, it might take between 3-7 different supplements to restore your health. A lot of my patients wonder why they still need supplements even if they are eating well. The sad truth is, even if you eat a healthy, predominantly plant-based diet with lots of fruit and vegetables, chances are good the food comes from soils that have insufficient mineral content. When foods are grown over and over again in the same soils, the mineral content of that soil becomes depleted over time. This is ANOTHER reason why it is so vitally important to consume organic foods as much as possible. Organic farming practices include "crop rotating" so that soil depletion does not occur. Unfortunately, even buying organic doesn't always mean you're going to get foods full of nutrition. Although organic soil can get depleted, buying organic remains the better, healthier choice. Also, if you are like me and live far from where the food is grown, a lot of nutrients are lost in the delivery time. I live in Colorado, six months out of the year the only thing we grow are hardy calves and ski bums. Sometimes, the foods we buy were picked weeks and even months before we see it on our shelves, so much for obtaining the maximum amount of nutrition. Also, if you are like me, you don't eat many raw veggies. Cooking does "kill" the food, resulting in lost nutrition. What's more, eating these depleted foods over time creates its own set of health problems. As we age, our bodies produce fewer enzymes, including all the important ones needed to properly digest and assimilate the foods we eat. Eventually, this results in "common" stomach complaints, like reflux, heartburn, upset stomach, and chronic constipation.

Stress + Stress + Stress = Compromised Immune System.

No question about it, we all lead busy, full lives, and some of us are busier than others! Between deadlines at work, taking care of your family, school, work, community, church, exercise, and other obligations, our lives are stressed. All of this stress takes a toll on our bodies, and as mentioned earlier, will weaken your immune system. Taking supplements can help to bridge that gap and give your body some of the nutrition it needs to function optimally.

Of course, nothing will take the place of eating a good and healthy diet. But taking quality, whole-food based natural supplements can go a long way towards helping you maintain a better level of health. Besides, if you're still working through some bad habits (skipping meals and not eating organic foods), you need them even more! Remember too, that it takes time to heal, you will feel better quickly but it is important to stay on and take whole food supplements daily. You are constantly making new cells to replace old cells. Old cells might have been made with insufficient nutrients, well now that you give the body the right nutrients, you will get new healthy cells. Any condition takes years to create, and although it won't take the same amount of time to feel better, be sure to give your body some time before you give up on nutritional healing. A rule of thumb is 1 month for every year you have had the condition.

I have known some people who take the needed nutrients and get very quick results. That can always be the case, but if it takes longer, just know that you will be a healthier person by continuing to give your body what it needs.

In the next several pages you are going to see a lot of big words and I apologize for that. There are so many brands and types of pills and supplements out there that the average person can become overwhelmed pretty easily. Also, some are better quality than others, having larger amounts of what you need and are looking for, not just trace amounts and extra filler. And while most employees in health food stores are fairly knowledgeable, how do you really know which ones they are, and remember, nobody is going to be as meticulous and careful to get the right supplements for you as, you guessed it, YOU. YOU are ultimately the one responsible for yourself and your health. Heck, you can even take this book to the health food store as a cheat sheet to help you on your way to tip-top health and well being. If I could make a list and say "go get these" that would be great, but unfortunately everyone is different. I'm going to educate you to pick the right ones you need, and don't forget the neurotransmitter quiz to help you select what you need. Also you can go to my website or see a health practitioner that sells Standard Process and take the Standard Process "systems survey," or contact myself. So here we go, let's learn about all those bottles on the shelves at the health food store and which ones to buy.

Use your results from the NEUROTRANSMITTER QUIZ in the beginning of this book to determine what supplements you might need. Remember, everyone is different and this is just a guideline, if you have a serious health condition find a Standard Process, Nutri-West, Nutrition Response Testing, or Biomeridian licensed practitioner to evaluate your body and see what you need exactly.

- If you scored high in PART 1, 2, 3, or 4, you really need to take a multi-vitamin and multi-mineral.
- If you scored high in PART 1, in addition to the multi-vitamin and minerals, you should try amino acids, the B vitamins, and 5HTP.
- If you scored high in PART 2, in addition to the multi-vitamin and minerals, you should take amino acids, extra

B vitamin complex, probiotics, iodine, and St. Johns Wart if you are not on any prescriptions.

- If you scored high in PART 3, in addition to the multi-vitamin and minerals, you should take extra stress supplements. You probably need a glandular and B vitamin complex for your adrenals, (I really recommend DSF from Nutri-West), and in addition, GABA or a cortisol balancer would be helpful. You could also try Stress Pan from Nutriwest.

- If you scored high in PART 4, you really need the minerals, especially magnesium and calcium, in addition to iodine. Also Kava-Kava (if you aren't on any prescriptions) and possibly a glandular such as Standard Process Symplex F for females and M for Males.

MULTI-VITAMINS–I recommend you take a really good multi-vitamin and mineral EVERY DAY. Remember the bucket, if you're not re-filling it, during the day you will lose your vitamins and minerals. These can also be taken alone for times when you need more strength and balance such as an extra busy month in your life or a time of grief. I really recommend Catalyn from Standard Process and Total Female or Male from Nutri-West.

GLANDULARS–meaning raw animal glandular and non-glandular tissues or extracts of these tissues that are normally dried and ground. There are many tissues, organs, and glands in the bodies of animals. Commonly available glandulars include the following: thyroid glandular, adrenal glandular, thymus glandular, testis, and ovary. Less frequently used glandulars are from the pituitary, kidney, liver, pancreas, spleen, lung, heart, brain, uterus, and prostate. You can find a glandular at your local health food store or on my website. Glandulars are great for healing the glands. When we take a supplement with the dried and ground animal tissue in it, it goes to our glands miraculously and heals our glands by making new cells. These extracts are used to replenish and eventually normalize adrenal function. An advantage over cortisol hormone replacement is that adrenal cortical extracts can be discontinued once they have done their job of repairing adrenal function. Glandulars can theoretically come from any animal, but most often they are derived from cow (bovine), while others come from pig (porcine), and sheep (ovine). I really like DSF from Nutri-West to heal your endocrine system.

AMINO ACIDS – are the building blocks for our bodies. When it comes to amino acid supplements–get one with all of them in it. I recommend a supplement called Amino All from Nutri-West; it has 18 different whole food aminos in it. Our bodies use amino acids to make many vital compounds we need to function every day. Amino acid therapy is a breakthrough in the treatment for neurotransmitter imbalance. Mostly people know about amino acids as building blocks for muscles, but aminos are more than just muscle builders; they also make up all those chemicals you learned about earlier.

Neurotransmitter imbalances have been linked to several diseases including Parkinson's, depression, insomnia, Attention Deficit Hyperactivity Disorder, anxiety, memory loss, weight gain, and addictive disorders. These neurotransmitters are formed in our bodies from amino acid precursors. Amino acids are the building blocks of proteins. Without the proper levels of these amino acids, we cannot survive, as proteins are responsible for the structure of our cells in addition to their function. It is important to supplement your diet with amino acids if you know you have low serotonin, but really, everyone needs to make sure they are getting aminos in their diet. Amino acids are also helpful to patients that have any kind of neurotransmitter deficiency. If you need more happiness and more balance, a good place to start is by taking an amino acid supplement.

Did you know that if you have neurotransmitter deficiency, and you go to the western medical doctor, you will probably be given a medicine that will only reduce the symptoms? Although effective to some degree in reducing symptoms, and helping you feel less depressed, in the long run, the medications can actually make the underlying neurotransmitter deficiency worse. These medications also have a side effect of suicide. For example, if you have depressive symptoms caused by low levels of serotonin, taking an "SSRI" medication such as Prozac, Zoloft, Celexa, or Paxil, is merely "tricking" the brain into thinking that it has more serotonin. These medications merely interfere with the body's normal metabolism of serotonin and do nothing to correct the real cause, which is not a neurotransmitter metabolism problem but rather a deficiency of the neurotransmitter itself. This is crazy to me. These medications do not stimulate the production of more neurotransmitters. In fact, there is solid scientific evidence that they accelerate the depletion of the neurotransmitters over time. This is why many of these medications only work for a short time and then stop being effective. There have also been deficiencies in several neurotransmitters associated with ADHD including dopamine, norepinephrine, and acetylcholine. Once again, conventional treatment of this disorder often involves the administration of a medication that alters transport of these neurotransmitters within the brain.

> *"On my 4th week of what I am calling my mood makeover, I feel like I am on Cloud 9, lately...and in Cloud City–Real and Sustainable Happiness is the Way to Go! I learned that I need to take care of me first, and how to keep my own gas tank full in every way and that is the difference."*
>
> *—Jenn*

Typically, amino acids can be obtained through proper diet in a healthy individual. However, in the presence of disease, such as depression or addiction, it may be difficult to obtain proper amino acid levels through diet alone. However, it is not as simple as eating the right foods. In most cases, patients with depression find that their depression lifts in 2 to 3 weeks. It is my recommendation that if you are on a prescription, that after you are on these for 4-6 weeks and are experiencing relief, that you work with your own personal medical doctor to taper your medications. When your body is working like it should, you won't need a high dose anymore and you can soon go off of all medications. Since all neurotransmitters are made up of proteins, the diet must contain adequate amounts of protein. PROTEIN. PROTEIN. PROTEIN. You must be eating meats and eggs daily.

Tryptophan, another amino acid, can be taken as a supplement too. This is the amino acid from which serotonin is produced; patients who have mixed neurotransmitter dysfunction probably do not get enough tryptophan in their diet. Supplementing with amino acids such as tryptophan, tyrosine, and glutamine, are important to take daily as we are feeding our bodies with the building materials needed to make the neurotransmitters serotonin, dopamine, norepinephrine, and GABA, among others. For this conversion to take place, however, we also need coenzymes and cofactors.

In the case of addictions, particularly to drugs and alcohol, an individual may have severe imbalances in their neurotransmitter levels resulting in symptoms of depression, anxiety, insomnia, and jitteriness, among others. This is often compounded by overt vitamin and mineral imbalances and poor absorption of nutrients through the intestines, causing problems in the body's innate ability to form neurotransmitters. By supplementing amino acids along with vitamins, minerals, and coenzymes, we can often re-establish proper levels of circulating neurotransmitters, thus minimizing or potentially eliminating side effects of withdrawal and healing the adrenal glands as well. Often, in the treatment of drug and alcohol addiction, medications for depression, anxiety, and insomnia are prescribed to quell these symptoms. Through altering brain chemistry these pharmaceuticals can be effective; however, the medicines themselves are affecting the body's own ability to produce and properly utilize neurotransmitters. By supplementing amino acids and supporting the body's ability to utilize them through nutrition, exercise, and adrenal support, the individual is closer to a balanced state of health rather than simply suppressing symptoms.

Anxiety? Most Americans that have anxiety and panic attacks that interfere with their day-to-day activities are treated with tranquilizers. In medicine today, most anxiety is treated with "SSRI" medications like Prozac, Zoloft, Paxil or Celexa. As noted before, these drugs merely trick the brain into thinking it has more neurotransmitters and does nothing to actually correct the problem. Anxiety, even if it has plagued you for a long time, needs to be fixed by fixing the cause of the imbalance.

And in case you have insomnia, PMS, or kids with ADD, all these symptoms are easily treated with amino acids.

PROBIOTICS–you can find them in any form at your health food store and you should take them daily. Probiotics are the "good" bacteria that normally reside in your gut. It is known that if these bacteria become imbalanced in some way (due to illness, antibiotic use, improper diet, or toxin exposure), a condition called "dysbiosis" results, which can have many dire consequences including decreased immunity, improper immune function, food allergies, Candida (yeast over growth), inflammation, indigestion, and numerous other physical disorders. However, until recently it was not known that these bacteria can also generate neurotransmitters that can also affect your brain, impacting your mental and emotional states. Researchers have recently discovered that good bacteria, such as ones found in probiotics, can produce neurotransmitters in the gut, yet another help in maintaining your neurotransmitter levels. This also proves true that many people with gastrointestinal disorders develop, or have one or more disorders, related to neurotransmitter imbalance and that correcting the underlying gastrointestinal disorder is imperative to long-term recovery.

"I was SO OVERWHELMED with the downward spiral my life was in. My marriage was on the rocks, my kids were not talking to me, I hated my job, heck I even hated myself. I was jealous of other people's happiness and success. Reading and using what this book taught me allowed me to be more effective in what I am doing and feel happy and fulfilled. My marriage is mending and my relationships with everyone are more peaceful. I realize now when momma's happy everyone is happy! I was hurting so bad, taking these supplements saved my life literally. It didn't happen overnight but every day I am a step closer and I am so thankful I know what to do now."

—Jill

VITAMIN C–This potent antioxidant has been shown to reduce the rise of cortisol and subjective response to physiological stress in human studies. Generally, a high-dose supplementation is recommended short-term as the bowels can tolerate. If you take too much or eat too much your bowels will become loose. Vitamin C is also good for the immune system, infections, adrenal and thyroid support, inflammation, and heavy metal toxicities. This is good to take up to 1000 mg a day if you feel you are getting sick or stressed. It's also great to help stop a cold sore (stress causes these too) when you feel it coming on. You can get it in your food from citrus, strawberries, kiwi, cruciferous vegetables, and green leafy vegetables. Women with fertility problems should take up to 3 times the dose as this helps prevent miscarriages. Vitamin C will strengthen the collagen and allow the egg to impregnate the woman.

VITAMIN B COMPLEX–B1, B2, B6, B12, niacinamide, folic acid, biotin, and inositol all should be in a good B complex. This is important to take when you are exposed to stressful situations, or daily if you are always stressed. This is great to take in the morning for energy and really helps with moods, fatigue, depression, stress, glucose control, skin, hair, eyes, and anxiety problems. It's also great for insomnia, hyperactivity, PMS (take extra a week before your cycle is to start), menopausal symptoms, alcohol withdrawal, and if you are on an antibiotic. So as you can see, most of us need it daily with extra on some days. Vitamin B Complex really helps to heal the adrenals also. All B vitamins are critical for all adrenal healing and daily health. You can eat liver, meat (pasture raised, grass fed sources), seafood (wild raised, no color added), seeds, and mushrooms as good food sources for B vitamins.

MINERALS—are very, very important. Minerals are the key to a blissful mind and body. The problem most of us have is that we don't eat the diets we know we should, and even if we try to eat healthy for a while, social pressure, work, family life, and temptation, will generally pull us back into a diet that is essentially inadequate for our body's needs and probably lacking in vital nutrients that could help keep us in peak condition and content.

Americans today are always in a hurry, eating refined food and processed food, refined products such as white bread, white flour, and sugar. These foods are heavily processed to suit our taste buds, but during processing, a lot of beneficial nutrients like fiber, minerals, and antioxidants are lost, especially in highly processed refined grain products. Manufacturers also add a lot of sugar and trans fats back in to improve the taste. They basically get rid of the good stuff and add a lot of bad stuff, and that's the reason those kinds of foods are really detrimental. In addition, the ground is very mineral depleted from years of crop growing. Even if we ate perfectly, our diets would still lack minerals. As a naturopath who sees patients every day who benefit from mineral supplements, I would highly recommend supplementing your diet with some today. Minerals are known as my highest-selling anti-depressant. In addition, if you are still asking, "Why put supplement minerals in your diet?" it's simple. Everything in your life depends upon you having enough oxygen and minerals. Energy, happiness, digestion, your immune system, your elimination system, your ability to use vitamins, and your body's ability to fully repair itself, are compromised without the natural plant minerals missing from our modern food. Minerals will also help you sleep better, and this will help your stress too.

Magnesium, Calcium, and Potassium are the most important ones we're going to cover. Magnesium is involved in over 200 bio-chemical reactions as a chelate for easy transport across cell membranes. Calcium and magnesium act synergistically in hundreds of reactions in the body, and they must both be respected and taken in balance. Magnesium is called the forgotten mineral by some. For instance, as important as calcium is in muscle function, the contraction-relaxation phase cannot operate without magnesium. Bones also need healthy balances of both calcium and magnesium. If you don't do anything else, take these ones. Magnesium is "essential to the production of the enzymes and the energy necessary for adrenal health." Be careful, some people experience diarrhea with doses of magnesium greater than 1,000 mg/day. A multi-mineral is a good choice for those wishing to supplement with higher amounts of magnesium and a higher Mg/Ca ratio than usually found. Potassium is a very important mineral because it's in every cell as an electrolyte. Potassium is needed for every cellular function and for metabolism. Potassium regulates the balance of our cells. Calcium works with magnesium for every function our body does. Maintaining balanced blood calcium is essential to our life. Calcium makes up 2% of our body weight and is not just in our bones and teeth, our whole hormone system needs calcium to be balanced. Calcium is very important for the neurotransmitters and is calming to the body and nerves. Calcium is good to take at night as it is calming and will help you sleep too. Milk, chocolate bites, or Tums, should not be your source of calcium, your calcium should come from dark green leafy vegetables and nuts. Look for a whole food that contains a balance of synergistic minerals. Look for the ingredients such as: Aspartic Acid Chelate (amino acid chelate), Phosphorus (as chelate), Calcium (as chelate), Magnesium (as citrate or chelate),

Potassium (as chelate), Zinc (as chelate), Copper (as chelate), Manganese (as chelate), Chromium (as chelate), Molybdenum (as chelate), and Selenium (as chelate). I really like Minchex or Mintran from Standard Process and Liga-PN from Nutriwest, remember, you can find these at a licensed professional office anywhere.

IODINE–The body needs iodine to live. Iodine is an element that is needed for the production of thyroid hormone. *The body does not make iodine, so it is an essential part of your diet.* Iodine is found in various foods such as fish, shellfish, and sea vegetables. If you do not have enough iodine in your body, you cannot make enough thyroid hormones. Iodine deficiency can lead to enlargement of the thyroid (goiter), hypo or hyper-thyroidism, and to mental retardation in children whose mothers were iodine deficient during pregnancy. Iodine is especially important in women who are pregnant or nursing their infants. Severe iodine deficiency in the mother has been associated with miscarriages, stillbirth, pre-term delivery, and congenital abnormalities in their babies. I really like Min-tran by Standard Process to help with the hormone balance because it is a mineral and iodine combination. A large percentage of people are iodine deficient and I believe it is because people are using less and less iodized table salt at home, because of the misguided medical advice to avoid salt. If you have any thyroid imbalances, mood imbalances, or menopause symptoms you probably need iodine. The great thing is that it works if you are hyper or hypo to balance you. Iodine deficiency is a major problem, I believe the drop in iodine intake might be contributing to many major health problems. Most of the patients I see are deficient in it. Low iodine can contribute to an increased risk of both underactive and overactive thyroid and hormone imbalances.

PHOSPHYTIDYL SERINE – cortisol balancer, great for weight control and athletic recovery, I recommend Pro-Cortisol Balance, from Nutri-west, is great to take if you took the test and your cortisol is too high or you are under stress, have anxiety, a recent surgery, you exercise or train too much, or you are gaining weight in the middle. To support normal cortisol levels, look for something like this or order online from me. Look for ingredients such as: Phosphytidyl Serine (supplying active phosphatides: Cephalin (Phosphatidylethanolamine) and Phosphoinsitides) 50mg, DMAE Bitartrate 50mg, Phosphatidyl Choline 22mg. You want to take this after exercise and before bed.

I wanted to do the "Race across the Sky", a marathon over the Rocky Mountains in Colorado. This is One hundred miles of extreme Colorado Rockies terrain — from elevations of 9,200 to 12,600 feet. I was exhausted from training so hard, I was frustrated that I had gained weight because I was going through some stress and training so hard too. I was extremely moody up and down to the point I thought I was bipolar. I would call my mom everyday crying an hour and angry or happy the next. I was very emotional, and I was sick with a head cold every other week. As I got my cortisol balanced I felt so much better. I wasn't bipolar I was just not balanced. The race was challenging, to say the least, but, I did it. My energy was great, my run was great, and my moods stayed great. In addition, when I got my cortisol under balance my joints started feeling better too.

—T

OMEGA 3–I recommend a liquid omega (Nutri-west has a good one), you want to look for one that contains: EPA, DHA, Flax Seed Oil, Black Currant Seed Oil, and/or Vitamin E. Get a good Omega 3 oil that has been molecular distilled, is pharmaceutical grade, is from cold-water wild fish, and has been independently tested for mercury. These are the absolute freshest oils available and should be refrigerated after opening to preserve this unique freshness. Omegas are good for everyone, and in addition to boosting moods, they can really help with chronic pain, inflammation, depression, osteoarthritis, and a healthy immune system. They also support the cardiovascular system, normal brain and nervous system development/function, kidneys, and the body's ability to regulate normal cholesterol and triglyceride levels. Fatty cold water fish: salmon, herring, and some tunas, are good food sources. Make sure you are eating good essential fatty foods and taking a supplement every day. Your brain is made up of 70% fat so make sure you feed it what it needs and it will work like it is supposed to for you.

VITAMIN D–is good for calcium assimilation and is good if you live where you have a lack of sun exposure. Vitamin D is the "mail man" that picks up calcium from your stomach from the food you eat and delivers it to your blood. Omegas are the "mail man" that takes the calcium from your blood to your bones and tissues. All the endocrine glands need calcium. This is why so many people have osteoporosis, they are deficient in calcium, vitamin D, or omegas; or the calcium is not being delivered properly. Your endocrine system is priority; therefore it will steal the calcium from your bones if it needs to. If you are getting canker or cold sores you are deficient in calcium, vitamin D, and omegas.

5 HTP–Is very helpful to take before bed or during the day. It increases tryptophan and serotonin levels in the body. From the essential amino acid tryptophan, it is the "immediate forerunner" to serotonin, a.k.a. the "happy hormone". It is great to help you lose weight and feel great. Taken before bed it will shorten the time it takes to fall asleep and will improve the quality of your sleep. It also helps stabilize moods and is great for kids or adults with ADD/ADHD. 5 HTP converts tryptophan into niacin (B3) and is great to alleviate depression and stress. It is also great for poor sleep, drowsiness during the day, restless leg, and bio-chemical imbalances. It will also help with weight loss and poor mental health. It is a great nutritional support for normal weight, brain balance, and normal sleep patterns. You can buy this at any store; just make sure it is a good brand. You can find it pure or with other ingredients, such as Total 5HTP from Nutri-west

(5-Hydroxy Tryptophan 50 mg, Pyridoxal 5 Phosphate 3 mg, Melatonin 1 mg, DL-Phenylalanine 12 mg, Pregnenolone 5 mg).

ADAPTOGEN HERBS–Adaptogen means that it responds to different bodies needs individually. If you're producing too much of a particular hormone, an adaptogen herb will regulate the production downward. However, if you're producing too little, it'll regulate the production upward. Whatever you need it will do for you. Isn't nature amazing!

CAUTION: Herbs should only be used if you are not on any prescription drugs.

GINSENG–Very good herb for chronic stress, both mental and physical. This is a great herb to take if you have fatigue and mental or physical exhaustion because you are stressing your body, or for any kind of stress. Ginseng will give you energy and it is a good adrenal gland helper. This is also a great herb for males or females; it is good for mood support but also really great for libido and ED. I personally have used it for adrenal fatigue and athletic endurance. It is a great herb to give you not just energy, but healing energy, not like energy from an energy drink, but actual strength because it is very healing for your body and mind. When I was in college I used this herb a lot in the morning to help with mental endurance. This is a good herb for your central nervous system and is good for shift work and if you are traveling into different time zones.

KAVA-KAVA – is a great herb to take for stress, but not necessarily good for depression. It is also an adaptogen herb that will help you adapt to mental and physical stress and help you sleep better. Kava-Kava can be taken by itself, in a blend, or with St. Johns Wort. This can be taken at any time of the day. It should not be combined with alcohol, or taken during pregnancy.

ST. JOHNS WORT–Is a great herb for mild to moderate depression and mood support. It is very effective in relieving depression without the harmful or dangerous side effects of anti-depressants and I have patients tell me it works better! St Johns is also an anti-viral and great to boost your immune system, and it's good when you are depressed because you have a virus. I have used this in patients with sexually transmitted diseases and found it to be very beneficial at getting rid of the viruses. Also, I have used this for Epstein-Barr virus and herpes and it works very well. You want to look for one with ingredients such as: Eleuthero, as it has been used for centuries as an adaptogen (balancer), this is a substance that regulates the homeostasis (balance) of the organs. Eleuthero also helps the adrenals function optimally and helps to increase the sense of well-being in psychological disturbances including depression, insomnia, and neuroses. I really like St. Johns Wort from Nutri-West or Standard Process. Or look for something that will supply you with: St. Johns Wort (hypericin) 400mg, Pyridoxal-5-Phosphate 5mg, Riboflavin-5-Phosphate 5mg, Folic Acid 100mcg, Vitamin B-1 10mg, Vitamin B-12 250mcg, Niacinamide 50mg, Calcium (as citrate) 20mg, Magnesium (as citrate) 16mg, Hyssop 15mg, Damiana 25mg, Blue Vervain 25mg, Ginkgo Extract 5mg, Ginkgo Leaves 30mg, Eleuthero 10mg (and take 1-4 tables daily). **Contraindicated when taking Anti-Depressants. Contraindicated (MEANS DO NOT TAKE) when taking Anti-Depressants. Do not take while taking any mood-altering drugs or prescriptions.** St. Johns Wort can also cause sun sensitivity, however, there is not as much concern with the whole herb. Ginkgo in large quantities is contraindicated with anti-coagulant drugs (only a small amount is used in this synergistic formula). Eleuthero in large quantities is contraindicated in hypertension. St. Johns Wort is also contraindicated in pregnancy.

MACA, MATCHA, and YERBA MATE – These are some of my patients favorites, you can find these at any health food store. If you are depending on to much coffee, try Maca instead. Maca is a root from Peru, it looks like a potato, and it offers an amazing energy boost for those with low energy. Maca however, unlike coffee, offers energy in a non-caffeinated way that supports the body. Maca is high in nutrition and contains high amounts of minerals, vitamins, enzymes, and all of the essential amino acids. Maca root is rich in B-vitamins, which are the energy vitamins, and Maca is a vegetarian source of B-12. In addition, Maca has high levels of calcium and magnesium. Maca root helps balance our hormones, and due to an over abundance of environmental estrogens, as you know, most people's hormones are a "bit out of whack". Maca stimulates the hypothalamus and pituitary glands which are the "master glands" of the body while it nourishes the whole body. Remember these glands actually are the boss of the other glands, so when they are in balance they can bring balance to the adrenal, thyroid, pancreas, ovarian, and testicular glands. Maca does not provide hormones to the body. Matcha and Yerba Mate teas, high in antioxidants, boost metabolism, decrease inflammation, and even have been shown to inhibit the growth of cancer cells, they also lower cholesterol and are good to reduce the bacteria in your body and teeth. Maca is the best for hormone balance but all these teas will give you a natural boost of energy and wellbeing.

KELP–is high in iodine, potassium, and iron, which are all essential for healthy menstruation in women. This herb also provides the body with many other nutrients, minerals, and vitamins which contribute to the overall state of wellness in your body. Kelp also has calcium, magnesium, and vitamin B.

ALFALFA–Not just for cows, is an herb which has eight essential amino acids. These acids are not made by our body so we have to get it from our food or supplements. Alfalfa is also full of vitamins C and K, iron, potassium, magnesium, calcium, and many other minerals and vitamins. This is a good green liquid or powder to add to your smoothies.

RED RASBERRY–drank as a tea, is very helpful, in general, to overall female health and balance. It helps to strengthen the reproductive system. It also reduces heavy bleeding during menstruation. It can help to prevent miscarriage situations, hemorrhaging during childbirth, and it is good for PMS, PCOS, morning sickness during pregnancy, as well as an increase in milk production during breastfeeding days.

EVENING PRIMROSE OIL (EPO) OR G a.m. LINOLENIC ACID (GLA)–are oils that come from seeds, like essential fatty acids but better. These oils help with PMS and weight loss due to the fact that they help water balance and cellular metabolism. They also help with depression where GLA is a deficiency, and are great for ADD/ADHA children and adults. They have also been shown to help all mental issues because they correct the balance of fatty acids in the brain.

BLACK COHOSH–is a natural estrogen and will not give any of the side effects which come with synthetic estrogen (cancer). The common problem of hot flashes and night sweats in menopausal women can be addressed easily with the help of this herb. It also regulates the bleeding during menstrual periods. Taken with ginger, black Cohosh also helps in getting rid of cramps during female cycles. Black Cohosh also benefits the other systems of the body. In addition, it helps to improve secretions from lymph glands, kidneys, and liver, and it also helps in the breakdown of mucous in the sinus cavities, and lungs.

TRIBULUS–another great herb for the endocrine system, is good to take if you are not on prescriptions and need a boost in energy, libido, or fertility. It is also good to take if you are an athlete and want to boost your stamina. This is the best herb for menopausal symptoms and male ED. I have also found this helpful in PCOS and other cystic ovary conditions.

RHODIOLA AND GINSENG – as a combination, or separate, these herbs work together to help with mental and physical fatigue and stress. Very good to help chronic fatigue, mental and physical exhaustion, depression, poor memory, concentration, adult ADD, and stress related headaches. Also good for high altitude sickness and jet lag or shift work.

BLADDERWRACK–an herb that is useful in stimulating the underactive thyroid is cases of hypothyroid (low) and slow metabolism.

VALERIAN–Is a good herb that is used for calming. It is a great natural calmative for anxiety or panic attacks, and is good for insomnia if taken before bed. It is also helpful for muscle tension and pain, especially stress related tension in the neck. In addition, it is good for headaches that are stress related.

WITHANIA or ASHWAGANDA – this is a great energizer and adaptogen. If you feel tired and wired or wound up and run down this is the herb you should try. This is my favorite because it is good support for the Type A personality (one who goes until they drop). This is good for men and women, teens and the elderly. It is not to be taken if you have high blood pressure. It works great with the multi-mineral and vitamins, and also with a glandular adrenal supplement for severe cases of stress.

FEVERFEW–is a good herb to keep on hand for migraines or headaches. Great to take for headaches associated with the menstrual cycle and even helps with cramps.

DONG QUAI – is a good herb for irregular menses in women and for cramps and pain with the menstrual cycle. It is also a big help to PMS and menopause when taken with Wild Yam.

CHASTE TREE–is a good herb for PMS, PCOS, Fibroids, Endometriosis, and Infertility. It's not just for women, in men and women it can help low libido, insomnia, and acne.

SARSAPARILLA–is one herb that works great for both *men and women*. It has natural progesterone, cortisone, and testosterone. Sarsaparilla helps in estrogen stimulation for women. This is a good one to start with for PMS and for male imbalances.

When experiencing a hormonal imbalance it is always best to consult an expert before attempting to balance these hormones using herbs. Whole foods anyone can take, they are just made from the food you eat, but, again make sure that you don't use herbs if you are on a prescription or pregnant unless you consult an expert. However, if you are sick of putting chemicals into your body, herbs are an excellent way to balance your hormones naturally. And sometimes taken with a whole food is the best help.

Other herbs are good at offering support during times of stress. My favorite is something with a combination of Valerian (root), Scullcap (herb), Passion Flower, Chamomile Inositol 40 mg, Choline Bitartrate, Niacinamide 15 mg, GABA 60 mg, Pyridoxal 5 Phosphate (coenzyme), and Thiamine Pyrophosphate (coenzyme). Also Ashwaganda root & leaf, Panax ginseng, Siberian ginseng, and Ginger root. All these herbs are adaptogenic herbs that can help to modulate cortisol levels, normalize blood pressure and heart rate, and increase metabolic rate by stimulating the production of digestive enzymes for protein and fat. You can take a combination or you can buy separately. You can also drink warm teas at night. For example, when I am really stressed I love to drink passion flower tea in the afternoon or before bed, it is a great stabilizer. The ginseng teas are great too and good for your adrenals, however, you DO NOT want to drink at night, as they will give you energy and keep you awake. It is best to do ginseng as a morning tea.

To support the Female body, I recommend something formulated to support the balance of the complete female hormonal system and corresponding organ systems, including ovaries, uterus, mammary, thyroid, and adrenal. Look for Standard Process Symplex F or Nutri-West Fem H, or Ingredients such as:

Ovary, Adrenal, Whole Pituitary, Uterus, Parathyroid, Stomach, Duodenum, Thyroid (Thyroxin Free), Mammary,and Placenta glandulars. In addition, you want to find something with Vitamin B1, Vitamin B2, Vitamin B6, Niacinamide, Vitamin E, B12, Vitamin D3, Biotin, Inositol, Calcium, and Selenium (as chelate).

And to support the Male body, you want something that is an all-around formula to support normal endocrine balance, male potency, libido, prostate, and testes. Look for Standard Process

Symplex M, Nutri-west Total Male, or something with bovine glandular or orchic, adrenals, pituitary, and minerals, in addition to: Vitamin A, Vitamin B1, Vitamin B2, Vitamin B6, Vitamin B12, Vitamin C, Vitamin E, Niacin 5 mg, Folic Acid 150 mcg, Selenium (as chelate) 20 mcg, Zinc (as chelate) 5 mg, Magnesium, Boron (as complex), Quercetin, Pepsin, Lipase (vegetable source), Amylase (vegetable source) 5 mg, MACA (lepidium meyenii), Panax Ginseng (root), Eleuthero (root), Damiana (leaf), Chlorella (plant), Passion (flower), Horny Goat Weed (plant), and Tribulus Saw Palmetto (berry).

L-THEANINE–As a calming amino acid, works by increasing GABA, which is a relaxer and creates a sense of well-being in the brain.

GABA–take at bedtime to calm the brain from over firing, or during the day if you are really having anxiety. GABA is another one of my favorites in times of stress. GABA is a great supplement to take if you cannot shut off your brain due to the fact that it is "over-firing" neurotransmitters. I use GABA a lot when I am going through a stressful time, or as my husband puts it, when I can't "turn off that switch on the back of my neck to shut off my brain." GABA is also great for menopausal insomnia.

MELATONIN–yes, a hormone, but also a supplement, is great to take if you are low in it. If you are not sleeping you are low in it. This helps with sleep and shortens the time needed to fall sleep. It is a natural hormone that regulates the biological clock, it is also great to help with jet lag and to take if you are working a job with shift work.

GINKGO BILOBA–a powerful anti-oxidant that helps to calm free-radical production and thereby protect the adrenals from the imbalance.

HORMONE SUPPLEMENTS–I recommend adding these last and only under the care of your doctor or natural doctor, but here are a few safe ones. **Definitely be checked with a saliva, or other lab test, to see if you need these before you start taking**

them, just because they are natural doesn't mean that they are safe.

Natural hormones for men and women–To keep one's hormone levels balanced, natural estrogen cream will sometimes be paired with progesterone cream or other products. Anyone who wants to begin using natural estrogen cream might want to talk to their physician about effective products, dosage, and whether additional hormone creams should be used. A physician will also be able to warn the patient of possible drug interactions and determine whether a natural estrogen cream will be safe to use.

Natural Estrogen for women–Natural estrogen cream is a cream containing estrogen made from natural materials. Many of these creams contain bio-identical estrogen, which means that the hormone is identical to naturally-produced estrogen on a molecular level. Natural estrogen cream is typically used to counteract the effects of menopause, reduce the symptoms of premenstrual syndrome (PMS), or increase low estrogen levels. These creams can be applied vaginally as well as on the wrists, inner thighs, stomach, chest, neck, and other areas. While it is possible to purchase natural estrogen creams without a prescription, users should carefully follow all dosage instructions and be aware of the dangers associated with using these creams. When an estrogen cream is said to be natural, the manufacturer typically means that the estrogen was derived from natural materials. Natural estrogen is not necessarily kept in its naturally-found form. In many cases, natural estrogens are manufactured from soy and yams. Some creams also contain estrogen extracted from the urine of pregnant mares (female horse). I recommend you look for a homeopathic water-based sublingual spray (under the tongue) at your local health food store or on my website. This is great for menopausal symptoms, PMS, crying, emotional bouts, menstrual disorders, hot flashes, depression, sleep disorders (especially due to grief, worry, shock, or emotional upset), fatigue, apathy, muscular pain and irritation, uterus/ovary conditions, infertility, nervousness, hormonal headaches, extreme sensitivity to pain and noise, cramps, and constipation.

Natural Progesterone-products I prefer to the synthetic progesterone (progestins) typically prescribed as part of hormone replacement therapy (HRT). HRT combines estrogen and progesterone to help relieve menopausal symptoms and prevent bone loss that could lead to osteoporosis. You don't need progesterone if you've had a hysterectomy and no longer have a uterus. If that is not the case, replacing estrogen alone can over stimulate the uterine lining, raising the risk of endometrial cancer. The problem with synthetic progesterone is that it can cause PMS-like side effects, which are usually less likely to occur if you use natural progesterone instead. Sometimes, natural progesterones are recommended to relieve premenstrual symptoms that may worsen as some women approach menopause. Natural progesterone creams are available over-the-counter.

DHEA (dehydroepiandrosterone) – for men and women, is a hormone produced by your body's adrenal glands. These are glands just above your kidneys. DHEA supplements can be made from wild yam or soy. Scientists don't know everything DHEA does, but they do know that it functions as a precursor to male and female sex hormones, including testosterone and estrogen. Precursors are substances that are converted by the body into a hormone. DHEA is a hormone that peaks in your mid-20s and gradually declines with age. Testosterone and estrogen production also generally decline with age. DHEA supplements can increase the level of these hormones. That's why a number of claims have been made about their potential health benefits. If you are low in DHEA it is helpful in building up the adrenal glands, strengthening the immune system, slowing natural changes in the body that come with age, providing more energy, improving mood and memory, and building up muscle strength for men and women. Since DHEA levels decline with age, some researchers speculate that supplementing your body's falling levels of the hormone might help fight aging. Also, some studies have reported positive anti-aging effects from the use of DHEA supplements.

Natural Testosterone—Is mainly for men but some women too. Many aging men with low testosterone report improved energy levels, sex drive, and mood, after testosterone treatment. Testosterone replacement therapy can have side effects, and the long-term risks and benefits aren't known. Only men with the symptoms of low testosterone, and saliva or blood test levels that confirm these symptoms are from low testosterone and not something else, should consider testosterone replacement. Talking with your doctor is the only way to know if testosterone therapy is right for you. The symptoms of low testosterone are sometimes obvious, but can be subtle. Testosterone levels decline naturally in men as they age over decades, and symptoms may appear slowly. Low testosterone symptoms include: low sex drive (libido), erectile dysfunction, fatigue and poor energy level, difficulty concentrating, depression, irritability, and a low sense of well-being. Some women are low in it as well, but a saliva test is needed to see where your levels are.

These are just suggestions and not a replacement for medical care. If you think your hormones are out of balance, you might want to be tested further for endocrine system issues.

I have several of these supplements from the company I use on my website www.happythenewsexy.com, you can buy them and they are already in the correct ratio for you. Take the quiz from the front of this book or online and see what supplements you need.

And, if you are curious about your own adrenal health status, again, contact myself or …Contact a naturopath, chiropractor, certified nutrition consultant, or other practitioner in your area to find out if they can run an adrenal salivary index test for you. NUTRI-WEST AND STANDARD PROCESS ARE MY FAVORITE AND TRUSTED COMPANIES FOR WHOLE

FOOD SUPPLEMENTS, THEY ARE SOLD ONLY THROUGH LICENSED PRACTIONERS ALL OVER THE WORLD. The practitioner you see will probably want to test you first to see what you need and I highly recommend that you are tested with NRT–nutrition response testing (applied kinesiology), a Biomeridian machine, saliva or blood test, or in other ways to determine what you should take.

> The person who takes prescription medicine must recover twice, once from the disease and once from the medicine.
>
> —William Osler, M.D.

KEY SECRETS TO BRAIN ALLERGIES

"Don't choose the one who is beautiful to the world; choose the one who makes your world beautiful."

Food allergies and intolerances cause more trouble than most people realize. Believe me, there is a strong relationship between gluten sensitivity and the hormones progesterone and estrogen. Additionally, most of my patients with gluten sensitivity have an adrenal hormone imbalance, thyroid problems, and blood sugar issues. Not to mention they are grouchy, and this becomes exacerbated for patients during menopause. With that said, let's learn more and talk about gluten (found in grains, wheat being the biggest problem since it is genetically modified) and the other culprits and their affect on the brain.

The most common food intolerances are dairy, eggs, soy, and gluten. Anyone can experience the physical symptoms to intolerances. These symptoms might include body aches and pains, stomach discomfort, headaches, mood swings, and diarrhea. People who are sensitive to gluten are also more likely to experience depression and anxiety. In fact, numerous studies indicate that people who are intolerant to gluten also experience more fear of normal life things, which can lead to increased depression and anxiety. **It's a vicious cycle that can, fortunately, be helped by removing gluten from your diet.**

Yes, food can give you the blues. When you eat food that contains gluten such as wheat (and even milk, eggs, or soy), the stomach breaks down the proteins into what are called peptides.

Those peptides in turn bind to the receptors in the brain, which then affect the central nervous system. When gluten binds to receptors, you experience a variety of "positive" feelings, such as mood elevation, numbed pain, decreased emotional sensitivity, confidence, and self-assuredness. Much like a drug, gluten-filled foods make you feel good in the immediate moment. But then, you will crash and you will feel more depressed. One of the challenges I have with many patients I see is they don't want to remove gluten from their diet because they have an emotional attachment to gluten food, such as bread and pasta. However, you can still have these foods gluten free, and research shows that it's not simply an emotional attachment, but it's an addiction. When we eat a food we are intolerant too it has a morphine-like effect on the body, much like endorphins. In short, the body becomes addicted to certain foods, like wheat, in spite of the fact that a person is sensitive or allergic to that food. In fact, many studies indicate that people with schizophrenia and depression may experience fewer symptoms if they stop eating wheat, as well as dairy products.

The good news is you don't have to live your life tired and depressed. All you have to do is remove gluten from your diet to help your depression and anxiety. Once you get over the "addiction" to these foods, you will experience a whole new life. I have heard it take 3 weeks to make a habit and 2 days to break it. Keep this in mind, I encourage you to eliminate all gluten from your diet for 21 days and then notice how you don't crave it anymore. In addition, I know this can be overwhelming for some, but don't worry; there is so much help out there to live gluten free (gf). All grocery stores carry foods labeled "gf" and even restaurants will show what foods are "gf" on their menus. You can even have gluten free pizza and beer, not to mention muffins, rolls, and pasta. You will be fine, I promise. Also, the internet is full of information, there are monthly magazines you can get with recipes in them, and there are thousands of other books to help you live gluten/allergy free.

> *"I quit gluten and dairy foods and I can now say I am living and enjoying life like I should be, I know I lost 10 years of my life in depression and most of the time in bed. Five months after stopping the foods I was intolerant to, I was able to go off of my thyroid, anti-depressants, acid reflux, and blood pressure medications.*
>
> *I now only take a multi- vitamin and mineral every morning, I have more energy and I have lost my melancholy, sad, face. I didn't know what happiness was until I got my body working right. I am now raising my grand kids and I know I wouldn't have had the energy to do that if I wasn't healthy."*
>
> —*Penny*

FOOD INTOLERANCES AND FOOD ALLERGIES

Food allergies and intolerances can easily be checked by an easy, non-invasive saliva test. Food intolerances are immunological in origin and cause different forms of hypersensitivity reactions. Food allergies are distinct from food intolerances—which are genetically dictated entities.

Food intolerances are diseases of childhood. Intolerances are more likely to be symptomatic in children but are found in adults of all ages, because they are genetic in origin. Food intolerances are perpetrators of ongoing intestinal inflammation, which may eventually exhaust the body's defenses.

Food intolerances are not only present in symptomatic patients. Food intolerances can be subjectively silent in many individuals. Nonetheless, they continue to drain our defenses and weaken our intestinal immune system. Food intolerance occurrence is underestimated in our symptom-driven heath care system.

Food intolerances are simply intestinal irritations. Food intolerances can be more than a local intestinal problem, and may increase the risk of autoimmune diseases and cancer as well as accelerate aging.

Manifestations of Food Intolerances include:

Malnutrition and Nutritional Deficiencies:

- Diarrhea or soft to loose stools are the most common GI tract (gastrointestinal, your digestive system) symptoms
- Intestinal hypermotility–accelerated intestinal passage of food which results in vomiting, spasms of the gut, and diarrhea
- Constipation
- Gastroesophageal reflux (severe or chronic heartburn)
- Malabsorption–inability to benefit from the food we eat
- Changes in intestinal wall integrity–allows foreign bodies and microbes access beyond the gut which normally does not occur
- Mouth ulcers
- Nausea/vomiting
- Gas
- IBS (Irritable bowel syndrome) Remember–You may have no symptoms and still have a food intolerance.

Beyond the belly:

Brain: Headaches, migraines, sleeplessness, irritability, anger, mood swings, depression, and schizophrenia

Skin: Hives, dermatitis, rash, eczema

Respiratory: Runny nose, asthma, nasal congestion, sinusitis

Anti-cancer defense: Folic acid deficiency

Changes in blood coagulation: Vitamin K deficiency

Anemia: Weakened red blood cells and/or reduced counts, which may result in fatigue

"The brain is highly sensitive to the wide variety of substances that gain entry to the blood, some of which can provoke undesirable effects should they cross into your amygdala, hippo-campus, cerebral cortex, or other brain structure. Once having gained entry into the brain, wheat polypeptides bind to the brain's morphine receptor, the very same receptor to which opiate drugs bind."

—Wheat Belly–William Davis MD

In menopause, especially as the ovarian output of sex hormones drops, the resulting hormone imbalance is worsened by over-consumption of gluten. The adrenal glands increase cortisol in response to the stress of unstable blood sugar and gastrointestinal tract inflammation caused by gluten. This causes increased body fat, fatigue, and unstable moods. PMS? It could be the wheat you are eating every day.

Do you know you could have a food intolerance and not know it? Do you know that this directly affects the brain? Do you know the brain is perhaps the most delicate organ of the body, and it uses 30% of all the energy we get from food? So it's no surprise, allergies to food can upset levels of hormones and other key chemicals in the brain, resulting in symptoms ranging from depression to schizophrenia. Sadly, our favorite foods are often the offending foods, so the patient is like an addict, eating the offending food to obtain a psychiatric high. For example, a patient of mine that had depression and a gluten allergy didn't want to give up her beer and pasta. She was addicted to the high, even at the cost of her health. I've lately been discussing with my husband, why don't people care about their health? It's so heartbreaking to me that people don't care more about their own health. Is cancer not a big enough scare?

"Because of wheat's incredible capacity to send blood sugar levels straight up, initiate the glucose-insulin roller-coaster ride that drives appetite, generate addictive brain-active exorphins, and grow visceral fat, it is the one essential food to eliminate in a serious effort to prevent, reduce, or eliminate diabetes."

—Wheat Belly – William Davis MD

Hay allergies runs in families and so do brain allergies. The allergic diseases have many presenting symptoms and common names, so the infant who cannot tolerate cow's milk may be starting a lifelong fight against allergies called colic, or eczema. You must know that studies show kids with ADD/ADHD have gluten and dairy intolerances and adults are also affected by food brain allergy. A study was done that examined 250 emotionally disturbed, depressed patients, for a possible presence of food/chemical allergies, using elimination and challenge diet, results showed that the highest percentage of symptoms seemed to occur in patients diagnosed with depression. For example, out of 53 patients diagnosed as depressed, 64% reacted adversely to wheat, 50% to cow's milk. I have helped many patients overcome mood disorders, panic attacks, and anxiety by eliminating the foods they are sensitive to. You can do a simple saliva food allergy test from my website or from any natural health care professional to see what your intolerances are. You can also just eliminate wheat, gluten, and dairy to start. I don't recommend these foods anyway. We are not meant to drink milk after we stop nursing and we are not meant to eat GM (genetically modified) grains either. In addition, the molecular structure of the protein portion of gluten closely resembles that of the thyroid gland. When gluten breaches the protective barrier of the gut, and enters the bloodstream, the immune system tags it for destruction. These anti-bodies to gluten also cause the body to attack thyroid tissue. This means if you have a gluten intolerance and a thyroid problem and you eat foods containing gluten, your immune system will attack your thyroid. For loads more information on wheat gluten and genetically modified grains read *Wheat Belly*, by William Davis MD.

In another study, 300 patients suffering from anxiety, depression, confusion, or difficulty in concentration were tested, using a placebo controlled trial, as to whether individual food allergies could really produce mental symptoms in these individuals. The results showed that allergies alone, not placebos, were able to produce the following symptoms: severe depression, nervousness, feeling of anger without a particular object, loss of motivation, and severe mental blankness. The foods/chemicals which produced most severe mental reactions were wheat, milk, cane sugar, tobacco smoke, and eggs.

Whole food supplements are good for reducing allergic symptoms. Vitamins C and B6 are probably the most effective, and the minerals calcium and potassium should be taken along with zinc and manganese. Elimination of the foods is a MUST for several months. I also recommend an HCL Pepsin and a Hydrocholic Acid supplement, you can find this at any health food store. This is good for essential absorption and aids in the digestive process. Usually people with brain allergies cannot digest properly in the stomach. The patient who is lacking enzymes because their pancreas has been overworked will experience brain allergies. I recommend you take this HCL enzyme with each meal and again you MUST avoid the foods.

Our daily bread is killing us now, or at least making us sick and crazy. Hidden sensitivity to one's bread can be the cause of depression, hormonal imbalance development, and mood and behavior changes. Our grains nowadays are fake, we can't digest plastic, in the same way we can't digest grains. I always thought I was fine and that I didn't have any food allergies, then I did a grain and dairy free diet with my husband when his saliva test came back positive for gluten and dairy allergies. I thought I was healthy, but in only a month I could tell a difference in my memory, energy, and joints. Most people cannot digest wheat, rye, and other cereal grains; this includes rice and corn, because they are genetically modified so they can be mass produced easier.

Some patients have a condition that is known as celiac disease; with this the grains just go through the gut undigested. Recent studies have indicated that celiac disease is responsible for many cases of bi-polar and schizophrenia. Evidence is accumulating which links various psychiatric disturbances with malabsorption caused by cereal grains, and it is becoming increasingly apparent that for many people their daily bread is really not so much a blessing. Of course, you should have the real daily bread and read your Bible to feed your soul.

I have seen many patients overcome depression and other mental disorders by not eating foods they shouldn't. I have seen it and believe mood disorders can result from an impairment of food absorption from the intestine, symptoms include IBS, acid reflux, or bowel movements that are frequent and are fatty, loose, large, and foul. Brain allergies make us dissociated from the world, weepy, and introverted. Celiac patients are also subject to mood disorders such as extreme depression and anxiety. These mood behavior swings occur after any grain is eaten and go away when such food is carefully avoided.

Even Some forms of autism may be linked to food intolerance, according to several studies. Researchers have found that a large proportion of autistic children, particularly those with late onset autism, respond well when fed a diet with no wheat, milk, or other products linked to food intolerance such as food colorings.

Gluten sensitivity is a common, yet little-recognized cause of female hormone imbalance that affects a significant percentage of my patients. The culprit is a molecule called gliadin, which is found in certain gluten-containing grains and causes symptoms in gluten-sensitive people. In really sensitive people, gluten destroys the villi on the lining of the small intestine, causing them to not absorb nutrients. This leads to chronic nutritional deficiencies and digestive problems such as bloating, gas, diarrhea, and constipation, as well as other symptoms such as fatigue, depression, moodiness, and anxiety. In addition, the

166

malabsorption of minerals causes other hormonal imbalances and the deficiency of calcium can cause headaches, muscle cramping and tension, skin rashes, and eventually osteoporosis. The thyroid will take what calcium it can, leaving the bones with none.

> "Just as the tobacco industry created and sustained its market with the addictive properties of cigarettes, so does wheat in the diet make for a helpless, hungry consumer. From the perspective of the seller of food products, wheat is a perfect processed food ingredient: The more you eat, the more you want. The situation for the food industry has been made even better by the glowing endorsements provided by the US government urging Americans to eat more 'Healthy' whole grains."
>
> —Wheat Belly–William Davis, MD

Food intolerances = malabsorption

Malabsorbtion = deficiencies

Deficiencies = mood disorders

Could it be that you are unhappy because your belly doesn't like what you are eating?

I really recommend that you have your saliva tested for food intolerances.

DO YOU HAVE TOXICITIES?

The first thing you should do on your quest for a healthier, happier life is detox. We are all exposed to toxins every day and the best thing you can do for yourself is detox. You need to detox before you can start to heal the cells. It is important to get the bad out, so that as you are healing the cells, your body is making new healthy cells. A hidden cause of mood swings, hormonal imbalances, and chemical and immune challenges are metal toxins. Symptoms can include insomnia, anxiety, tremors, impaired judgment and clumsiness, impaired cognitive function, mood swings, headaches, fatigue, loss of libido, and depression.

Did you know that what you are exposed to every day can be harming you. Do you spray perfume on your neck each morning? Men do you use aftershave? If you do, DO NOT DO IT ANY MORE, the chemicals in these could be the cause of your thyroid issues. It is best, if you must wear it, to spray it on your clothes and let it dry before getting dressed. Do you know deodorant with aluminum is the cause of breast cancer? Some other things you may not realize are causing your hormonal imbalance that you use everyday could be:

Fabric softeners, hair color, gel nails, aerosol hairspray, spermicides, feminine douches, and plastics. The following information is a little scary, but you should know it. Exposure to polychlorinated biphenyls (PCBs) in the womb can lead to reductions in the level of infant thyroid hormone.

Triclosan, an antibacterial chemical added to soaps, toothpastes, bath towels, and many other products, interferes with thyroid hormones. Plastic-softening phthalates have been found to reduce thyroid hormone levels in men. These chemicals are commonly found not only in plastics but also in consumer products (whose labels may list them as "fragrance"). Because they are so broadly used, phthalates may affect a large number of peoples health and hormone balance. Perfluorooctanoic acid (PFOA) is an industrial chemical used to make nonstick cookware, microwave popcorn bags, and many other products. Research has linked PFOA to low thyroid activity. Plastic has been found in the blood of most people in this country and is linked to behavioral and developmental problems. BPA is found in plastics and the liners of food cans, including baby formula, it can alter the function of thyroid hormone in the brain, potentially leading to the development of ADD/ADHA and other issues. Try to avoid these chemicals as much as possible.

Mercury poisoning can cause depression by directly killing and damaging neurons (nerve cells). It also blocks the synthesis, release, and binding of brain neurotransmitters such as dopamine, noradrenaline (norepinephrine), and serotonin, which control moods and promote feelings of wellbeing. It can cause widespread oxidative damage and inflammation throughout the nervous system. On top of that, it interferes with the actions of essential minerals such as magnesium and zinc, which are important cofactors in a lot of enzyme reactions. Subnormal levels of zinc have been associated with treatment-resistant depression and low levels of magnesium have been associated with a wide range of psychiatric symptoms. Directly damaging the structures of the cell such as the DNA, mitochondria, and cell membranes, mercury also activates the microglia cells in the brain; which produce large amounts of neuro-toxic substances such as glutamate, which promote inflammation of the brain and stimulate the region associated with anxiety. Not to mention that it causes deranged glucose metabolism. This in turn leads to cravings for substances such as carbohydrates and alcohol, and the brain is highly sensitive to low or poorly controlled glucose levels, which are a direct cause of depression and poor mood modulation. And lastly, it stops your body from making noradrenaline (norepinephrine), causing you to feel exhausted and depressed.

Exposure to mercury has long been documented to cause depression and anxiety, and acute exposure can cause chronic depression, chronic anxiety, and chronic fatigue. There are also many studies of people suffering with depression and major neurological diseases that are linked to chronic mercury poisoning from dental amalgam fillings. In particular, those suffering with depression are often found to have a lot of high negative current dental fillings, which indicates that these fillings are highly electrically active and emitting large amounts of mercury. Several metals, such as mercury from dental amalgam fillings, and nickel and gold containing crowns, have all been shown to be major factors in reduced pituitary gland function. Mercury settles in the brain, mostly the pituitary gland, and in fact, studies show that suicidal thoughts are a direct symptom of low pituitary function and appear to be a major factor in suicides in teenagers. Mercury toxicity also reduces amounts of the posterior pituitary hormone. I have found when I do a metal detox, give pituitary glandulars, and the patients have the metals in the mouth replaced, mood disorders are gone.

So how can you detox? Every store has a detox program now, you can even order one from Amazon now, and many actress are endorsing a favorite cleanse. Many patients come into my office asking me if I think that they should do a cleanse. And Yes, it is where I like to start; for some people, it can be a very important step into improving their health and changing their life.

The fact is, unless you live in a bubble, we live in a toxic world; our bodies are weighed down and bombarded by toxins every day. Toxins enter the body through the digestive tract by food additives, contaminated soil (heavy metals; especially cadmium), soft drinks, our cook ware, the fish we eat, even some supplements and vitamins contain dangerous metals. We get metals in our dental work, our vaccinations, and from drinking from aluminum cans. We get metal toxins from the air we breathe and the water we drink. Sadly, the U.S. allows over 10,000 chemical additives to our food supply. In 2008, the Toxic Release Inventory Report revealed 3,849,793,153 lbs. of toxins were released in all industries for all chemicals. Another way that toxins enter the body is our skin, through every day products like hair dye, perfume, hairspray, shampoo, lotion, and cleaning supplies. When you breathe in air, this is also a way that toxins can find their way into the body (exhaust, toxic fumes, second hand smoke, etc.). The body does three things with toxins, it either hides them in body fat (causing cellulite), deposits them in glands and cells, or removes them. Our liver, blood, skin, kidneys, colon, lungs, and lymph systems, work 24/7 to clear the body of toxins. Unfortunately, our bodies weren't designed to handle the exponential amount of toxic elements that modern day life has produced. Many people are in a state of toxic overload. Our bodies can only handle so much before inflammation and disease appear.

I recommend you find and do a Standard Process 21 Day Cleanse.

(Standard Process is sold through licensed health care providers all over the world)

The Standard Process 21 Day Cleanse is one way to safely detoxify the body. Not all cleanses achieve this goal safely, gently, and effectively. A cleanse that claims to detoxify the body in under three weeks is usually too good to be true. The key factor in an effective and safe cleanse is that it supports phase two liver detoxification. Toxins are generally fat soluble, meaning they are stored in fat cells of the body. The more fat that our bodies contain, the more likely it is we are storing toxins in the body.

Chances are your body is full of toxins, which do have an effect on how your body performs. Detoxifying your body with the right cleanse is a sound practice for optimum health and well-being. Many cleanses only support the liver or the bowels, but the 21 Day Cleanse is a whole body detox. The problem with some generic cleanses is that they don't really remove toxins from the body, they only move toxins around. I found the Standard Process 21 Day Cleanse meets the goals to safely, gently, and effectively detoxify the body. What I like about this program is that it lasts for three weeks, is not based on starvation, you can add in meat, fish, and good fats like oils after a few days, it has healthy phytonutrients, and is a whole food based program with nothing synthetic or processed.

This program was also studied and reviewed in a top health journal. The conclusive results showed an average weight loss of 9-15 lbs. for men, 6-9 lbs. for women, and a significant reduction in cholesterol (on average 30 points), as well as lipid (fat) profiles. Many patients of mine have great success stories with the Standard Process 21 Day Cleanse. I also recommend adding cholacol 2, parotid, and chlorophyll supplements to help detox specific metals.

FOOD IS JUST FUEL

"Healthy citizens are the greatest asset any country can have."

—Winston Churchill

"What is on your fork? What is going in your mouth?" I ask all my patients. My profession is nutrition. My happiest patients are the ones who watch what they put in their bodies. This chapter is probably one of the most important in the whole book, along with the supplements. By just eating a healthy diet you can solve most health problems that people have in today's society. Probably the biggest problem is not what people aren't eating, it's all the bad things they are eating. On a daily basis, I see patients with medical problems and I help them care for their own bodies with whole food supplements and diet changes. When I was growing up, my dad drove a diesel truck and my mom drove a car that required unleaded gasoline. Whenever my sister or I would borrow one of their cars, my dad would lecture what fuel to put in it. He would remind us every time that if the wrong fuel was used we would ruin the engine and the vehicle would not run. In the same way, your body is like a vehicle. If the wrong gas is put in, you cannot run efficiently.

I see people in my office every day who feel stressed with life and are down in the dumps. After testing them, I find that the reality is they are just starving for nutrients. Most of the patients I see are famished for nourishment. In my experience, the American family is ordering way too many Happy Meals but their bodies are asking, "Is this really a happy meal?" Modern life is tough.

You have deadlines to be meet, appointments to be kept, errands to be run, groceries to buy, laundry to clean, kids to take care of, a husband to keep happy, a sister who needs to talk, a dog that needs walking, and a house that needs sparkling. It's no wonder our stress levels are in constant overload. And it's no wonder we have adapted certain coping habits like comfort foods, drinking coffee during the day, and a glass of wine at night. However, stress is aggravated rather than remedied by the excessive consumption of caffeine, alcohol, sugar, and saturated fats. If you are constantly feeling tired, worn out, fatigued, stressed, or run down and/or if you are suffering from a lack of motivation, there is a good chance that your body is malnourished.

> *"I did the saliva food test and it showed I had a gluten intolerance, I didn't want to give up my pasta or beer so I kept eating it. Two years went by and I was in worse shape. My marriage was a mess and I was so depressed I decided to give it a try. I started eating gluten free and after just one week I am happier. Just do what she says, it works"*
>
> —*Sarah*

We have in our cells more to make us happy than any drug could ever reproduce. Our cells are just chemical. The key is to keep your cells happy and your happy hormones in balance so you feel them working for you. Medical textbooks don't lie, and I have spent years studying nutrition. There are several things you can do today to make your cells happy, and they will make you happy and keep your happy hormones in balance. You can start today by feeding your cells what they need. Are your meals really happy meals?

Serotonin is our happiest hormone of all. We all have it in us, but if we don't keep it going, we become low on it. Just like a gas tank in your car, you have to keep it full or the car won't run properly. Eating the right food is the key to a better mood, and it's simple. It boils down to this, control your blood sugar by eating every four to five hours throughout the day. Eat a diet rich in soluble fiber. Soluble fiber is soluble in water. When mixed with water, it forms a gel-like substance and swells. Soluble fiber has many benefits, including moderating blood glucose levels and lowering cholesterol. Incorporate foods rich in omega 3 fats, folic acid, B12, and vitamin D–four nutrients that researchers have found to be mood lifting.

4 FOODS THAT PUT YOU IN A GOOD MOOD, AND EVEN THE MOOD

Food and sex: we need both, and as it turns out, they're closely linked. A poor diet can lead to a poor sex life, while a good diet has the power to make you feel sexier and "in the mood". A healthy balance of vitamins and minerals keeps your endocrine system humming, which in turn regulates the production of the hormones estrogen and testosterone, essential for sexual desire and performance. Enjoying an active sex life is essential to our wellbeing, and the foods we eat play a large role in ensuring we feel in the mood. So you could call good food and good sex a positive feedback loop. Here are four foods that are proven to put you in "the mood."

CELERY

It may seem like all this crunchy veggie has going for it is its low calorie count, but trust me, it's sexy, too. Celery contains chemicals called androsterone and adrostenal, which make us feel more sexually attractive. Celery also contains a small amount of male hormones, which can boost female arousal.

LOBSTER

A good source of lean protein, copper, zinc, and selenium. Zinc, in particular, has been linked with a healthy male libido. Lobster is also chock full of the mineral phosphorus, which boosts *both* your sex drives.

RAW CHOCOLATE

This melt-in-your-mouth delectable has been called irresistible, wicked, and divine — no wonder eating it makes us think of other pleasurable indulgences. Raw dark chocolate contains a compound called phenylethylamine, or PEA, that stimulates the nervous system, increases blood pressure, and makes your heart beat faster, giving you all is well feelings similar to being in love.

BRIGHT FOODS

If someone's diet is a junk-food debacle, their love life may be too. That's because the quality of sexual experiences fluctuates with overall health. Reversing the effects of poor nutrition improves energy, mood, and even conception rates. And since brightly colored fruit and veggies are the most nutrient-packed foods you can eat, consuming the recommended 5-a-day could turn up your sex life.

For more information see my story in Women's Day Magazine http://www.womansday.com/sex-relationships/ sex-tips/improve-your-sex-life#slide-2

I believe that food should only be used for fuel and not for any other reason. YOU need PROTEIN, FATS, FRUIT, VEGGIES and Herbs (spices). Oh, you think I forgot the "whole grains"? NO, I didn't. We are controlling our hormones here and the best way to do it is to cut the fake, genetically modified, over processed, chemically made, food. That is all any grain is these days sadly. Also you should eat multiple meals at lower calorie levels this will result in greater cortisol control than less-frequent meals, and we know keeping cortisol in check yields less fat, more muscle, better recovery, and more energy. And when your blood sugar is in balance, your moods will be too! Remember cortisol is a steroid hormone produced by the adrenal glands during stress. Overproduction of cortisol is associated with dangerous health implications, including excess abdominal fat. A healthy diet to balance cortisol, therefore, is one designed to lower cortisol production in the body. High-quality sources of protein, healthy fats, and fresh fruits and vegetables are all part of a cortisol control diet.

Cortisol also assists with regulating blood pressure, inflammatory response, and proper use of fats and nutrients. When cortisol is released, it helps the body respond to and cope with trauma and stress. Normal levels of cortisol are considered good and even beneficial because they increase energy and metabolism. Elevated levels of cortisol due to chronic stress can potentially lower immunity, cause cognitive impairment, and cause an imbalance in crucial blood sugar levels. In addition, too much cortisol in the blood is a suspected cause of abdominal fat as well. Healthy fats may offer multiple health benefits, including anti-inflammatory and heart-protective effects on the body, while potentially decreasing cortisol. I really recommend fats; remember fat will not make you fat! Omega-3 fatty acids from certain fish and flax seed oil, for example, may prevent surges of stress hormones. Monounsaturated fats from nuts and seeds, egg yolks, olive oil, and avocados may help reduce cortisol as well.

Fruits and vegetables are thought to combat both cortisol and weight gain. These contain essential phytonutrients and vitamins that may work in numerous ways within the body. Vitamin C, for example, may suppress cortisol production, promote healthy immune functions, and also combat free radicals. Magnesium, as found in spinach, may help regulate cortisol levels while also preventing headaches and fatigue. A cortisol balancing diet in some cases not only works at lowering cortisol, but it may boost feelings of well-being as well.

Healthy eating begins with learning how to "eat smart"–it's not just what you eat, but how you eat. Your food choices can reduce your risk of illnesses such as heart disease, cancer, and diabetes, as well as defend against depression. Additionally, learning the habits of healthy eating can boost your energy, sharpen your memory, and stabilize your mood. **Disease is not a drug deficiency it comes from nutritional deficiencies**. You can expand your range of healthy food choices and learn how to plan ahead to create and maintain a satisfying, healthy diet, and don't forget, this isn't only a diet change, it's a lifelong lifestyle change.

To set yourself up for success, think about planning a healthy diet in baby steps rather than one big change. If you approach the changes gradually and with commitment, you will have a healthy lifestyle sooner than you think. I do one-on-one nutrition counseling with all my patients and these guidelines I'm giving you are no secret, but they are in my professional opinion, the best way to fuel your body. We all need a balanced diet of protein, carbohydrates, and fats, to be healthy and to be happy.

- Variety. Instead of being overly concerned with counting calories or measuring portion sizes, think of your diet in terms of color, variety, and freshness–then it should be easier to make healthy choices. Focus on finding foods you love and easy recipes that incorporate fresh veggies. Gradually, your diet will become healthier and more delicious.
- Start slow and make changes to your eating habits over time. Trying to make your diet healthy overnight isn't realistic or smart. Changing everything at once usually leads to cheating or failure. Make small steps, like adding a salad (full of different color vegetables) to your diet once a day or switching to real butter or olive oil when

cooking. As your small changes become habit, you can continue to add more healthy choices to your diet and new lifestyle.

- Every change you make to improve your diet is important. You don't have to be perfect and you don't have to completely eliminate foods you enjoy to have a healthy diet. The long term goal is to feel happy, feel good, have more energy, and reduce the risk of cancer and disease. Don't let your mistakes upset you—every healthy food choice you make counts. If you mess up a food choice, forgive yourself and do better the next day.

People often think of healthy eating as an all or nothing, but a key foundation for any healthy diet is moderation. Despite what certain fad diets would have you believe, we all need a balance of carbohydrates, protein, fat, fiber, vitamins, and minerals, to sustain a healthy body. I do not like or recommend fad diets at all, however, if you are wanting to follow a diet plan I believe it should be one of variety and wholesome foods. And keep in mind that fad diets are usually short term; we are here for the long term lifestyle change.

- Try not to think of certain foods as "bad." When you ban certain foods or food groups, it is natural to want those foods more, and then feel like a failure if you give in to temptation. If you are drawn towards sweet, salty, or unhealthy foods, start by reducing portion sizes and not eating them as often. I like to tell my patients they can have one bad day a week to splurge on unhealthy foods. For example, if you know you are going to a birthday party on Friday, don't eat cake on Monday. Later you may find yourself craving them less or thinking of them as only occasional indulgences. It takes a few days of eliminating the foods you crave, and then you should notice your cravings will be gone.

- Think smaller portions. Serving sizes have supersized recently, literally, particularly in restaurants. When dining out, choose an appetizer instead of an entrée, split a dish with a friend, and don't order extra anything. At home use smaller plates; think about serving sizes in realistic terms.

Healthy eating is about more than the food on your plate; it is also about how you think about food. Healthy eating habits can be learned, but it is important to slow down and think about food as nourishment and taste rather than just something to gulp down in between meetings or on the way to soccer practice.

Protein is our get-up-and-go. Protein in food is broken down into the twenty amino acids that are the body's basic building blocks for growth and energy and essential for maintaining cells, tissues, and organs. A lack of protein in our diet can reduce muscle mass, lower immunity, and weaken the heart and respiratory system. Happy people eat at least half their body weight in grams of protein a day. For example, if you weigh 130 pounds, your body needs 65g of protein a day. I also recommend supplementing with amino acids.

Here are some guidelines for getting enough protein in your healthy diet:

Try different types of protein. Whether or not you are a vegetarian, trying different protein sources—such as beans, nuts, seeds, peas, tofu and soy products—will open up new options for healthy mealtimes.

- Beans: Black beans, navy beans, garbanzo beans, and lentils are good options.
- Nuts: Almonds, walnuts, pistachios, and pecans are great choices.
- Lean meats: Beef, chicken, fish, or wild game is a good idea. When you are having meat, buy some that is free of hormones and antibiotics.

It is also my recommendation you cook for yourself whenever possible and avoid processed and packaged foods. In addition, try to eat organic whenever possible. By adding a few changes to your diet you will not only be healthier and look younger, but you will be one step closer to a happier, sexier lifestyle.

- Don't eat in front of the TV or computer, this often leads to mindless overeating.
- Take time to chew your food and enjoy mealtimes. Chew your food slowly, savoring every bite. We tend to rush though our meals, forgetting to actually taste the flavors. Experience your own joy of eating.
- Listen to your body. I use the acronym–H.A.L.T., Ask yourself if you are really Hungry, or if you are Angry, Lonely, or Tired. Try having a glass of water to see if you are thirsty instead of hungry. During a meal, stop eating before you feel full. It actually takes a few minutes for your brain to tell your body that it has had enough food, so eat slowly. Sometimes you don't know you are full until twenty minutes after you are done eating.
- Eat breakfast, and eat smaller meals throughout the day. A healthy breakfast can jumpstart your metabolism, and eating small, healthy meals throughout the day (rather than the standard three large meals) keeps your energy up, your cortisol stable, and your metabolism going. I like protein for breakfast. Try eggs or fish with fresh fruit, or a protein smoothie. You can even add your herbs to your smoothie.

Fruits and vegetables are the foundation of a healthy diet. They are low in calories and nutrient dense, which means they are packed with vitamins, minerals, antioxidants, and fiber. Fruits and vegetables should be part of every meal and your first choice for a snack–try for a minimum of five portions each day. The antioxidants and other nutrients in fruits and vegetables help protect against certain types of cancer and other diseases. I tell my patients the brighter, deeper colored fruits and vegetables contain higher concentrations of vitamins, minerals, and antioxidants—and different colors provide different benefits. Some of my favorite choices are:

- Greens: Greens are packed with calcium, magnesium, iron, potassium, zinc, vitamins A, C, E, and K, and they help strengthen the blood and respiratory systems. Be adventurous with your greens and branch out beyond the norm, try bright and dark green lettuce, spinach, seaweed, kale, mustard greens, broccoli, and Chinese cabbage. Spinach is my favorite. In addition, if you are not getting enough greens because you don't like the taste, you should supplement your diet with a green or vegetable pill or powder.
- Vegetables: Naturally sweet vegetables add healthy sweetness to your meals and reduce your cravings for other sweets. Some examples of sweet vegetables are corn, carrots, beets, sweet potatoes or yams, winter squash, garlic, and onions.
- Fruit: A wide variety of fruit is also vital to a healthy diet. Fruit provides fiber, vitamins, and antioxidants. Leave the skin on for the highest dose of fiber. Don't worry about the sugar content in fruit, it is natural and your body knows what to do with it.

A quick definition of healthy carbs and unhealthy carbs:

Good carbs include fruits, and vegetables. Healthy carbs are digested slowly, helping you feel full longer and keeping blood sugar and insulin levels stable. You will not gain weight eating healthy carbs. You should get your carbs mostly from vegetables and fruit, if you must have a carb meal, it should be gluten free and eaten just every so often.

Bad carbs are foods such as wheat, gluten, white flour, refined sugar, and white rice that have been stripped of all bran, fiber, and nutrients. Unhealthy carbs digest quickly and cause spikes in blood sugar levels and energy. These carbs will also make you gain weight.

Tips for eating more healthy carbs:

- Try to eat foods low in glycemic index. These are healthy carbs and your body knows what to do with them. The glycemic index or GI is a number given to foods as an indication for how they affect your blood sugar. Choosing low GI carbs—the ones that produce only small fluctuations in our blood glucose and insulin levels—is the secret to long-term health. Reducing your risk of heart disease and diabetes and is the key to sustainable weight loss. This is the way I eat all the time.
- Avoid: Refined foods such as breads, pastas, and breakfast cereals, anything with wheat and gluten in them even if you are not gluten intolerant. Avoid anything with white flour or white sugar in it. If you bake at home, this is a good way to know what is coming out of your oven and going in your mouth.

Good sources of healthy fat are needed to nourish your brain, heart, and cells, as well as your hair, skin, and nails. Foods rich in certain omega-3 fats called EFA and DHA are particularly important and can reduce cardiovascular disease, improve your mood, and help prevent brain and memory problems. Omegas and good fats will help you stay focused at work, feel full, be beautiful, and be happy too. Sometimes when I am feeling down, I will just eat an apple with lots of natural peanut butter on it.

Add to your healthy diet:

- Mono-unsaturated fats, from plant oils like coconut oil, peanut oil, and olive oil, as well as avocados, nuts (like almonds, hazelnuts, and pecans), and seeds (such as pumpkin, flax, and sesame). You can use avocados in your baking as the oil.

- Poly-unsaturated fats, including Omega-3 and Omega-6 fatty acids, found in fatty fish such as salmon, herring, mackerel, anchovies, sardines, and some cold water fish oil supplements. Other sources of poly-unsaturated fats are unheated sunflower, soybean, and flaxseed oils, and walnuts.
- Reduce or eliminate from your diet:
- Trans fats–found in vegetable shortenings, some margarines, crackers, candies, cookies, snack foods, fried foods, baked goods, and other processed foods made with partially hydrogenated vegetable oils.

HERE ARE FOODS I RECOMMEND TO COMBINE TO MAKE HAPPY MEALS

Proteins:
Eggs
Bacon
Beef
Clams
Chicken
Shrimp
Tuna
Turkey
Oysters
Scallops
Sausage
Duck
Bison

Lamb
Fish
Salmon
Lobster
Pork
Sardines
Veal

Nuts and Seeds:
Walnuts
Almonds
Cashews
Macadamia Nuts
Pecans

Pine Nuts
Pistachios
Hazelnuts
Brazil Nuts
Pumpkin Seeds
Sunflower Seeds
Sesame Seeds

Vegetables:
Onions
Shallots
Spinach
Acorn Squash
Delicatta Squash
Arugula
Asparagus
Artichokes
Carrots
Kale
Bok Choy
Broccoli
Daikon
Jicama
Mushrooms
Scallions
Rhubarb
Garlic
Sweet Potatoes
Butternut Squash
Spaghetti Squash
Pumpkin
Mixed Greens
Beets
Celery

Zucchini/Summer Squash
Chard
Cabbage—Red,
    Green, Napa
Peppers—All Kinds
Turnips
Lettuce—all types
Cauliflower
Parsnips
Leeks
Cucumbers
Fennel
Eggplant
Radishes

Fats:
Coconut milk
Olive oil
Lard
Coconut Oil
Ghee
Bacon Fat

Fruits:
Lemons
Oranges
Avocado
Blueberries
Blackberries
Strawberries
Raspberries
Tomatoes
Frozen Fruit
Apples

Apricots
Grapefruit
Figs
Plums
Kiwi
Peaches
Grapes
Limes
Plantains
Persimmon
Pomegranate
Bananas
Mango
Pineapple
Pears
Cherries
Melons
Nectarines
Papaya

Condiments/Spices:
Raw Apple Cider Vinegar
Baking Soda
Cinnamon
Cumin
Allspice
Basil
Cilantro
Coriander
Emeril's Essence Seasoning
Oregano

Cayenne Pepper
Cardamom
Chili Powder
Ginger
Rosemary
Curry
Paprika
Dill
Turmeric
Tahini
Balsamic Vinegar
Red Wine Vinegar
Tomato Paste
Dijon Mustard
Capers
Horseradish
Canned Tomatoes
Tamari—Wheat
    Free Soy Sauce
Canned Chipotles in
    Adobo Sauce
Broths—Chicken,
    Beef, Vegetable
Sun Butter, Almond
    Butter, Cashew Butter
Red Pepper Flakes
Thyme
Marjoram
Sea Salt
Black Pepper

You can find some really great recipes online using these foods, Google paleo recipes. As a Christian I believe in creation, not evolution, so I don't like the background for the paleo diet. However, as a PH.D naturopathic and from my own experience, my husband's success eating this way, and my patients' progress, I definitely do recommend it. In addition the recipes are deeeeeelicious! I recommend you read the Paleo Solution and Wheat Belly books. I didn't personally test for gluten intolerances, however I feel better when I avoid eating them.

GET OFF THE ROLLER COASTER

"If you really want to do something, you'll find a way. If you don't, you'll find an excuse."

Are your moods on a Roller Coaster? Do you feel your energy is going up and down, up and down? A big connection to our moods being on a roller coaster is our blood sugar being on one too. Blood sugar is the glucose (sugar) that circulates in the blood. Taken from your food, glucose is one of the body's main sources of fuel; it is the energy to your cells and brain. This is why your fuel (food) is so important. Glucose that is not taken up by cells (your whole body is just cells making up organs, muscles, and bones) for energy use is either converted in the liver into glycogen (an extra gas can for later) and stored for later use or is put in the stock pile as fat. This is why you gain extra weight if you don't use the food you are eating as fuel. Really, note that only a small amount of glucose is stored as glycogen for short-term energy use; most excess glucose is stored as fat for long-term energy use.

In a perfect world, our digestion should look like this. When we eat our blood sugar naturally rises, making the pancreas work and release insulin. Insulin is a hormone made by the pancreas to move the glucose into our body for energy use and converts excess glucose into fat; it is what metabolizing our food. Carbohydrates in particular, more than fat or protein, will start the release of insulin. The insulin allows glucose to enter cells throughout the body, and as glucose enters the cells, blood glucose levels normally fall back to a normal range. Cortisol as you know, goes to work here too (adrenal gland hormone with many important functions), as one job of cortisol is to regulate blood glucose. Cortisol is used to bring blood sugar UP when the body is under stress caused by the blood sugar roller coaster ride.

The blood sugar roller coaster caused by over eating of too many carbohydrates or the wrong kind of carbohydrates (refined and processed, and whole grains) produces scary and elevated levels of insulin. High insulin levels cause the cells to take longer to respond than normal. As a result, the extra glucose is stored as fat and even more insulin is released by the pancreas. The pancreas is working overtime now and will soon be overwhelmed and call in sick to work (diabetes). A balanced meal is referred to as a meal that contains all the health-building macronutrients (protein, healthy carbohydrates, fruits and veggies, and healthy fat) in ratios and amounts that support blood sugar stability for approximately 4-5 hours after consumption. You should eat these foods, and eat them often, 6-7 small meals a day and you will be on a flat ride like the carousel.

Symptoms that your blood sugar is bringing on these roller coasters:

Increased appetite shortly after eating

Food cravings

Feeling fatigued (tired and sleepy)

Feeling hyper, angry, irritable, or jittery

Brain fog and spacey

Depressed mood

Pessimistic thoughts

Anxiousness, and/or obsessive thought patterns.

SWALLOW MORE WATER

"Each day is a new day. Seize it. Live it."

—David Guy Powers

If you don't know, our whole body is made up of cells; all our organs, skin, and brain are made up of cells. Up to 60% of the YOUR body is water, and YOUR BRAIN is composed of 70% water. Your lungs are nearly 90% water. Your muscle tissue contains about 75% water by weight, body fat contains 10% water, and bone has about 22% water. About 83% of our blood is water, which helps digest our food, transport waste, and control body temperature. So we must replace water by drinking it every day.

Remember in eighth-grade science class when you learned that cells make up tissue and tissue makes up organs and organs make bodies? Every single living cell is made up of water (intracellular fluid)—including our own body cells—and surrounded by water (extracellular fluid). Every one of our body's tissues and organs, as well as every one of the body's sustaining processes, such as thinking, nerve function, blood circulation, digestion, locomotion, and elimination, requires water in order to function properly. When we were in the womb, we were surrounded by water, and our bodies are more than 75 percent water. If you go on day after day drinking coffee, tea, and soda, and you're not drinking enough water, you are starving your cells of the water they crave to replenish themselves and reproduce into new, happy and healthy cells. Could it be that you are not depressed, you are just thirsty?

Dehydration, even if it is very mild, causes your stress hormones to multiply because the body thinks dehydration means you are in a life-threatening situation. When your stress hormone cortisol increases, it causes many changes to your thyroid and adrenal hormones, as well as your insulin. You may know that you can pour yourself a glass of water anytime, but your body still thinks in terms of basic survival. Just like you go into flight or fight with something as simple as a phone call nowadays, and not a bear chasing you. I recommend you drink 1 oz. of water for every 2 lbs. of body weight per day. This means if you are 120 pounds, you should be drinking 60 oz. of water every day to maintain your hormone balance. And, with the food you eat, especially proteins and fats, your bodies use water to transport it to your bloodstream.

Dehydration = Cortisol

Cortisol = Hormonal imbalance

Hormonal imbalance = Depression.

CUT THE CAFFEINE

"Caffeine. The gateway drug."

—Eddie Vedder

Yes, we all love to go get a coffee. I think it's more of a social thing for most. The saying, "Let's grab a coffee," can just make you feel good for a moment. It's time with your friends. It's a great start to your morning, a great start to your meeting, or a way to cope with a painful situation. It's a way to meet colleagues or relax before your day starts. I agree it is great to sit on the deck in the morning and sip my caffe Americano. However, day after day, caffeine will start to deplete your adrenal glands where your happy hormones and adrenaline come from. You give your body the energy it needs from the cup of joe, and then your body stops producing the adrenaline itself. This is how we become addicted to the innocent coffee bean. Have you noticed how every day; you need your caffeine vitamin to get you going? Does your body know how to function before that first cup? If not, you might need to cut back on the caffeine and replenish your adrenal glands with supplements. Yes, the caffeine makes you feel good for the first hour or two, but then you will drop, and it won't be pretty. The ups and downs of your adrenal glands and hormone balance could be a large cause of your emotional ups and downs.

Now, you don't have to explain a caffeine addiction to me, I lived off of it in college, remember. But the truth is that just a few hours after consumption, when the high goes down, many people may reach for more coffee or something sugary to get another lift, leading to daily fluctuations in energy, mood, and alertness, and possibly to eventual chronic adrenal exhaustion. You probably don't drink as much coffee as I drank, but just two caffeinated drinks–whether it's a soft drink, caffeinated tea, or coffee–will put your body on the caffeine rollercoaster. When you consume caffeine, the drug begins its effects by initiating uncontrolled neuron firing in your brain. By stimulating your adrenal glands to produce adrenalin, caffeine puts your body in the "fight-or-flight" state, which is useless while you're just sitting at your desk. When this adrenal high wears off later, you feel the drop in terms of fatigue, irritability, headache, or confusion. So what do we do, grab another when we get tired. If you have mood swings you should reduce your caffeine use.

A REAL SWEET FIX

"Food high in bad fats, sugar, and chemicals, are directly linked to many negative emotions, whereas whole, natural foods, rich in nutrients, contribute to greater energy and positive emotions."

—Marilu Henner

It might be your comfort food of choice. Craving comfort foods is different for everyone because we have different views of comfort foods and which comfort foods work for us. For instance, when I'm sad or sick and I'm craving comfort food, I choose animal crackers. I spent my freshman year of college with animal crackers always in my dorm. One of my close friends craves chocolate ice cream, and I know others who crave potato chips. One thing many people have in common when they're craving comfort food is a yearning for sugar and fat. Sad people are usually craving comfort food to overcome their feelings. One reason food is comforting is that a snack filled with sugar and/or fat can give them a fast bump of euphoria that makes them feel good. When eating gets out of control, overeating can develop easily. I have found people link comfort foods with happy memories, people they love, or feelings they want to recapture. It's not the food itself that provides comfort, it's the feelings that the food stimulates. If your mom always fed you homemade chicken soup or freshly baked brownies when you were ill or upset, you might crave them as an adult when you are ill or upset. This might be why the next time you're sad you will be craving

Mom's pie. On the other hand, the bump of euphoria will only last a few minutes, and it is wiser to save yourself the calories and try healthy alternatives to sugar. Added sugars such as cane sugar, beet sugar, high-fructose corn syrup, glucose, fructose, evaporated cane juice, fruit juice concentrate, and honey, are used to sweeten packaged foods like sodas and fruit drinks, cereal, candy, cookies, and baked goods. Sugar will not only pack on the pounds, but has been shown to cause heart attacks, diabetes, and high cholesterol.

So what happens when you eat sugar, well it stimulates the pancreas to release insulin. Insulin's job is to lower blood sugar, by moving it into cells to be used for energy, or stored for later use. We store sugar for energy in two ways. Sugar can be stored as fat, or in the liver as an energy reserve. Cortisol is insulin's partner. Among many other functions, cortisol takes sugar stored in the liver and puts it into the blood stream. To keep things simple, insulin lowers blood sugar, and cortisol raises blood sugar.

This is what may sound confusing at first. When insulin goes up to lower blood sugar, cortisol goes up as well. It may sound odd. Why would the body raise cortisol, which increases blood sugar, at the same time insulin is going up to lower blood sugar?

The answer is very complex but the body, you know, regulates itself to keep homeostasis. Too much insulin will lower blood sugar too much. This is called hypoglycemia (low blood sugar). So when insulin goes up, cortisol goes up a little also. This is not to raise blood sugar, but to make sure insulin does not drop blood sugar too much. In simple terms, if you are eating sugar, you are putting your body into "flight or fight" from the inside. Not to mention the "flight or fight" it is already in from worries, fears, kids to feed, and deadlines. So you can see, we should avoid too much sugar. Really, we should just get sugar from our fruits and veggies. When your blood sugar is balanced, your moods will be too.

In addition, I have noticed that athletes are sponsored by various energy drinks. If you look close to what they are actually drinking, you will see it is a water bottle with a sponsor label on it. These athletes know how bad the stimulants found in energy drinks are on the body and they choose the water for their greatest performance, and you should too.

Start today to cut back on your sugar.

1. Eliminate all drinks with sugar in them: coffee, juice, sports drinks, soda, and all energy drinks.
2. Sweeten your foods and drinks sparingly. Use half a teaspoon or less a day, added by you.
3. Check the label, and buy and choose packaged foods with less than seven grams of sugar per serving, and watch your serving sizes.
4. Watch your sweet tooth. Eat less than a hundred calories a day in desserts or only allow yourself one dessert a week.
5. Don't be fooled by advertisements. For example, some yogurts have more sugar than a can of soda.

We must have a balance in our blood sugar levels.
Too High = Imbalance.
Too Low = Imbalance.
Imbalance = Stress.
Stress = Hormonal imbalance.

So we fight to keep our blood sugar/insulin levels at a level that will keep us just right, rather than too low too fast, or too high and then falling off back into the low area. Just like Goldie Locks' porridge, it should be just right.

IT WORKS, STOP STRESSING

"God will never give you anything you can't handle, so don't stress."

—Kelly Clarkson

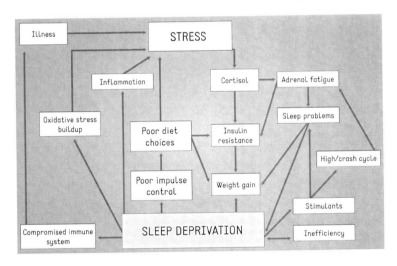

I sn't it time you stopped stressing. Enough is enough, come on now, really. 75% to 90% of all doctor's office visits are for stress-related ailments. Stress is what you feel when you try, or have to handle, more than your body can. When you are stressed, your body responds as though you are in danger. It makes hormones that speed up your heart, make you breathe faster, and give you a burst of energy. This is called the "fight-or-flight" stress response. The dictionary describes it as "mental, emotional, or physical tension; strain, distress, or pressure." We get stressed when we are under mental, emotional, or physical pressure. Stress is the body's reaction to any change that requires an adjustment or response. The body reacts to these changes with physical, mental, and emotional responses.

Stress is a normal part of life. Many events that happen to you and around you, and many things that you do yourself, put stress on your body. You can experience stress from your environment, your body, and your thoughts.

The human body is designed to experience stress and react to it. Stress can be positive, keeping us alert and ready to avoid danger. Stress becomes negative when a person faces continuous challenges without relief or relaxation between challenges. As a result, the person becomes overworked and stress-related tension buildsStress that continues without relief can lead to a condition called distress, meaning a negative stress reaction. Distress can lead to physical symptoms including headaches, upset stomach, elevated blood pressure, chest pain, anxiety, and problems sleeping. Of course, all of this is because when we stress we throw our hormones off. Research suggests that stress also can bring on or worsen certain symptoms of diseases.

Stress also becomes harmful when people use alcohol, tobacco, or drugs to try and relieve their stress. Unfortunately, instead of relieving the stress and returning the body to a relaxed state, these substances tend to keep the body in a stressed state and cause more problems.

In a Rating scale the top 10 stressors of Americans are:

1. Untimely death of anyone close, especially a spouse or child
2. The economy
3. Finances
4. Loss of a job or fear of losing a job
5. Loss of a home
6. Moving
7. College

8. Serious illnesses / cancer
9. Debt
10. Bankruptcy

Stress is a killer. It contributes to death from strokes, high blood pressure, and heart attacks. Stress can make virtually any medical condition or disease worse. But, more than that, stress is a killer of dreams and it robs us of our joy. There will always be stress in life, and we will always have the task of coping in the ways that we choose. We can keep at it or give up. You can drink a fifth of scotch or you can re-organize your life and come out fighting for survival.

One thing that I have really learned that helped me with my stressing is to live in the moment. If you are in the moment you don't have to be stressing about the past or about the future. I used to stress about things that weren't in the future and worry about the past so much that I would make myself crazy. Mountain climbing really helped me learn to live in the moment. All the mountains I have climbed with my husband have taught me to be mindful. When climbing you have to be climbing in the moment and thinking of nothing else but your next hand hold or your next step. I have also learned from my husband and the mountains that in order to have a successful climb, my mindset must be right. The same is true with our daily lives, if my mind is not in the moment, I am stressed. If my mind is not on what I am doing, I mess up. If I am scattered and all over the place, I am stressed and I am a mess, and I always catch it, but it takes me a few days to simmer myself down and become balanced again.

Mary or Martha? I just recently read the story of Mary and Martha, the one where the two sisters let Jesus into their house.

As Jesus and his disciples were on their way, he came to a village where a woman named Martha opened her home to him. She had a sister called Mary, who sat at the Lord's feet listening to what he said. But Martha was distracted by all the preparations that had to be made. She came to him and asked, "Lord, don't you care that my sister has left me to do the work by myself? Tell her to help me!" "Martha, Martha," the Lord answered, "you are worried and upset about many things, but few things are needed–or indeed only one. Mary has chosen what is better and it will not be taken away from her."

Luke 10:42

Mary sat still and listened and Martha was a busy bee, cleaning the house, scrambling to get food ready, and making sure everything was in its place. Sometimes (a lot of the time), I have to remind myself to be like Mary, even though we live in a Martha world. If we just sit and listen and enjoy the moment, I have learned we will be a lot happier every day. I think mountains teach me what is important and really put things into perspective for me. When I come to a serious spot when I could fall to my death, I don't think so much about bills, patients, deadlines, worries, or really anything else. Living and my next breath and my next step become all I am aware of. It helps me to be happy when I remind myself how to be mindful and in the moment, in this busy world. I encourage you to do something that is a mindful moment for you. Maybe just think about everything you do every day, drive in the moment, play at the park in the moment with your kids (that means no cell phone), have dinner with your family without the TV on or cell phone near, go for a walk and just enjoy the air, the sky, the flowers, and breathe. Work to make your heart and mind like Mary's in this Martha world.

The Maroon Bells are admired every year by thousands of tourists, and offer a post card perfect view that I'm sure you have seen somewhere. My wonderful groom and I share a love of climbing Colorado's 14ers, for those of you that don't know, they are all the peaks over 14,000 feet. Last September, we left the truck at 4:20 a.m. (at 9600 ft) to climb both North Maroon (14,014 ft) and Maroon Peak (14,156 ft). On this September day I learned several personal lessons in mindfulness. To me, mountain climbing and life share a common denominator in that *it's all mental.* The person whose mind is stressed and not thinking correctly will never be a good climber. Mentally, many people defeat themselves on the mountain and in life. Any negative beliefs we have are powerful and are deeply ingrained into our subconscious. However, I believe all things can be overcome. Both these peaks are known for being dangerous and claim several lives each year, including one a week after we were there. However, I had to stop stressing of the danger; negative thinking only causes a physical reaction and will make your muscles tired from the tension in them. Now, I consider myself a good climber, I'm comfortable with exposure, and have done class 4 mountains before and I trust my guide/husband to take very good care of me, however, this turned out to be an adventure in which I had to conquer more than just the summits, I had to conquer myself. We started walking in the dark like we always do and easily reached the summit of Maroon Peak at 7:50 a.m. Maroon Peak has 4850 feet of elevation gain and is a class 4 mountain, which means that it is more technical climbing. You are not just using hand-holds, you have to search for them, and these mountains are rotten rock so we had to test and select each hand and foot hold. My husband has taught me to climb with focus and to be mindful and slow down; I think that is what I love so much about climbing. As we descended to the saddle towards North Maroon the terrain became looser, steeper, and more exposed, this definitely made it more dangerous. As we started up North Maroon there were three more difficult parts, all of which are class 5, where actual technical climbing moves and techniques are used. At the first one I began to feel the fear and knew I had to finish anyway. For the first time ever I started to get emotional as I felt the fear on the first of the 3 difficulties. On class 5, I am past my comfort zone, and I get nervous and stress a little when my movement involves straight up climbing on loose rock with a pack on and exposure behind me, not to mention that we weren't using ropes.

Being the great guide he is, my husband helped me back to safety and found a better way around. I knew the best thing I could do was make myself relax and get rid of my stress. When doing anything, if you are tense you will unconsciously hold your breath and tighten your neck and shoulders, if you do this, you will lose focus and your climbing will become careless and dangerous. I had to compose my mind, I had to take a deep breath, I had to picture myself safe and relax. I made myself calm and each small movement occupied my mind. Until we were safely at the truck, I was in a state of mindfulness. As we approached the 2nd crux I smiled to my husband and myself. It was a real smile and I had a good mind set and felt more comfortable, although it was more dangerously exposed. However, when in a difficult spot, if you can't smile for real, fake it. The brain associates a smile with pleasure. Smiling while climbing something hard with your muscles burning will trick your brain into thinking that you are not in as much pain as you are. At this point, we had to get out the webbing, and although I wasn't tied into it as a life line, it helped mentally just knowing it was there if I needed a hand-hold. The 3rd class 5 part was an open chimney, and although a fall may have killed me, since my mind was right it was actually a fun challenge. After all this, I took a deep breath because I could see the summit and I had made it. By 11:20 a.m. we had summited both peaks safely, but as every climber knows, you are not safe until you're down. We sat for a bit and enjoyed the summit views, ate a quick bite, and began the 4 mile descent. At 2:40 p.m. we made it to Maroon Lake and took off our shoes to soak our feet in the cold mountain water. I had a great feeling of knowing that I could climb class 5, and I had a great feeling knowing that we had made it safely to the truck alive. The 3 big things I learned for anyone wanting to conquer a real mountain or the mountains in life are that you must be positive, stay relaxed and composed, and don't forget to do it all with a smile on your face!

When your hormones are balanced you will automatically not stress as much, if you eat the diet I recommend and you take the supplements you need, your hormones will be balanced. And as a Christian, I'm so thankful that I know I don't have to stress. *John 17:16, we are not of the world!* Yes we do live in this world in the flesh, but it's comforting to me to know we don't have to function like the rest of the world in stress. We don't and shouldn't think, talk, or act like the world. In fact, our attitude and approach toward situations should be entirely different from the world's. We should approach our days ahead with joy and peace even though we live in this world. In John 16:33, Jesus said,... *In the world you have tribulation and trials and distress and frustration; but be of good cheer For I have overcome the world.*

Some things we can do are look at our problems differently; we can have a better attitude. With a good attitude, I know I have learned, I don't have to get upset if someone isn't treating me right, I have an extra expense, or get work added to my day. I can decide to enjoy myself right where I am, even though I'd rather not be there, or I can become upset trying to do something that I can't do anything about. It's my decision! If I have a plan and it's not working, I can get upset and angry, or I can also choose to adapt and overcome. It's my decision! Just as I was writing this book today, I've had to deal with about five stressful circumstances. It's been one of those testing days. One of those days where everything that can go wrong has, but before I got stressed out, I stopped myself. It's my decision. I'm not going to let anything take my joy!

We tie ourselves up in ropes with good knots when we stress. Picture a man tied to a chair with his hands in ropes behind his back and his feet tied to the legs of the chair. Sound familiar? Is this how you feel? To stop stressing, to get untied from the ropes, we need a change of attitude. I've learned that the right attitude can completely turn a situation around. If I attack something in dismay, I'm setting myself up for unhappiness before I even begin, because dismay creates stress. But if I decline to dread it, I set myself up for happiness. The choice is yours.

Happy people know how to handle stress and stop stressing. First, you need to figure out what is it that sparks your stress. Is it the workload at your job, frustrating relationships with family members or friends, driving in traffic, fear revolving around your health condition, or maybe fear of something else? After you know what sparks you, figure out ways to either avoid those sparks or cope better with them through improved communication, deep breathing exercises, anger management, or even talk therapy.

Next, you need to take a timeout. It can be as easy as taking twenty minutes to simply sit and think, to take a bath or engage in an activity that soothes you, like reading, doing a crossword puzzle, or practicing some yoga. Timeouts ease the stress, and remember that it is a good way to fill your own gas tank. Sometimes I find that an area doesn't stress you if you're ready for it. Again, find an activity you enjoy that is physical. Jogging, cycling, swimming, and walking a dog, are examples of physical activities that are not only good for your overall health, but are also smart ways to reduce stress. Another thing that you can do to relieve stress is soothe yourself with music. Music can go a long way in improving your mood on your commute to work, at the office, while working out, or even while shopping. When you're starting to feel the effects of stress, turn to your favorite songs, playlists, or station on the radio. Listen to calming music. My favorite satellite station is Coffeehouse. Turn your radio to it and see the effects of soothing music.

Our bodies were created to withstand a certain amount of stress; but when we push ourselves beyond that limit, we begin to experience problems. Are you pushing yourself too hard? One day, while climbing a mountain, I came to a creek with a log bridge to cross it. As we walked across, the log creaked under the pressure of our weight. It was on the verge of collapsing. Many unhappy people are living this way. Day in, day out, they continue stretching themselves to the limit until, like a log, one day they will snap. It's so important not to over commit ourselves. Do you have too much to do? This seems to be the number one complaint I hear today. "There's just too much to do and not enough time to do it all." This is often the result of not saying, "No," often enough. If you have too much to do, I encourage you to examine what is priority for you to do and drop the rest. Start saying no to people, activities, and meetings, which are not a priority to you. Be true to yourself. Happy people don't stress.

Be prepared. When I was fifteen, a good friend, Dan, once told me a story of when he was in college. He spent all morning preparing and studying for his finals. Around three in the afternoon, his roommates came in, asking him if he wanted to go to the beach. He agreed, but the beach afternoon turned into dinner and then a party. Everyone was out until 2:00 a.m. As they were going home, all his buddies were stressed because they still had finals to study for. However, Dan went to bed without worry, knowing he was prepared. He also told me something I will never forget. He would say, "Perfectly prepared makes perfect." This story has stuck with me since. I am always prepared for what I know is coming. Being prepared will instantly relieve stress. On the days I see patients; I always get to work early to make sure that I am prepared and ready for the day. When my patients come in, I am ready to see them and not stressing in a time crunch. Before Kyle and I leave for a mountain climbing trip, we double check to make sure we are prepared for everything. We take plenty of food, rain gear, snow clothes, and sandals. We take extra water, propane, and firewood. We take our hiking shoes along with books to read. We are prepared for whatever. This leaves the trip stress-free. When I or any teacher teaches a class, we have a class plan to follow. When you have guidelines all ready and you are organized, then you are all set for anything and you will be happy and stress free. If you start any project prepared the best way you can for it, you will eliminate a lot of your stress.

OBTAIN ESSENTIAL OILS

"If all the medicine in the world was thrown into the sea, it would be bad for the fish and good for humanity."

—O. W. Holmes (Harvard Medical Professor)

E ssential oils are oils produced in the cells of aromatic plants and are held in specialized glands. They are released from the plant and collected (concentrated) most often through steam distillation. Essential oils have great therapeutic benefits to the body when applied directly to the skin or inhaled as in aromatherapy. Essential oils, also called aromatherapy, because when the oil molecules enter through the nose, they reach the lungs, brain, and go into the blood stream and every part of the body. Chemical interactions occur between the oils and our bodies that begin physical adjustments. Hormone and enzyme responses to the oil molecules immediately take place.

In Oxford, England, hospitals are using essential oils known for their sedative or anti-depressant qualities to release endorphins (neurochemical analgesics and tranquilizers). Lavender, marjoram, geranium, mandarin, and cardamom have replaced chemical sedatives in these hospitals. These and other oils relax people, lower blood pressure, increase mental acuity, normalize body functions, reduce stress, and even act as aphrodisiacs.

—Aromatherapy Scent and Psyche: Using Essential Oils for Physical and Emotional Well-Being

Jasmine is my favorite oil. When I was going through a very depressing, grieving time, I was introduced to essential oils, and jasmine became my most desired. Jasmine is a very special oil because it is one of the best-known oils for helping ease depression. Jasmine is very soothing and kind. It is consoling to the nerves and tender to the emotions, producing positive feelings of self-confidence. I don't think that there is any other oil that I have personally had so much success with in emotional healing as I have had with jasmine. When I was in a sad state, I wore jasmine as perfume daily, and it helped warm my feelings.

Essential oils can help bring you happiness by helping you clear away your negative and stressful thoughts and relax. Essential oils can definitely lift your spirits and emotionally lift you up. Other oils that have the same effects are rose, orange, ylang ylang, and jasmine. Any oil that is citrus or cooling might be of help to you. I would recommend wearing it as perfume, carrying it to smell regularly, and using a plug-in diffuser. You can try any oil by itself or as a blend.

Here is a recipe you can try that I have discovered: in a saucepan, boil water on the stove and add a few drops of orange, rose, and cinnamon oil. Let the steam diffuse all over your house; and enjoy the happy, relaxing benefits.

I also love orange or lemon oils, you can use in a diffuser, place on a tissue, add to your lotions, and even put a few drops in your drinking water.

Certain oils can also stimulate certain hormones, oils are great because they can be kept on your desk or in your purse or briefcase and can be used at any time you need some extra balancing. There are a number of oils that can be stimulating and uplifting or calming. Essential oils are also great because they can be relaxing and clarifying to the mind. These are good oils to use topically, I recommend you rub on your neck and behind your ears and make sure you take a big whiff of them as well.

If you are feeling:	Use this oil:
Sad	basil or jasmine
Restless	bergamot, chamomile, or ylang ylang
Anxiety	cypress, lavender, or sandal wood
Irritable	chamomile, jasmine, rose, or clary Sage
Tension	geranium or ylang ylang
Tired and fatigue	eucalyptus, lemon, or orange
Stress	bergamot, chamomile, marjoram, or neroli
Hormonal imbalance	rose or geranium
Insomnia	chamomile or lavender

BATHS AND MORE

PMS tension	Make a bath and add 4 drops geranium and 4 drops rosemary (or apply to a warm wash cloth and apply to the abdomen for pain and cramps).
Insomnia or if you need calming	Take a bath with 6 drops of lavender in the water Before bed.
Tension relief	Take a bath with 6 drops of geranium in it.
If you feel off	Take a bath with 6 drops each geranium and lavender and relax and breathe for 20 or more minutes.

POSSESS A PET

"A house is not a home without a pet."

—Anonymous

If you are like me, it's hard to not be happy when those big brown eyes gaze at you with love. Not to mention, that cold wet nose nudging the arm that is near the edge of the bed in the early morning, the wagging tail, the happy greeting at the door when you come home from work, and having someone to always walk with. You are probably not surprised to know this, but now there is scientific proof that our bodies have hormonal changes when we interact with dogs. Research shows that dogs do help people cope with depression and stress-related illness. Preliminary results from a study show that a few minutes of petting a dog prompts a release of a number of "feel good" hormones in humans, including serotonin, prolactin, and oxytocin. In addition, petting our pooches results in decreased levels of the primary stress hormone cortisol. Could a dog help raise your serotonin levels in order to help you be happy? I believe as long as they aren't adding more stress to your life, such as a new puppy chewing up everything in sight, the answer is, yes.

I have had a pet all my life, in addition to horses and livestock, since I had the privilege of growing up on a ranch. For me, coming home and being greeted with a wagging tail and kiss is just like taking a fur-coated Xanax. There really is something incredibly comforting about coming home after a long day at work and being greeted by a hairy friend. For many people, interacting with a pet is the ultimate antidote to a stressful day. In fact, in one study, when people were presented with stressful tasks in four different situations–alone or with their pet or with both their spouse and their pet–they experienced the lowest stress response and the quickest recovery in the situation where they were only with their pet.

There is no doubt about it. Pets are a big responsibility. Not only do they demand regular meals and endless fresh water, but they have to be cleaned up after constantly too. In addition, when you try to leave town, you must find a place for them to go, and, depending on the breed, they might also require frequent walks–not to mention the added cost of food, vet bills, grooming, and licensing. I don't have children, but I believe that caring for a pet is like raising a child. However, despite the responsibility, an astonishing number of furry friends have managed to work their way into our homes. Research shows that in the United States, 63 percent of households–about 71.1 million homes–harbor at least one pet.

The numbers are insane, but why? With all the attention and money lavished on them, what do pets offer us in return? If you have a pet, you know and agree with me plenty, actually. If you ask me, pets are a pretty wise investment. Research shows that what pet owners sacrifice in terms of time and money they get back in better health and increased happiness. The pet prescription appears to work in a number of ways. For one thing, pet ownership tends to prompt people to adopt a multitude of healthy behaviors. From my own experience, owning animals all my life, I know that on some days, they were the only thing that got me out of bed. Walking the dog, watering the horses, and feeding the steers, gave me a sense of purpose. I believe the responsibility improves our human self-worth. To this day, my dog keeps me off the couch, and exercising with him improves my health and happiness every day. In addition, studies also show that interacting with a pet helps reduce levels of harmful neurochemicals in the body and raise the good ones. This is why dogs are allowed in hospitals and nursing homes.

If you aren't ready for the responsibility or your living conditions don't allow it, don't worry. While stronger pet-owner bonds usually lead to the greatest stress relief, even brief encounters can create improvements. Research shows that patients who spend just a short amount of time with a dog before an operation experienced a 37 percent reduction in their anxiety levels; I believe this is because the animal's presence helped distract them from their fears.

Indeed, multiple studies indicate that pets are powerful forms of stress relief, lowering not only blood pressure, but also harmful stress hormones like cortisol, which is associated with depression and anxiety, and elevating beneficial ones like oxytocin, which is linked to happiness and relaxation. Some people experienced increased output of endorphins and dopamine after just five minutes with an animal. If you don't have a furry friend, try volunteering with a pet organization, start a dog walking business, or just borrow a pet from a friend. In addition, while it's usually the four-legged critters that get all the credit, other pets can help, too. Simply watching a fish tank versus a bare wall for thirty minutes lowers blood pressure significantly. Research has shown that meditation into a fish tank can be an even more dominant relaxant than several proven meditative techniques alone. If you are in a space where you can allow a pet to join you, I encourage you to try getting a buddy of some kind. Do some research of your own. Maybe look into adopting a pet from the pound that needs a friend too. Fish might be the easiest and a good place to start. However, from my experience, they don't give very good sloppy kisses.

LET'S GET PHYSICAL

"Those who think they don't have time for exercise will sooner or later have to find time for illness."

—Edward Stanley

Have you ever needed to blow off some steam? Not only does a walk help you calm down, it also will help you get rid of anger. I've heard that anger is one letter short of danger. Being physical gives us all many benefits from improving self-esteem to blowing off steam. In order to make happy and sexy happen everyday, you must be physical every day. Yes, I said every day. Have you ever gone on a great walk and returned with a smile on your face? Well, now you know how you can feel so good after exercising? I love doing anything that requires movement; however, I understand that for some, exercise is looked at to be torment and distress. There's a reason I love exercise. Exercise releases endorphins, and endorphins are the happy hormones. Happy and sexy people know this secret. The gym is full of happy folks. Endorphins are the well-known feel-good factor in the human body. Endorphins are in the brain. They are a family of endogenous morphine-like peptides present within the central nervous system. The term *endorphin* is generic, referring to all the opioid peptides. Opioid peptides are the reward mechanism inside the brain, by which the brain is signaled that something good has happened and the brain should register a state of pleasure or happiness. They can also act as pain relief, when the body becomes too hurt to handle things. It's not only exercise that makes us happy; I don't know about you, but fresh air makes me twice as happy. You can get moving today for free. You don't need a gym membership or expensive equipment. Just start walking. Exercise releases endorphins in our brains, lifting our spirits and lightening our moods. And for most of us, being outside–soaking up the natural light (good source of vitamin D), breathing in fresh air–also makes us happy. So what if you combine the two and exercise outside? Would you be twice as happy? I know I am. Exercise is not just to lose weight or stay thin. For me, exercise is my daily stress reliever. When I am having a really bad day, you won't find me at the bar; but you will find I have my Merrell hiking shoes on. Just as you get more energy from exercising, you also get happier. You will feel good; and if you don't already appreciate all the good things in life, then you might start. When you move, your body gets rid of stress and you don't feel as stressed as before exercising. Research shows that people who exercise daily are less prone to get depressed than people who don't. Research also shows that people who participate in outside activities–walking, gardening, farming, riding bicycles– see greater positive effects from the exercise than did others. Any kind of natural environment, even parks in big cities, is enough to provide the mental benefits. You don't have to spend long outside to experience these benefits. The researchers concluded that just five minutes of outside activity is enough to improve your mood and self-esteem. Exercising for longer than five minutes is obviously important for reaping the utmost health benefits, but it's nice to know that a short walk around the block makes you feel better, especially when you might only have a short break at work. If you find that you are depressed after working inside at your cubical all day on your computer, make yourself happy today and take a five-minute walk around the block and get some fresh air. Plus, if you make a habit of it, you will acquire the benefits every day. Not only will the endorphins make you happy, but you will look good in your jeans!

The other side of needing to exercise is that it can be harmful to you. Yes, anything we "over do" can be harmful. And I'm not just telling you this, I am talking to myself here. I am known to over train. Remember my story of being in college waking up early to exercise? I didn't know the damage I was doing; now I do. Take it from me overtraining is just as bad as under training.

Overtraining = high cortisol

Overtraining has been shown to affect blood levels of important neurotransmitters such as glutamine, dopamine and 5-HTP, which can lead to feelings of depression and chronic fatigue. The stress caused by intense, excessive exercise can negatively affect the hypothalamic-pituitary axis, possibly causing conditions such as hypothyroidism. Hypothyroidism is known to cause depression, weight gain, and digestive dysfunction along with a variety of other symptoms. As we know, high stress in general can cause symptoms of hypothyroidism, and the stress caused by excessive, intense exercise is no exception.

Another major effect that extreme exercise has on our bodies is an immediate increase in cortisol, the hormone that is released when the body is under stress. Heavy-resistance exercises are found to stimulate markedly acute cortisol responses, similar to those responses found in marathon running. Chronically high levels of cortisol can increase your risk of other health issues, such as insomnia, IBS, acid reflux, depression, weight gain, and brain fog. Excess cortisol makes us gain fat, particularly around the abdomen. This is why I was exercising and stressed and gaining weight, and why maybe you can't lose weight while exercising. REMEMBER, everything has to be in balance, even something that is good for us can be bad if it's overdone.

SHINE IN THE SUN

"He is rich who can walk in a sunrise undisturbed."

—Anonymous

The above quote is one of my favorites because I run on solar power. Yes, sunlight is believed to affect the production of endorphins. While I love to climb mountains, sometimes forty-five minutes can feel like four hours. My hardest mountains are when I am feeling cold. Somehow, the discomfort is magnified. The cold makes me more tired and makes my body ache more. But my favorite thing is when the sun comes up and shines on my cheeks and forehead. I recall a really hard mountain where I was trying to find a rhythm of breath and steps, trying to catch my breath and making sure my footing was good. As we came to a place where the path was less steep, I was breathing in the cold air and looked up to my climbing guide and husband, Kyle, with an exhausted look on my face, frozen eyelashes, and a red nose. As I looked up, he was pointing over my shoulder. When I turned around, I saw the large, orange, warm sun so big I felt I could touch it. As the temperature rose, so did the corners of my mouth. Because Kyle has seen the smile on my face in the sunrise, it has become like a tradition for him to point to the large, orange ball of sun whether we are fishing in a lake, floating down a river, sitting in a chair in Hawaii, or climbing a mountain. My favorite feeling is the morning light and the yellow glow on the snow, water, or mountainside as it comes up. I believe that sunshine can lift anyone's spirit. I know that living in Colorado where the winters are long, a sunny day can make my day. Whether I am exercising or just lying in it, there is something about that big, orange ball in the sky that also brings endorphins to our bodies.

We also get natural Vitamin D from the sun and it is important to the body in many other ways as well. Muscles need it to move, neurotransmitters need it to carry messages between the brain and every body part, and the immune system needs vitamin D to fight off invaders. Vitamin D is found in cells throughout the body. Together with calcium, vitamin D also helps protect older adults from osteoporosis. It does so by helping the body absorb calcium, a main building block, from food and supplements. The body makes vitamin D when skin is exposed to the sun. Most people can get at least some of their vitamin D needs this way. You have to be outside; sun through a window will not produce vitamin D. However, despite the importance of the sun to vitamin D synthesis, it is of course smart to limit exposure of skin to sunlight in order to lower the risk for skin cancer. When out in the sun for more than a 20-30 minutes, wear protective clothing. I don't recommend a sunscreen unless you know it is chemical free, remember you absorb everything through your skin. Tanning beds also cause the skin to make vitamin D, but of course have similar risks for skin cancer.

Have you ever noticed how when kids draw a picture of the sun, they have a smiling face? If you are not getting all your natural vitamin D, try shining in the sun and carry the shining smile all day with you. We have been told that too much sun is bad for us, causing skin cancer and other health problems, but as it turns out, there's another side to the story. Sun exposure isn't all bad. In fact, it's mostly good. This is no surprise to me, since the big, orange orb always brings a smile to my face. In addition, I believe my mom knows something, because whenever we would visit my great-grandma in the nursing home, she would always open the curtains. That's great news to me. After decades of being told to avoid it, researchers are finding that we might have been doing more harm than good. The evidence is substantial. A chronic lack of sun exposure has been linked to fertility problems, several forms of internal cancer, general poor health, and varying degrees of depression. People actually get depressed, with symptoms like sadness, fatigue, and hopelessness, from a lack of sunlight. The form of depression most often associated with variations in sunlight is SAD, seasonal affective disorder. The disorder runs in cycles of depression and wellness that follow the seasons. SAD is most common in Alaska, where some days are only one hour of daylight. But even in Colorado, the gray days can affect people. This is why spring break vacations are so important to everyone here. However, if you want to be happy every day, try to get a little solar power.

BEGIN BREATHING

"Inhale peace, exhale problems."

—Cammi Balleck PH.D

Your breathing becomes faster and shallower when you are under stress. By slowing down and concentrating on your breathing, you can reduce your stress levels and your cortisol levels. Cortisol and other stress hormones will speed up your heart rate, causing undue stress on the walls of the blood vessels. For instance, when you are stressed or in a panic, you take fast, shallow breaths. Yoga recommends deep breathing exercises that will counteract the effects of stress and cortisol by slowing down your pulse rate and blood circulation.

Air. It's free, and it will make you happy. We can survive days without water and even more days without food. However, we can't live any time at all without oxygen. As a yoga enthusiast, I have learned that it is important to breathe and breathe deep breaths. It is especially important when you are stressed or depressed. Breath is the best way to center yourself. Whenever I have a problem I inhale peace and I exhale problems. I find inhaling harmony and exhaling chaos instantly changes my mood. In order to make happiness happen in your life, you must breathe. Breathing is powerful, our life force, and is a major factor influencing our state of mind. (If you are uncertain about this, hold your breath for two minutes and reread this sentence.) I have learned that to be happy and centered, we should sit and breathe comfortably but deeply in through our noses and out through our mouths. Imagine you are breathing from that area of your abdomen just beneath your bellybutton. Make the in-breath last to a count of five and the out-breath to a count of six or seven. Continue for at least two minutes, and notice what you feel. Remember that most people don't breathe nearly enough. Every day, take at least five deep breaths. Start to breathe more deeply and notice how much better you feel. Have lots of fun with this. Notice how good you can make yourself feel when you just breathe. Try to remember when you are in a stressful situation to take five deep breaths. It is great to start your day with breath; start your meetings with breath. Try this exercise when you are sitting in traffic or dealing with a difficult situation or people. Remember, the benefits double when you combine air with movement. I would also suggest, if you have never tried, trying yoga for the same reason.

A few weeks ago, I bought the newest and best smart phone to help me run my business. I had just learned how to use it when it quit working. I went to my cell phone store, and after three hours of sitting in the office, I was told I would have to get a new one by mail in a few days. Very frustrated about not being able to work, I left the store early. I was almost in tears, starting to let stress overwhelm me. I went home and changed my mind right away. I knew I couldn't let a cell phone company embezzle my happiness. I put on my hiking shoes and decided I needed some air. I got outside and took a few deep breaths and instantly felt better. I decided I was breathing in delight and exhaling tension.

SWITCH ON YOUR SMILE

"Birds sing after a storm; why shouldn't we?"

—Rose Kennedy

Did you know that when you smile your body makes more happy hormones than when you eat chocolate or have sex? It's a fact. Research shows that smiling actually releases serotonin, your happy hormone. Studies have shown that people with depression can be completely cured with daily 20 minute sessions where the patient just sits and smiles! In addition, smiling will make you look better, lower your blood pressure, and of course, it reduces stress. Our bodies don't know the difference between a real smile and a forced smile. If you need a boost of serotonin all you have to do is smile, and it's free too. Plus, smiles are also free of sugar and calories so they are completely guilt-free. So you better switch on your smile. Smile until your cheeks hurt, let your liver smile and let your adrenals smile, smile until you feel every cell in your body smiling.

Going from unhappy to happy can be as easy as turning on a light switch. Have you also heard that it only takes eighteen muscles to smile and forty-three to frown? I encourage exercise, so, of course, I am going to encourage you to build the muscles in your face as well. A frown leaves us with wrinkles around our lips and a puckered brow. A smile only leaves smile lines. Happy and sexy people make it a point to smile. The more you smile, the happier you will feel, and the happier you will make others feel. Your smile will not only make you feel more confident, it will give others confidence. A smile is like the word *no*; everyone, everywhere understands a smile. Happy people make it a point to smile. Switch on your smiling.

When I see patients, I make it a point to smile at them when they enter my office for the reason that I truly am happy to see my patients, because I love them all. But in addition, my smile gives them a feeling of ease and confidence in me. When I see people I love, I always smile because seeing them brings a smile to my face and shows them I am happy to see them.

Look around at people today as you are working or doing errands. You will note that you are able to tell which people are confident in themselves by the way they carry their head and shoulders. The same is true with a smile. Notice the people who look happy and the ones who look miserable. You can tell with just a facial expression what is going on inside.

However, the good news is you can switch on a smile. As the clowns say, turn your frown upside down. If you wear a smile, you will not only look better but feel better. You will win friends, not wrinkles. Start smiling now.

MAKE TIME TO PRAY

"Let us never forget to pray. God lives. He is near. He is real. He is not only aware of us but cares for us. He is our Father. He is accessible to all who will seek Him."

—Gordon B. Hinckley

A new science "neurotheology," has done a new research in the U.S. and Canada. Scientists have found that the brains of people who spend untold hours in prayer and meditation are different. For example, scientists have learned that people that pray develop more antibodies to a flu virus than did others who did not meditate. Meditation by definition is what we think, ponder, and turn over and over in our minds. Meditation or prayer can be anything you want it to be for you. Meditation or prayer is your own journey and practice. It is done in your own mind and your own body. Even though meditation is usually done in a comfortable position or yoga pose, it can be done in any position or movement. You actually meditate every day; it's what you mull over. In order to make happy happen every day you must pay attention to what you are turning over and over in your brain. A good way to do this is to sit quietly so you can reflect on your thoughts, but positive thinking can be done anywhere at any time. To me, meditation is an intimate meeting with my own body and heart. Meditating is nothing more than entering an altered state of consciousness. So no, you don't have to sit like Buddha and say *Om* all day to enjoy the benefits of meditation. Anyone can meditate. Happy people know how to stop and focus on life. If you can think, you can meditate. Meditation can be practiced in many different ways. While there are numerous different meditation techniques, the common is to quiet the mind. With meditation, your thinking mind becomes quiet. You stop focusing on the anxiety of your day or your life's problems as well as the solution to your problems. You just let that voice in your head be quiet, which is easier said than done. For example, start thinking about nothing now. I think this is the main reason I love to climb mountains so much. Sometimes with the cold and the exhaustion there, I realize I am not thinking about anything else but my next step. Going to the mountains is my way to heal, for it is not the mountains we conquer but ourselves. When I am climbing, I think in the now moment; my mind is quiet. I don't think about what the mountain is thinking of me, what I am wearing, or if the mountain cares I have snotcicles on my face. My mind is quiet, and I can meditate. I allow myself to slip into an altered state of consciousness. For me, focused meditation is the easiest, and I find that focusing on my breath or next foothold is the best for me. I encourage you to find what is best for you. You don't have to become a mountain climber to feel this feeling. Meditation can be done anywhere at any time. If you're not practiced at quieting your mind, it probably doesn't take long before thoughts creep in. I used to teach a local yoga class; and at the end of the class, I would tell the students to calm their minds. This was always hard. My students would lie in the corpse pose and think of their grocery list, what they had to do when they went home, and what tomorrow would bring. Hint: if you're thinking, your mind is not clear. Even thinking about not thinking, you are still thinking. The best way I have found to quiet the mind is a yoga technique called focused meditation. With this technique, you focus on something like an object or the inhale–exhale of your breath, but don't engage your thoughts about it. If you are like me, you might find it easier to do this than to focus on nothing. But the idea is the same. Every minute, you are allowing yourself to slip into an altered state of consciousness.

Lots of studies show that religious people tend to live longer lives, but not until recently did scientists have any idea why. Scientists have done studies that confirm that individuals who were religious and prayed were more likely to live not just happier, but longer lives. Scientists think it's because religious people are more friendly and grateful, and they worry less. In other words, for these individuals, religion is a core and stable part of who they are and how they behaved. Furthermore, studies show that the least religious group of people were, on average, depressed and least likely to live a very long life. They were generally productive and successful but they were less likely to be very extroverted and trusting, less likely to get and stay married, and less likely to have children or to be extensively involved in helping others. The group of non-believers had shorter depressed lives full of worry, fear, and loneliness. The core of the finding showed overall it was not religion that was so important to long happy life, although it helped many people. Rather, it's the lifestyle that tends to go along with being religious that explained why these people lived longer and happier.

I pray every day, sometimes I don't even know I'm doing it fully, and sometimes I'm fully in the moment of prayer, either way it is helpful to me. I give away my anxiety, I am thankful, I give away my worries, and I am hopeful, and this makes me happy. To me prayer is just like journaling, it is a way to get your feelings off your mind and heart and get them out. It's a way to be grateful, to live in the moment, and to be happy where you are while expecting more blessings. Prayer is not a mysterious practice reserved only for clergy and the religiously devout. Prayer is simply communicating with God, listening with your heart and mind and talking to Him. Believers can pray from the heart, freely, spontaneously, and in their own words. There is no correct or certain posture for prayer. In the Bible people prayed on their knees, bowing on their faces, and standing. You may pray with your eyes open or closed, quietly or out loud—however you are most comfortable and the least distracted. You don't need to have a certain prayer; neither do your prayers need to be wordy or impressive in speech. A prayer is a conversation with God just like you have a conversation with your best friend or spouse.

FILL YOUR OWN GAS TANK

"Never hesitate to hold out your hand; never hesitate to accept the outstretched hand of another."

—Pope John XXIII

Hormonal balance is really about taking care of yourself. You need to do anything for yourself that will fill your own gas thank, like get a massage, go for a walk, take a bubble bath, drink a cup of hot tea, listen to music, or read a good book. If you are a caregiver, this is especially important. I have been a certified massage therapist for thirteen years, in addition, I am also the director and instructor of the massage program at Colorado Northwestern Community College. I learned fourteen years ago at my first day of massage school the benefits of keeping your gas tank full, and it's the first lesson I teach to my students. We all have a mental measure of where our own energy or gas is. When we are on F, or full, we feel good generally and are able to give to others. However, when we are running on E, or empty, we feel depressed, tired, brain fog, stress, and don't have the energy to take care of ourselves, let alone others. Getting a massage is a really great way to fill your tank, and also an endorphin releaser. A whole-body massage can relax those stiff muscles that might be causing tension headaches. It can help to free your mind of stressful events or difficult emotions, at least temporarily. Having a massage puts the focus on you and the present, taking it from problems and the past or future. You can escape challenges and problems by languishing in the care of a trained therapist whose firm hands will roll the tension right out of your body. In addition, massage is a great pain reliever when you have an injury or sore muscle. Massage is also a way to increase your circulation when you are sluggish or you have been sitting at your desk for too long. For me, massage is a great way to fill my own gas tank. Being a care giver, it is important when you are giving and giving all the time to sometimes be the receiver. Your car can't run on empty, and neither can your body. Let's face it; many of us are hard workers and caregivers, looking after children, aging adults, and our own careers or relationships. All of these things can be demanding, so escaping for an hour to get a massage is a terrific way to step into another world, at least briefly, to enjoy the luxury of relaxation and endorphin release. Just like when you exercise, afterwards you'll be ready to re-enter the everyday world of stress and strain because you have stepped outside temporarily to take a breather. It's hard to stay in a bad mood when a professional massage therapist is using techniques on your body in a way that releases natural substances from the brain that evoke a pleasurable response. Plus, just getting away from the hectic pace of everyday life and enjoying a personal indulgence can give you a calmer, happier, frame of mind.

I have found that many joys in life come from paying attention to personal needs and making time to do things that we usually let pass by. To be happy, you must pay attention to your own personal needs. Make sure you take time to refuel yourself. Make sure you are doing one or more of these endorphin releasers every day.

Happy people know how to fill their own gas tanks. They take time for themselves and nurture themselves with body work, acupuncture, chiropractic, a facial, or a whole spa day; and yes manly men, it's ok to go to the spa. Most everyone I know is driving their own body around on empty. Your car won't run on empty, and neither will your body. If you are constantly giving and never receiving, or never taking care of yourself, you are driving with an empty tank. You are at risk of running out of fuel at any moment. Happy people know when they are on E, and they stop to refuel.

INTIMACY IS NATURAL

"I am not afraid of my femininity; I am not afraid of my sexuality."

—Goldie Hawn

SEX MAKES YOU HAPPY AND HEALTHY

Happy people are physically healthier, they live longer, and they enjoy a higher quality of life. If you didn't already know, having sex is a great way to unleash your happy hormones. Being intimate is a natural necessity for all humans. Sex is a basic need for us, it is a great way to help your body be happy and release endorphins. If you are feeling a little blue or stressed, having sex is a great way to calm down and cheer up.

Here are the top seven ways sex can make you happier and healthier.

Unleash Happy Hormones–When you have sex or physical contact, your body releases hormones such as dopamine and norepinephrine. These endorphins produce a general sense of well-being, including feeling soothed, peaceful, pain free, and secure. Engaging in sexual activity with a loved one will not only give you a release of endorphins after orgasm, but it gives you a natural high. The endorphins released during sexual intercourse and orgasms are naturally calming and not only ease depression, but will prevent it. In your brain, serotonin and dopamine levels increase in response to positive social interactions. In women, positive social interactions cause oxytocin levels to rise, and, in men, vasopressin levels rise. Oxytocin and vasopressin are the chemicals that drive people toward feeling connected and happy. People with strong, supportive partners live healthier, happier lives. Endorphins are also what our body releases for pain relief. Sex can lower levels of any pain, especially headache pain, yes I said headache pain, no more excuses ladies! Hormones that are released during sexual excitement and orgasm can elevate pain thresholds.

Reduce Stress–A big health benefit of sex is lower blood pressure and overall stress reduction. Sex will help you reduce stress, calm your nerves, and feel happier. Letting your mind go and relaxing is a natural part of sex. When you relax, your body is naturally happier. When you reduce stress in any way you will naturally have an "all is well" feeling. Stress happens, it's an ongoing problem and you can't expect to solve it in a day. But by relaxing and enjoying one another, you'll find your stress levels declining.

Sleep better–Sex is also a great way to help you sleep, and when you get enough sleep you will be happy. And getting enough sleep has been linked with a host of other good things, such as maintaining a healthy weight and blood pressure. Getting enough sleep is a great way to keep your body happy. Most people need seven to nine hours of sleep every day. When you are sleeping your body is able to repair itself and get ready for tomorrow.

Glow–The glow of good sex is a real thing. Women who have more sex have higher levels of estrogen, which is essential to having shiny, clear, and healthy skin. Knowing your skin looks great is a confidence booster. When we feel good about ourselves we are naturally happier.

It's Exercise–Sexual activity is a form of physical exercise! Making love three times a week burns around 7,500 calories in a year, that's the equivalent of jogging 75 miles! A night of love can raise the amount of oxygen in cells, helping to keep organs and tissue cells functioning at their peak. Any kind of physical exercise is going to increase testosterone. Testosterone is believed to help keep our bones and muscles strong. Any exercise has a number of mood-enhancing physiological effects. Exercise releases endorphins that make us feel happy. Also, a good workout helps detoxify the body from the inside out via the lymphatic system, making all body systems function more effectively.

Lowered Cholesterol–Making love regularly can lower levels of the body's total cholesterol slightly, while positively changing the ratio of good-to-bad cholesterol. The movement is also great for your circulatory system.

DHEA–Is a popular supplemental hormone that is released naturally during lovemaking. This hormone is important because it balances all the other hormones. Just before orgasm, DHEA spikes to levels three to five times higher than usual. DHEA is used for slowing or reversing aging, improving thinking skills in older people, and slowing the progress of Alzheimer's disease. Athletes and other people use DHEA to increase muscle mass, strength, and energy. DHEA is also used by men for erectile dysfunction, and by women who have low levels of certain hormones to improve well-being and sexuality.

So as you can see, a little, or lot of, love making is great for your health and happiness. This should put a smile on your face. The basic fact is that a good sex life also means in the bigger picture, a good relationship with one's partner, happiness, less stress, and by virtue of all that, physically healthier.

Again, not every chapter is for everyone. However, if you are physically healthy and in a healthy relationship, being sexual can be another great tool to help you release endorphins. Being intimate is a natural necessity for all humans. Sex is a basic human need for us all. If you are in a healthy relationship, research has shown that having sex not only releases happy hormones, but it also has many other benefits. Studies show having an orgasm on a regular basis boosts confidence, reduces the risk of heart disease, improves fitness, is a natural pain killer, and boosts your immune system. Having sex during PMS or menstruation is known to relieve a woman's cramps and is even suggested during labor to relieve the pain of contractions. In addition, thirty minutes of sex burns about 150 calories. This makes sex healthier for you than yoga, which burns 114 calories per half hour. So, having sex twenty-three times for just thirty minutes will burn off one pound of fat and be much more fun than exercise. And considering that people gain weight gradually, this benefit of sex can help you maintain your ideal body weight over time. So you have nothing to lose but your clothes.

So why aren't you doing it more often? I believe that there are a few reasons people aren't in the mood. First, you might have let yourself get too busy and overloaded with kids, jobs, and housework. Our brains are on information overload, and we are just too tired physically and mentally. Also, medications can lower your libido, and any low levels of hormones can reduce your sex drive, another reason to keep your happy hormones bio-chemically balanced. If you have low libido, see a professional who can help balance your hormones. If you are not having sex because you don't feel great about yourself or have self-confidence issues, I can almost guarantee your mate doesn't see any flaws if your clothes are off. Depression is another cause for low libido. If your libido is low, it is due to your body running on empty for too long. When you are stressed for a long period of time your adrenal glands or stress glands shut down and all your hormones, including the happy ones, are at a low level. If you are experiencing a low libido and do want to be physically sexual, I would recommend adding the vitamins and supplements suggested in the chemical chapters. Low libido is a sign you are not happy and you are too stressed. When you are too stressed you body takes all its energy into just giving you energy, this leaves no energy left over for intimacy. It's a bad continuous cycle. If you are depressed, you don't feel in the mood, but when you're happy, you want to have sex. And win-win: if you have sex, you are happy. Therefore, I suggest you stay happy. It's a win-win for all. Not only is it good for your relationship but good for your health too. In addition, people's home lives can either help alleviate stress at work or make more stress. Having a good relationship is a great way out from your stressful day. Cuddling, touching, holding hands, and sex, are things you can come home to. Sex is something that gives you leeway to rewind, relax, and recover from your work day. Or better yet, a great way to start the day!

In addition, if you are withholding sex from your mate as punishment, stop this right now. Sex is not a weapon, nor is it a reward. Do not use the two-week penalty. In order to be a happy, you must never go to bed angry. In order to be happy, your relationship has to be happy, and in order to have a happy relationship, you must not control or reward your relationship with sex. Making love is sharing pleasure with your partner. It is not a payment for good behavior or a punishment for bad actions. Withholding sex is a manner of control. You cannot control your relationship or how your mate behaves by withholding sex from them. You are not your mate's mother. You should not punish them in any way, especially by withholding sex.

Personally, I think the only time that it is within reason to withhold sex is if you just had surgery, you're unhealthy, or your mate has cheated on you and you need time to think clearly about the situation. Also, if you have been hurt, you might not want to get intimate. It is understandable to withhold while you work out your problems. However, it is best to communicate, and then have makeup sex! If your partner shows you love, affection, compassion, respect, and attention, then you do not have a justifiable reason to withhold sex. In addition, having a headache is not a reason to say, "Not tonight." I have already told you that pain relief is gained from the endorphin release. Withholding sex feels like rejection, and you know rejection hurts. If you have ever been denied something, you know it hurts. Denying sex to your mate is hurtful. When the one you love is the one rejecting you, it hurts even more. Using sex as punishment is not only inappropriate, it is wounding to the one who loves you and the one you love. You would never on purpose physically hurt the one you love. If you realized how hurtful withholding is, you wouldn't do it. I'm here to bring light to you and help you realize that using sex as a weapon is a big gash to the heart of the one who loves you. If you have a problem with your partner, then do something about it. But don't be petty by withholding sex. Grow up. Don't withhold sex just because you didn't get your way. Don't withhold sex because they missed something. Don't withhold sex because they need a shower. Take one with them. Don't withhold sex because you want to. Don't withhold sex because you're annoyed. Partners need to know that the other is vulnerable and that they are trustworthy of respecting that vulnerability. Find another way to communicate your needs with them. In conclusion, if you've got a good man or woman and have a healthy relationship, then don't use sex as a weapon. Have sex with love. Relationships will endure many problems, and every relationship has ups and downs. Don't let this be an issue to make it worse. Although sex isn't the superglue that holds relationships together, it sure does help strengthen the superglue that does.

GET SOME BEAUTY REST

"I love sleep; my life has a tendency to fall apart when I am awake."

—Ernest Hemingway

Sleep is not just for beauty. They don't call it beauty sleep for nothing though; sleep does help us look good. Just ask anyone who's woken up with dark under eye circles. Happy people know that they need to get rest. Sleep deprivation plays a huge role when it comes to high levels of cortisol. It is also a reason many people struggle so much with weight-loss. Imagine compounding all of the above mentioned cortisol raising agents, it would go something like this. *Woke up for work with 7 hours of sleep, went to work tired, drank four cups of coffee, had a bad day, stressed out, ate a bunch of bad carbs, and flipped out in traffic on the way home.* Stress is high and cortisol is flying high. Where does all this cortisol go? If you don't sleep, it goes to your muffin top and spare tire. We need sleep in darkness with the TV off. When we sleep, in darkness, our bodies convert cortisol to melatonin. We need sleep!

No sleep = No Melatonin.

No Melatonin and High Cortisol = Very dangerous chemical imbalances.

Dangerous chemical imbalance = Very unhappy you

Also, stay away from melatonin supplements. If you take them to sleep, your body will sense the increased amount of melatonin (from being outsourced) and take a less serious role in the production of melatonin, making your body less efficient at the conversion of cortisol to melatonin.

During sleep, your body turns into a repairman for itself and releases repair hormones. These repair hormones set to work fixing all damaged tissues, including the skin (can you say beauty rest?). If you don't get enough sleep, not only do you shortchange yourself of the repair hormone, but you're also at risk for boosted levels of stress hormones, which can wreak havoc on your organs; and the largest organ happens to be the skin, which causes premature aging. The relationship between stress and sleep is a vicious circle. Too much stress, be it regarding financial concerns, health problems, or relationships, makes it harder to sleep. A lack of sleep, however, only increases the amount of stress you feel because your sleep-deprived body churns out more stress hormones. Insomnia due to stress has been linked with increased risk for anxiety disorders and depression.

LAUGH ON PURPOSE

"A day without laughter is a day wasted."

—Charlie Chaplin

Proverbs 17:22 says a joyful heart is good medicine, but a crushed spirit dries up the bones. Studies show that an hour of 'laughter-yoga' decreased the group's cortisol levels pretty dramatically. Laughter literally is medicine–and without the nasty side effects! Laughter yoga is fun, you make yourself laugh on purpose for a whole hour long class, and of course, if you can image watching others trying to make themselves laugh, is enough to make you laugh. I recommend you laugh every day. Have a joke app. on your phone or a joke calendar on your desk. Do whatever you need to do to laugh from your belly and when it hurts laugh some more.

The other day, I was worrying and stressed a bit from a long day at work, and when I walked into my friend's house, her first response was, "What's wrong with you?" How did she know I was upset? If I asked you to describe what a depressed person looks like, could you do it? The answer to both these questions is hunched shoulders, slouched posture, eyes looking down, frowning, no energy, etc. The human body is wired this way. When you feel depressed, you'll act/look this way. In addition, when you act/look this way, you'll feel depressed. There is a physical neurological connection between the two. So, similarly, we have a connection between happiness and laughter. When you're happy, you make yourself laugh. When you laugh, you're making yourself happy. How happy we want to be partly depends on how often we choose to laugh. Happy people laugh a lot with childish joy.

Not only does laughter make us happy, but it also has its health benefits. Laugher triggers positive chemical and hormonal changes in the body. Here is how research has shown it affects one's health.

LOWER BLOOD PRESSURE

After the initial burst of laughter, our blood pressure drops to lower-than-usual levels. We also breathe deeper and fuller after a good bout of laughter.

BURNS CALORIES

By laughing, you are exercising the various muscles in your body, including the diaphragm, face, abdomen, chest/lungs, and back. This is known to help several bodily functions, including our digestion process. Another benefit is that laughter burns as many calories as a few minutes of real exercise such as walking, etc. Now is that great or what?

PAIN RELIEVER AND FEEL-GOOD FACTOR

Laughter releases those fantastic happy hormone endorphins, which gives a sense of well-being.

STRESS RELIEVER

Laughter releases pent-up emotions. Stress, tension, worry, anger, etc. can be reduced through a good bout of laughter.

Have you ever been at a funeral and let out a chuckle and then felt unsure if you should laugh or cry, but you were glad the speaker lightened up the situation a little? I remember, when I was at my grandma's funeral (the first close relative I had lost), the speaker joked of the way she would cover her walls in pictures instead of wallpaper. This made everyone chuckle, because it was so true. To understand, you would have had to go into my grandma's house just once to know that her entire walls were covered ceiling to floor with family picture collages and funny signs. I remember feeling unsure if I should laugh or cry. But I automatically let out a chuckle and realized that it felt good to let it out. This is normal and good. When you laugh, what you're doing is telling yourself that you can handle the situation. Unconsciously, that's what you are telling your brain. While you're laughing, your brain thinks, *"Wait a minute. I'm okay. I'm laughing. I guess I can do this."*

Sometimes we laugh with nervousness, silence, fear, or sometimes it's when we are agreeing. Try to notice when you laugh. As a kid, I remember pregnancy-checking cows. If you don't know how this is done, the vet actually inserts his hand into the anus of a cow to feel the uterus. As I was helping get cows into the chute, I was splattered with cow manure all over my face. As gross as this was, I remember laughing hard even though my mouth was closed. I remember the vet commenting that this type of laughter was good for your health. Actually, this is the concept behind laughter yoga and laughter therapy. Little did I know that the manure on my face was good for my health. By silently laughing, a smile was still brought to my face. I encourage you to laugh for happiness. Laugh when you have fear. Laugh when you are nervous, if your kids are sleeping, or your coworkers are near and you need a boost, anytime works. Imagine you have manure on your face, and laugh silently to yourself. The benefits will be the same.

I have found that by responding to our challenges with laughter instead of worry, we can put ourselves in a state to tackle whatever issues we are facing. I know that when I am feeling stressed or angry, my judgment will often lack accuracy. I know that when I am in a frazzled state, a little joke goes a long way.

I am a personal witness that we take life too seriously. We all tend to perceive things as being worse than they actually are. If I let myself worry unconsciously, the ideas my head can come up with are outrageous. Even scarier is if I let my head believe these things. Laughter is the best way to bring things back into perspective. When I am in a difficult situation, I will naturally make a joke. Maybe it's because I'm uncomfortable and maybe a little insecure of the situation, but it always helps me lighten up a little. Laughter encourages positive thoughts and feelings, and these have an impact on the body. I am a firm believer of the phrase "What you think, you become." Negative thoughts create dis-ease, and dis-ease in the body will create diseases. I don't know about you, but my health is more important than letting negative thoughts make me sick. Nevertheless, laughter and positive thoughts regenerate and heal the body. In addition, I believe we should be able to laugh at ourselves. When we can laugh at ourselves, we don't take ourselves too seriously.

> With the fearful strain that is on me night and day, if I did not laugh I should die.
>
> —Abraham Lincoln

Now that I am an adult, I realize that stress is on every adult. Everyone I know is reflecting on the things we haven't done. We start each day worrying earlier over coffee and end each night staying up late with worry. I once heard a story of Buddhist priests who patented a method for making holy water. He took a pot of water, placed it on a hot stove, and boiled the devil out of it. He patented that the bouncing of the bubbles released the bad. Now, he wasn't the first to discover boiling water. As an instructor of massage, I teach my students that laughter boils the lymph system. I think that if we giggle more, we can boil out our worries. I know sometimes we feel like the world is on our shoulders. Every week, I talk to people who are battling the heavy load of life. The number of people who are dealing with depression, oppression, loneliness, and barrenness saddens me. People hold the weight of heartaches and disappointments on their shoulders. However, notice that when you giggle hard enough, your shoulders can't help but bounce. Happy people know that in order to be happy, they must boil the stress away. Let the disappointment bounce off like bubbles. Find a good joke book, watch a funny movie or comedian, or spend time with a friend you know will make you laugh. Just start laughing over nothing until your shoulders bounce. Watch yourself in the mirror. (Doing this, I promise you will start to laugh at yourself.) In the midst of the battles we face, we can still choose peace. Happy people know that the ammunition of life doesn't have to penetrate the soul.

We all have times when there doesn't seem to be enough to go around. Bills pile up faster than the checks come in, and anxiety creeps into your mind. I know that giggling doesn't make the bills go away any faster. But in order to be happy, we can't let worthless worry steal our daily joy. I had a patient the other day tell me she carries Ziploc bags to hide the germs. She uses them on hotel remotes, door knobs, and ATM machines. She had a Ziploc over her own phone so it didn't have her own germs on it. I explained to her how I am hardly ever sick and I never worry about the germs on a remote control or my own phone. We laughed about this. But this made me think how we can have fear of the unseen and worry about the potential harm. Happy people know how to keep everything in perspective and rest in laughter. Happy people know how to keep peace and enjoy the day even when the bills are on the counter and it's a week before a check comes.

You have the power to move on in life through the contagion of laughter. My grandma has spent years collecting jokes and sayings that make us all laugh. She has quotes on dieting, age, mothers, husbands, wives, kids, jobs, wrinkles, love, and cleaning—you name it; you know, all those hot spots in a person's life that would kill us if we didn't laugh about them. The secret she says "is to not get down, and the secret of not letting them get you down is to laugh about them." My grandma says, "We can cry, or we can laugh." Both of these responses create a release in us. Sometimes I've found I need to do both. But the laughing is certainly the more fun. I love Tanya Tucker's song "Strong Enough to Bend." I think when we bend over from laughing so hard it's so we don't break. I know laughing is like changing a baby's diaper; it's only a temporary fix to the problem, but it makes life stink less for a bit. Happy people know that they need to giggle for life to be acceptable for a while. So get giggling and laughing.

FORBID TO LIVE IN FEAR

"How we spend our days is, of course how we spend our lives."
—Annie Dillard

I'm sure you already know fear triggers the "fight or flight" response, characterized by increased heart rate, breathing, and muscle tension. Our emotions are hard-wired, bio-chemical functions of the brain, and our feelings, from the conscious mind, give us emotions. When we are in real danger, and our eyes see danger, for instance if you are hiking and have a bear encounter, the nerves from the eye send an emergency red flag directly to the hypothalamus (brain) to produce a stress hormone. The release of this stress hormone triggers the pituitary glands to release another stress hormone (ACTH), which in turn stimulates the adrenal gland to secrete cortisol. Cortisol in the bloodstream causes an increase in glucose production, providing the necessary fuel for the brain and muscles to deal with stress. This is all great, except when it's just a fear and not a seen danger. When we have fear in our minds our body does the same assembly line of chemical reactions. We think up a problem that could, might, maybe occur and then we put our hypothalamus, pituitary, pancreas and adrenals to work. We make our body stress and overwork just by thinking up a problem, no wonder we are exhausted and overwhelmed. No wonder $300 billion is spent on stress in the USA. Most of us are living in fear every day and the news doesn't help. Recently, we are aware that our government is a mess, we are in debt, food and fuel are going up, and we are making less money. We are afraid to send our kids to school, we are afraid of what we eat, we are afraid of the weather, we are afraid of tomorrow. YUCK! No wonder we are all stressed. Just thinking fear thoughts makes your body make cortisol. Do you know there are phobias for just about everything? There is the even the fear of bath soap, sunlight, and even the fear of fear. Holy-moly, let's stop this.

Fear = Cortisol

So how do we stop this downward spiral? FEAR NOT, do not be afraid, do not fear, is in the Bible 365 times, I don't think that is a coincidence, I think God knew us humans would be tempted with fear. I believe FEAR NOT is in the Bible 365 times so that we remember to "not fear" every single day of the year. Fear is not from God but from Satan. See 2nd Timothy 1:7. Every time you feel fear it's from the kingdom of darkness. The devil is real and he uses fear to keep people from enjoying life. Fear brings distress, according to the Bible, and you really can't enjoy life and be in distress at the same time. I know it is so hard, but we have to learn to face the fear and do it anyway. Last year I was on my first LIVE TV show, I was so nervous and had so much fear in front of all the cameras, but I knew deep down that what God had called me to do, he would help me. I prayed for strength with my husband and I did it, I faced the fear and did it anyway. No it wasn't easy, and yes I was sweating bullets, but I did it anyway. I want to encourage you to stop fearing. Face your fears, whatever you are fearing right now let it go, and believe me God will help you. I have now done 7 live TV shows and I'm a pro on camera. If I would have never done the first one, I would never be where I am today. The time is now to face your fears and not run away from them. Just ask Jesus for strength and acknowledge that He is with you, and go do it. Don't let your heart be troubled, stop being anxious. After all, many things are not worth getting worried and upset over. Most things are just part of life and not the end of the world. What are you worried about today? Worry is just another word for fear; for us to be happy, we must forbid having fear in our minds. In my experience, most people worry too much. If you are one of them, start by asking yourself what you are worried about. In my experience, we worry about stuff that is never even going to happen, and we lose today in the process.

If you want to be happy, you need to live each day from sunup to sundown. The next time you find yourself worrying, pause and ask yourself, *What's the worst that could happen?* By doing this, I have found that when you think of the very worst, you will find that you are still going to be okay.

Stop fussing. Start enduring. If you are one of those people who fuss at the little things and gets upset over minor things, you need to start recognizing that it is so. Sometimes things in life are just so. Take for instance the snow. I hate the cold weather and the slick roads that come with it, but it is just so. A lot of things we can let ourselves worry about are really out of our control. Just like I can't change the weather, you can't change the economy, other people, or the height of Mount Everest. Some things are just so. In addition, the past is also just so. You can't change the past. It is dead. You can't burn ashes. If a circumstance is beyond your control, let it go. You can't change the predestined.

Something you can do to help with any situation is getting the data in details. Once you have all the specifics, then write several resolutions out on paper. In my experience, I have found that when a patient or friend comes to me with worry and stress, most of the time, they lack details to a decision. By getting all the facts and clearly coming up with a result, you will be able to choose the way out. If you are losing sleep over a situation, ask yourself, *What are the odds of this really happening?* In my experience, we, as humans, worry over too much that isn't even in the odds.

The next step is to prepare yourself mentally to accept the worst. If you are worried about money issues, for example, think of the worst that could happen. Maybe it would be losing your house to foreclosure and filing bankruptcy. Yes, I admit those are scary circumstances that happen sometimes in life. On the other hand, you are still going to be okay—uncomfortable, yes, but okay. If you prepare yourself mentally—imagine living in a camper at the KOA, showering in the public shower, and folding the couch out to make your bed—you might realize that it isn't ideal but it's not the end of the world and you could do it. You can do anything if you are intellectually prepared.

Lastly, calmly try to perk up the worst that you have agreed to accept. Last month, I had a trial in this area. I was stressing about a meeting with someone, and I had fear in every area I could imagine (literally). As I was writing this chapter, I realized that I needed to take my own advice. I started to think of the worst that could happen. I prepared myself mentally for the meeting and decided to get honest with myself and accept the worst. I decided to not believe lies, but every day leading up to the meeting, I decided to put on clothes of strength. I decided I couldn't dwell in the fear, and I decided to live one day at a time. In addition, I decided to perk up the worst. I decided that I was going to make the best of it. The month leading up to the meeting was a growing process for me, and when the day actually came, all my fears proved to be false and the meeting didn't even take place.

My grandma always told us to make the best of it. She was a great example to us all. It's very simple but important if you will make the best of what life throws you, even the worst that could happen can be perked up a little bit. I recall one time while on a camping trip with my grandparents it rained more than had been expected. All our clothes were soaked with water, and to top it off, we had to stay an extra day so we didn't get the truck stuck trying to get through the new mud. None of us had a change of clothing, but my grandma looked at us all and said, "Well, we will just have to make the best of it." This meant that we all had to wear towels from the cabin's closet as clothes—not ideal, but we did make the most of what we had. The only food we had was pancake mix and water, but we all made the most of it. We all still laugh today how we wore towels for clothes.

If the worry you have is what others think of you, I am going to be frank with you and tell you to grow up. If you are worrying about criticism of others, know first that most people are so worried with their own issues that they really don't care about yours. If you go to the store and worry about what others will think about what you are buying, wearing, or driving, you need to realize that most people really don't care. They are not looking in your cart but worried about what is in their own. If others are really criticizing you, know that criticizing is often a compliment in disguise. If others are talking about you, it is usually in their own jealously that you are on their minds. In this instant, you need to ban this fear.

ARE YOU READY TO QUIT WORRYING?

"I never worry about diets. The only carrots that interest me are the number you get in a diamond."

—Mae West

So the other day while I was on my stationary spin bike I realized it is just like worrying. When we worry our stress hormones do the same as if we were in real danger. Our brains and bodies don't know the difference in a real problem or when we worry about a problem. Worry is like riding a spin bike, your brain spins and spins and it's always in motion but you don't get anywhere. So why do we struggle with it? I myself used to worry and worry. I would make myself sick worrying over things. And what good did it do me? I have learned that to worry is the opposite of having faith, and it steals our joy and it takes our peace. The constant stress on us physically wears us out, and is hard on the immune system so it can even make us sick. Chronic worrying affects your daily life so much that it interferes with your appetite, lifestyle habits, relationships, sleep, and job performance. Many people who worry excessively are so anxiety-ridden that they seek relief in harmful lifestyle habits such as overeating, cigarette smoking, or using alcohol and drugs. When we are on the spin bike of life spinning our mind in circles, we put our mind and body into overdrive as we constantly focus on "what might happen." We are making our hormones go out of whack and we wonder why we feel so stressed. When we worry, we are just torturing ourselves. We are putting distress on our own selves. Why do we put ourselves through this anguish? Really, As a Christian I have learned that when we worry we are listening to the enemy. I used to worry so much as a kid my grandparents bought me a worry stone for Christmas. I am now sad about all the time I have wasted worrying about the next day and things beyond my control. I was only putting myself in distress. I am so thankful I have learned to do something else with my fears. Worry is caused by not trusting God to take care of us and our situations. Too often we trust our own selves and rely on our own abilities, believing that we can figure out how to take care of our own problems. Yet sometimes, after all that time worrying and effort to go it alone, we come up short, unable to bring about suitable solutions. Now I ask you, knowing that you are doing the enemies work for him, are you ready to quit worrying?

In The Bible Peter says, "humble yourselves under the mighty hand of God, that in due time He may exalt you, casting the whole of your care. All your anxieties, all your worries, all your concerns, once and for all on Him, for He cares for you affectionately and cares about you watchfully." Since Jesus invites us to cast all of our care and worry on Him, why do so many of us refuse to let go? Apparently, I think it's because we like to be miserable. We like to worry and tell others about our worries. We like to call friends and talk about our latest worries and fears. I can tell you, I am much happier now that I have learned to cast my anxiety on him. I've learned that my attitude has a lot to do with living a worry-free life. There will always be situations that cause us concern, but with God's help, we can live above all of it and enjoy a happy life. My favorite verse that I had to have up on my bathroom for years is Philippians 4:6-7: "Do not fret or have any anxiety about anything, but in every circumstance and in everything, by prayer and petition, with thanksgiving, continue to make your wants known to God. And God's peace which transcends all understanding shall mount guard over your hearts and minds." I believe this means that if we want to have peace we must stop worrying. If we want to be happy we must not let the devil whisper lies to us, we must learn to give away all our worry. This comes with practice; don't get me wrong, I have spent the last five years building my spiritual muscles up so I don't worry now. But I did it and you can too. Learn to control what you can and give and trust God with what you can't. So stop worrying about everything, give it to God, and live in grace. Grace isn't just divine favor – it's power! Don't waste another day of your life worrying.

ENJOY THE SUCCESS OF OTHERS

"One man cannot hold another man down in the ditch without remaining down in the ditch with him."

—Booker T. Washington

Have you ever tried to hold another person back? If you will live unselfishly and help others get to the next level, you will not only be happier but you will reach your next level too. I read about this professional mountain climber who was with a group on Mt. Everest. The group was almost to the summit when they encountered a blizzard and were near frostbite. Five hundred feet from the top they came upon another climber who had fallen down and went to sleep with hypothermia. The professional climber stopped and started to shake his limbs, rub his face, and massage the fallen man to help circulate his blood and warm him up. The climbers group left him, thinking he was crazy, and kept climbing to stay warm. But the moral of this story is that not only was the man who was freezing warmed up and alive, but the professional climber kept himself from frostbite, the massage and movement increased both their circulation. You see, in order to make happy happen we must stop to help others. The truth is, when we take time to help others win, we help ourselves win. Fill your mind with peace, joy, courage, hope, and trust, for our life is what our thoughts make of it. One thing that I have learned is a happiness stealer is thinking negatively about our enemies. Probably the hardest lesson I had to learn was to love others who have done me wrong. I used to get so upset and feel threatened by others who were successful in my same profession. It used to drive me crazy to see other women be successful, looking good, or in a happy relationship when I wasn't. I know women who have lost the friendship of others when one lost weight. I know of women who lose friends over fertility issues when one tries to have a baby and the other has several. I remember being so upset that my younger cousin was engaged when I was still in my internship and not even dating someone. I have learned that envy is ignorance. We need to find ourselves and then be ourselves. When we are good to others, we are greatest to ourselves.

When I was in my internship, the doctor, from whom I learned a lot, did me wrong in a business deal. I spent months being angry with the whole family. I recall wishing bad luck upon them. It's not something I am happy about now, but I admit that I remember wishing that they would go out of business, get flat tires, and the like. However, once I learned that this was only hurting me, I stopped. I now wish good fortune upon them. I now wish a blissful life for those I feel threatened by and those who are my contenders. It's not easy, and it takes some time to really mean what you are wishing for. I have learned that trying to get even with our enemies is just putting negative thoughts out there, and if we think negatively we will feel negative; however, if we wish blessings to our enemies, we will get blessings in return. Trying to get even only steals precious time from us. I have taught myself to only send out positive thoughts to my opponents. I admit it's hard, but I wish everyone the best now. And to prove this, I even pray for happiness and success for my bad boss, who I see as my enemy, my rivals, and anyone who is an enemy. Start today. Start wishing good to those you are competing with in business. Today, start wishing your enemies good luck. It might be hard, but go easy on yourself. Give it time, and soon you will really mean it from your heart. In addition, soon you will reap the benefits of the positive you are putting out there.

MAKE TIME TO CHILLAX

"The best eraser in the world is a good rest."

—O. A. Battista

L ife is hard. There is no doubt about it. There is no "easy" button to push when things get tough. Life is tricky, demanding, and sometimes grueling. But once you accept this and relax, it instantly gets better and you will instantly be happier. Another thing I have learned is what I like to call chillaxing (chill out + relax). Chillaxing is a word we made up for being super relaxed and having a stress free time. A chillaxing time is a time without any pressure, doing what is pleasing to you. What is your idea of chillaxing? Maybe your definition of chillaxing is reading a good book in a lawn chair, maybe it's shopping, maybe it's cloud watching. Whatever your idea is, have a cheerfully chillaxing day and feel the benefits of being anti-stressed. I spent my childhood being a grownup and my grownup life being an old person. Determined is one thing, but I invented being serious. But now that I have learned to work hard and play hard, that's exactly what I prefer to do. I love to have a weekend of climbing mountains after a week of seeing patients. In addition, I love to sit by the campfire and watch the stars and just relax. A few weeks ago, we went to Lake Powell, a fantastic place to chillax. I spent the days on the boat and the evenings watching shooting stars. I encourage you to relax, and wherever you are, spend the evening under the stars and try to see a shooting star. Up until about five years ago, I had not taken a vacation just to have a vacation.

After school, I went on trips, but they were always for continuing education or work-related reasons. I have learned though that chillaxing is not only enjoyable but it is necessary. The first time I understood relaxing completely, I was in Vegas with my friend on a girls' trip. We spent the entire day at the day spa in white cotton robes, listening to soothing music by the waterfall and receiving various massages, body scrubs, and facials. It was so peaceful and replenishing that I knew I had to do more. The next month, I was on a small weekend getaway, snowshoeing the Continental Divide. After a great day hiking to the summit, we spent the afternoon in Creede, Colorado. It is an old silver mining town with a population of four hundred. We had a very chillaxing day with friends, walking through antique stores, eating snacks, and just doing zilch. It always makes me happy to have a day without pressure, activities, or a schedule. I enjoy every minute of my tranquil days, and I make sure I chillax more often.

BE OF SERVICE

"Be kind whenever possible. It is always possible."

—Dalai Lama

S ervice with a smile is what is important for happiness. Service should be with love. I grew up being of service. I am a helpful person and credit my parents for teaching me this skill. I find it easy to be of service. I am always the first to say, "If you need help, let me know." And I mean it when I say it. However, being of service is sometimes hard for others. If you have ever been to an AA meeting, you know this is as a step to recovery, and it is, in my book, a step to happiness, because by serving and helping others, we help ourselves. When you serve others, you will find amazing things in the process. I don't know about you, but I cannot be sad when I make someone else happy. I cannot find my depression when I'm serving others. I have discovered gifts that I never dared to share or even knew I had by helping others. I have found in serving others the desire to give, the trust to take risks, the strength to bear others' burdens, the courage to confront evil, and the grace to forgive. I have found that knowing others and their gifts as well as their needs teaches us about what is important and what we need to live for. When we serve, we find ourselves becoming a new people. We find that when we help others, not only is the smile contagious but we learn that we are new people. We learn that we are strong people.

Giving should be done for the joy of giving, not for gratitude or appreciation. If you are giving so others will appreciate you, you will never find the happiness that is meant to be found in giving. True happiness is found in giving when you don't want the gratitude or the pleasure from admiration.

DECREASE SOME DUTIES

"Make everything as simple as possible, but not simpler."
—Albert Einstein

"So today, first, I'll go to exercise class. Then I'll blend a protein shake. Then I'll run to the grocery store. Then I'll have lunch with my friend. I have to call back my messages, and then I'll meet friends at the movie. I also have to check my e-mail, and then I have to get ready for our yard sale and find something to wear to my friend's party this weekend. Oh, I have my own BBQ to plan for mom's birthday next week. And I need to take the dog to the vet, and then…" Sound familiar? Is your life run by your "and then's" and your smart phone? Are you stressed by your to-do list? I believe that happy people know that the first step toward being happy is living simple. Happy people know how to decrease duties. Happy people do what they want and say no to the rest. When you have a schedule full of things to do, you overwhelm yourself and your brain. If you are overwhelmed, your body doesn't know where to start. Your contentment is hidden. When you schedule fewer things, you create space in your day for the natural contentment that's always present. Simplify. Do what you need to do for yourself, your health, your loved ones, and your money situation, and stop scheduling what only adds anxiety. For me, living "simply" is to live content. If I am not spending money on things I don't need, I don't stress about making more. I used to live alone in a 2600-square-foot house with two living rooms and three bathrooms. I can only use one toilet at a time. I was constantly stressed about the mortgage and cleaning it. Now I live in half the space and I don't stress at all. Instead of stressing over a job, find the easiest way to get it done. Hire help or simplify. If you are planning a party, do you really need to stress over the balloons? If you are cleaning out closets, do you really need to spend a Saturday having a yard sale, or could you just drop it off at Good Will and go fishing instead? If you are meeting friends and being social and it's getting in the way of your time, simply say no. Simply simplify. Being simple doesn't mean you are content and not improving. Simple doesn't mean stop striving, but just live with an acceptance of what is and celebrating the good of each moment (refer back to the Chillax chapter you just read if needed). Depression comes when you are so busy you don't see the good of each moment until a few days later. I grew up thinking we always had to be busy to be successful. However, I have learned the hard way that success and happiness come from both striving and acknowledging that we are humans. True happiness is found when you are not so busy that you can't enjoy every moment of your life.

I believe technology is a distraction to this simplicity and happiness. Yes, I probably couldn't live without my phone these days. However, after being honest with myself about the stress it puts on me, I definitely have boundaries with my smart phone. I don't know about you, but most of my stress comes from my cell phone. Technology leaves us feeling like we must be available for others at all times. We feel like we must reply to texts, e-mails, and social media pages quickly. I have used my cell phone so much my wrists hurt, and my stress level rose every time I would check my messages. With the growth of smart phones everywhere, we are the most united disunited country there is. If you are unhappy and stressed because you are constantly checking your computer or smart phone, start to have a set time and limit for connecting with others. Shut your phone off sometimes and get back to it when you are ready. Happy people know that they can't let the distracting phone cause anxiety. In order for you to be happy, you must get rid of the desire to not miss anything. If you are overwhelmed by your little piece of technology, I suggest you get reconnected with something uplifting. Close your eyes for a minute, meditate, shut it off, and go for a walk outside. Reset yourself any way you need to. Simplify your life, but be the boss of your phone, not the other way around. Is there an app for that? I'm sure there is somewhere an iNoStress download for your iPhone. However, I have a free app for you. Push power, and turn your phone back on only after relaxing and rebooting yourself. Reply only when you have found peace. Set a time to check messages and reply when it's on your time. And, please, I beg you; don't stress yourself out with social networks. It has been proven that Facebook, MySpace, and such, are just as addicting as other bad habits. If you are addicted to Farmville, Quiz Me, Baby World, or whatever game you play, it's time to walk away from the computer. I agree it's great to be in contact with family and old friends, however, the anxiety that comes with posting and replying and the games is too much added stress for anyone. Use the thirty minutes you reply meaningless messages back for something to better yourself. Try a warm bath, meditate, stretch, or pick up the phone and talk to the person, voice to voice. Happy people know how to reset, relax, and reflect.

Today, we are attacked by three times more information than our parents were in the 80s. With the overflow of constant information coming at us, in addition to being constantly connected to everyone, I am sure that we are increasing our stress levels, losing creativity, potentially, and creating addictions. How many times a day do you check your email and Facebook on your phone. Can you say addiction? When we do something over and over it becomes an addiction, we cause our body to release dopamine, and evidence shows that you can become addicted to the rush you receive when the dopamine is released. This is why we continually return to something that gives us a rush, but this can disrupt normal, healthy patterns in your life.

Some studies show that being constantly connected to e-mail, social media sites, and your cell phone, may cause increased stress levels. Yes, I agree, because I know it increases mine. When I stop doing what I'm doing to check an e-mail/voicemail/text message, I experience stress. I know that I release cortisol whenever I look at my notifications. I believe my brain needs downtime, and I'm sure yours does too. In the middle of working on this book, my husband and I took off for a day of hiking and fishing without cell service to give our brains some down time.

When we're not doing anything, our brains are able to create on their own; I know I have more creativity when things come at me. When we constantly feed our brain information, it doesn't have time to recharge and regenerate. This doesn't just include your phone; it is also TV commercials coming at us. The great news is that when your brain is not having messages come at it, it continues to work, creating new ideas, and thoughts. It is through downtime that I can increase my creativity and learning. I just got a hot rock massage and the therapist put a rock on my forehead, the weight of it literally grounded me to the table and made me stay still and quiet. In yoga, a good grounding is to sit on your hands. So my advice; turn off your phone, lie down, put a small rock on your forehead, sit on your hands, and breathe sometimes.

Can you simply do one thing by itself and nothing else? We are all great multi-taskers. I was just writing this and listening to music. This morning, I put the dishes away and talked on the phone. In fact, the other day, I just burned my arm on the curling iron trying to fix my hair and brush my teeth at the same time. However, I believe this is why I love mountain climbing so much. For one, it is always just one task–keep on climbing–and another thing is I usually don't have phone service. Recently I spent a few days in a tent at Lake Powell. My biggest worry was applying more sunscreen. The peaceful trip was not expensive, but it was simple. The simplicity of doing nothing was so distressing that it got me thinking. I realized that I get unhappy and stressed when

I rush too much. I realized at one point that I was just lying in the tent, reading, and later that night, I realized I was just cooking dinner. I wasn't cooking, doing laundry, feeding the dog, talking on the phone, and worrying about my hair. I was happy, and I was simply warming up food on the propane stove. As we went on the boat to fish, I was mindful the whole time about my line in the water. I was just waiting for a tug on my bait. I wasn't answering e-mails, sending my thoughts to Facebook, or scrubbing toilets and folding towels. I was simply sitting in Zen, waiting for a bite. I realized at this time how happy we can be when we diss our duties and do one thing at a time. Multi-tasking is okay sometimes, in fact, it's a must on your job application. But the truth of it is, we need to be able to simply do one job at a time and be satisfied just as it is. You will be surprised at the mental space you find from simplifying your actions, schedule, and way of living. Happy and content people live simple.

Happy women simplify the time in the bathroom. Last month, a good friend and I were getting ready for a wedding when I laughed as I realized she was curling her hair and I was straightening mine. Not that we aren't happy with what we have, but we were looking for a new formal look. To be honest with you, I did the math and I have spent over 5500 hours straightening my hair since I was a teenager. That's 230 days in the bathroom. I'm not proud of this, but I believe you can learn my lesson only if I share truth with you. I have always had curly hair, but I liked the look of long layers straightened out, so I had my hair cut in layers and bought a Chi iron. It's upsetting now to me the hours I have lost in front of the mirror. I got honest with myself and started to simplify. I now spend five minutes in the bathroom with a little gel and I go out looking hot. In order for your mind to find space, you must simplify every action you make. If it's possible for you to simplify your time in front of the mirror for something more important, I suggest you try it. Go with what God gave you and get on with your day girl. Life is too short to be spent in front of your own reflection.

DISCONTINUE DISHONESTY

"Be truthful; nature only sides with truth."

—Adolf Loos

Stop lying to yourself. Happy people don't lie to themselves, and they don't believe the lies they think. Happy people don't live in fear. Happy people aren't dishonest with themselves. If you are like me and most people I know, you probably have a few negative thoughts going on in your head. Our minds are made up of thoughts. Some are good, and some are negative. In my first book, *Get Real*, I explained how thinking negative is reeking thinking. Like trash that is left in the house starts to reek and needs to be thrown out, in order to be happy, your reeking thinking needs to be thrown out.

How many times each day are you attacked by reeking thinking? Unless you are being conscious of your every thought, it's probably more than you realize. That is why it's important to start thinking about what you are thinking about. And if it's a lie, stop believing it.

How often do you think, I am not good enough. He/She doesn't really want to be with me. I am fat. I hate my hair. I'm scared about money. I'm so stupid. They don't like me. I hate my job. I hate where I live. I don't know what to do. I can't take this anymore. I'm being lied to. I wish…

No wonder you are so tired at the end of the day. Scientists say that women think an average of sixty thousand thoughts a day, men a little less. Of this, an untrained mind, not thinking, will think 80 percent negative thoughts. That is 48,000 negative thoughts a day, and you wonder why you aren't happy. When I do kinesiology muscle testing and something poison is placed on the body, the entire nervous system goes weak. Likewise, if you have a negative thought in the body, the entire nervous system will go weak. This is why the entire body is tired, has pain, and is sick with depression. On the other hand, if I was to place a positive vitamin on you, one your body likes and needs, your nervous system immediately would get strong. Likewise, when you think positive, your body gets calm, strong, and sturdy. Therefore, negative thoughts are the same as poison. You would not play with a venomous snake because the poison is fatal. Don't play with negative thoughts. They are toxic and fatal.

Your thoughts aren't always true. Have you ever had a sleepless night, thinking the same thing over and over? Have you ever replayed a situation over and over either what you should have done in the past or what you are going to do in the future? If you are like me, you have. I have spent a few sleepless nights with my own reeking thinking. I have had polluted thoughts playing the day before over and over in my head. In addition, I have had more restless nights letting toxic thoughts in of what I am going to do, say, wear, or be in a situation I am fearful of. However, years ago, I made a discovery that I lie to myself. And I'm sure you do it too. The truth is reeking thinking of the future is worry. We don't know what is going to happen in the future, and most of the time, I have found that what we worry about never happens anyway. Worry is toxic to our bodies too.

Sometimes we lie to ourselves. I remember when I had this breakthrough many years ago. I was house-sitting a very large hunting lodge in the mountains that was thirty miles from the nearest town. One night, I awoke to noises outside. I was immediately in fear of what the noise could have been. My thoughts went directly to *bear on the deck*, or was it maybe the lonely sheep-herder who knew I was very cute and very alone?

I lay awake and listened to every clatter and clang. I heard the deck boards rattle, and my thoughts got worse and worse. When I heard the glass in the door window shatter, my heart skipped a beat. I was in fear of whatever it was and wondered if it could come up the stairs to my bedroom. I jumped from my bed to go see what I needed to do. Could I find a way out the back door to my truck? Could I lock my bedroom door? I tried to turn the lights on, but the electricity was out. I instantly shut and locked my bedroom door, and then I ran into the bathroom, locking that door behind me too. I sat on the toilet, wishing I had a gun and a flashlight. I worried, as I was listening to every sound I could hear in the silence of the dark mountains. I sat in the bathroom for several hours and listened to every jangle and bang. When I couldn't hear any more noise, I got the courage to open the bathroom door. When I saw the sun coming in the bedroom window, I was relieved to see that it was morning. The house was quiet, so I bravely opened my bedroom door to look downstairs. What I saw was that a tree had fallen through the deck roof and the glass window of the front door. What I had feared was a massive mammoth coming to kill me was only the wind, nothing more. It wasn't the end of the world. It wasn't a gigantic man-eater. It was only wind. The moral to this story is I stayed awake all night in fear of the worst. I started to believe the lies I was telling myself. I lied to myself, and I believed the lies for hours. I thought my life was in danger.

However, that night, I learned a simple lesson. It's a revolutionary idea actually. I learned that we cannot believe everything we think to be true. All the negative thoughts are lies to us. All the thoughts of *I can't*, *I am*, and *I hate* are just lies we can't believe anymore. In the same way you wouldn't trust a friend or mate's lies, don't trust your own.

A few nights ago, I couldn't sleep because I had anxiety about what someone had said. I had a sleepless night, thinking over and over in my head what I was going to do and say. As I realized

I was in a nightmare awake, I instantly asked myself if what I was thinking was true and if I knew it to be 100 percent true. The answer was no. In my mind, I was making a mountain out of a molehill. I was embellishing and overstressing on a lie I was telling myself. I stopped in an instant when I realized this, and you can too. In order to stop believing your lies, you have to do more than just stop thinking negatively. The first thing you need to do is start to think about what you're thinking. When you do this, you will become conscious of all the toxic thoughts you let run through your head in a day. In addition, the next step is to do exactly what I did and ask yourself, *Is this accurate?* If you don't know your thought to be 100 percent factual, you are wasting your time trying to find a solution. Next, notice how you feel when you think the thought. When I was thinking negative in my sleepless night, I asked myself, *Is this accurate? Is this real? Is this confirmed?* My answer was, *No.* I didn't even need to think negatively anymore because I already knew that my thinking wasn't spot on. Then I tuned in to see how I was feeling. Heart racing, fretful, and uneasy is not a good combination. By my feelings, I knew I was unquestionably thinking negative. I changed my thinking and at once became calm. As I changed my thoughts, I found myself feeling empathy toward the situation and only respect for the one who had said the sentence. Thoughts and feelings aren't facts, and they are not you. If you don't have proof, you are probably lying to yourself. Stop drinking the poison.

WATCH YOUR WORDS

"Watch your thoughts, for they become words.
Watch your words, for they become actions.
Watch your actions, for they become habits.
Watch your habits, for they become character.
Watch your character, for it becomes your destiny."

—Anonymous

I'm sure this is not the first time you have heard this. Watching your thoughts and words is taught by many, many people. I am certainly not the author of this. Even the Bible says to watch your tongue. It has been proven in many ways that your words become your habits, leading to your future. It has been shown over and over that when the sick repeat, "I am sick," they just get worse; and likewise, when the sick declare out loud, "I am getting better and better every day," they do just what they say. Happy people know how to watch their words. Happy people know not to declare, "I'm depressed," out loud, nor do they let it in their thoughts.

It is hard to understand an energy we cannot see. I turn on the light switch, and the light comes on. I don't know how it works or even think about it. I just use the electricity. Your words are the same. They carry an energy we cannot see. Your thoughts, words, and mental pictures have strength to manifest in your life. The scary truth is that our words and our imagination is the source of our futures. Happy people watch their words, thoughts, and feelings. If Kyle or myself says something negative, the other one of us always makes the offender re-say it in a positive way so it's not put out there negatively, sounds silly, but it also helps make you think about what you say when someone else holds you accountable.

STOP SATISFYING

"The supreme happiness of life is the conviction that one is loved; loved for oneself, or better yet, loved despite oneself."

—Victor Hugo

I have learned from owning my own business that everyone expects us to keep them happy and give them what they want. However, this doesn't only happen in business. Your best friends, mom, sister, husband, kids, and cousins, expect the same thing. In order to be happy, we can't let people around us determine our value by what we do for them. Most of the time, the expectations put on us are too much and unreal. For years, I tried to be Superwoman, pleasing everyone who knew me by name. I became tired and overwhelmed very quickly. I tried to be Superwoman for everyone. I tried to make sure that everyone liked me. I spent many weekends taking care of my great-grandma so the rest of the family could have it off for fun. I did a lot of activities that weren't appealing to me to make others' lives easier. I couldn't say "no" for fear of criticism or making life hard on others. A happy person does not allow the moods of others to change theirs. In order to be happy every day, you must be single minded enough to have your own thoughts. Do not live under the dictatorship of anyone else. Be your own person.

Awhile back, my mom was invited to a wedding she felt obligated to go to. She is not fond of flying or traveling alone and didn't have peace about going; however, she felt obligated to go because she received the invitation. I shared with her the same advice I'm giving you. After she thought about it and said no, she told me she felt a weight lift off her shoulders. Wanting to make others happy is a great trait, but sometimes we find that we purely can't be what everyone wants us to be all the time; and quite frankly, it's exhausting and foolish to try. A lot of people fake everything they do. Unhappy people are phony and pretend so they don't upset anyone. Happy people don't spend their life being phony. Happy people don't mock or imitate to be accepted. True happiness comes from being yourself. Don't spend your life being with people you don't like. Don't spend your life doing things that you really don't enjoy. We should be nice to everyone, but we don't have to spend our days with them. I used to do things I didn't enjoy day in and day out; until I learned that I am a lot happier when I do what I want to do. Yes, there are always days we have to bend a little, always people we have to work with who we might not choose to if we had a choice. A little bend is okay. It is healthy to compliment your husband at the bowling Christmas party when you despise bowling. Or maybe sometimes you go to a guy's action film instead of your chick flick, or vice versa. Give and take is always good. But far too many people I know are pretenders. Make sure that you are around people who allow you to be yourself. If you have friends you are always pretending around, they are probably not true friends. In addition, if truth be known, they are probably pretending too. How sad. If you need to say no, do it. Anyone who says, "Okay," "Sure," "All right," "Why not," "No problem," or, "Yes," all the time is heading for sorrow. Happy people know how to say no. Maybe you will disappoint someone with your no, but they will get over it. You must decide that you are not going to spend your life making others happy all the time if you want to be happy yourself.

The world is full of people who are made-up performers and artists. I know too many people who pretend to be happy when they aren't. I know too many people who are in jobs they hate. One reason for divorce, I believe, is that too many people are pretending and you can only make-believe so long. If you are living false, inventing, or acting, stop now. Happy people don't act. Be yourself, and you will always be happy.

FINISH FORGIVENESS

"Always forgive your enemies–nothing annoys them so much."

—Oscar Wilde

Sometimes it's hard to let things go and forgive, but not forgiving is like trying to saw sawdust. You can't do something that's already been done. Not forgiving is trying to change what was done. The truth is that whether the wound is big or small, you can't be happy until you truly forgive. No one can deny that sometimes life is mean and sometimes we are treated unfairly, yet even in instances like these, forgiveness is possible and necessary. Most people believe that forgiveness is essential to mental health. I also believe that it is essential to physical health as well. In addition, I believe that you can't be truly happy without forgiveness. It doesn't matter if it is yourself, someone you will never see, or someone you love. Forgiveness is necessary to be happy and healthy. We often hear that it is important to let go of the anger and forgive, but if you don't know how, you might be stuck.

Anyone have trouble with their in-laws? Well I have had a run in with one of my sister in-laws. I won't go into details, but as a PH.D that preaches forgiveness to my patients, this situation made me think about forgiveness in a completely different way. Every time we go through something, I believe we can learn from it and let it shape us. I had such an issue forgiving her that the thought of seeing her would make me cringe and her name spoken would give me a stomach ache. If you have these feelings toward someone, it's a good sign that you haven't forgiven them.

It all started four years ago when I said something I shouldn't. This was my fault; I admit God has done a lot of work on me and controlling my tongue. However, I didn't mean any harm, I was speaking my truth, had I known it hurt her, I would have asked for forgiveness back then. But, I didn't know I had done anything wrong. You might think this is a story where she needed to forgive me, and you are right, however, I also had some forgiveness to do. I had to forgive myself and I had to forgive her for not handling it as I thought she should have.

I believe that many people ruin their health by holding bitterness and resentment. I had to practice what I preach and I had to handle this conflict as best I could. So what do I do when someone hurts me? I forgive them. To this day she has said she will hold a grudge forever, but I am glad that I don't have that weight on me and I am thankful that as a Christian I am free, and that I know how to forgive.

To actually forgive is hard, because as humans, we feel that if we forgive someone they are free, the truth is, when we forgive someone we become the free one. It's easy for me to tell others to forgive, but when I actually had to do it, for days I felt it was unfair. It feels unfair to us that we get the pain and they get the get out of jail free card. It took me over a year to be able to say I can truly forgive her and not let her scare me. Forgiveness is hard but it is so worth it to you. DO IT FOR YOU!

Our brain tells us not to forgive because we feel we are letting the other person off easy, But the truth couldn't be further, the truth is, when we forgive we are the one who is set free. In addition to letting the pain go with forgiveness, we also allow ourselves to be healthier. Studies show that when we hold the stress of pain we develop diseases in our cells. I think to really forgive we must really know how to forgive.

There have been times in my life that I thought I forgave someone or something, and then a problem arises again and I realized I must have not really forgave them. So how do you really, really, really forgive and take the weight from *your* shoulders?

Forgiveness does not mean what they did to you was right, alright, or that you have to be in a relationship with them. It simply releases the debt they owe to you and FREES you from the stress of it.

The dictionary definition of forgive is:

for·give

1. To excuse for a fault or an offense; pardon.
2. To renounce anger.
3. To absolve from payment.

There are 3 steps to true forgiveness and really truly letting things go.

1. Make a decision. First, before you do anything, you must make a decision that you want to be set free. You must choose to make up your mind that you want to be at peace and that you know that you are the one that it is fair to. You must make the decision for you and not for them. You must come to a decision that this is what you are going to do for you.

2. Let yourself off the hook. One of my hobbies is to fish, if you have ever fished you know when you have a fish on the hook they are powerless. When we haven't forgiven someone, we become powerless; we let them control our thinking and actions.

   We have this thinking that when we don't forgive, it gives us the control, but we're wrong. The truth is, when you forgive you are actually in control, "of yourself." When we really forgive we are also able to release the anger so we can live free. Become the powerful one by letting go.

"Forgive," only means to let go of that person or situation so that it, or they, no longer rob you of precious time. Your mind is no longer on the situation. The people you need to forgive are the ones you keep playing mental dialogues with, you know, those times when you're driving down the road and discover that for the last three miles you don't remember anything, because you have been thinking of what you are going to do or say?

Forgiving someone does not mean they didn't do anything wrong, or that they did not do something really mean to you. Forgiveness does not let them off the hook for anything they have done. It lets you off the hook of having to remember, avoid, and or, resent them. Let the situation fall away from your life and thoughts so you can be free, so you can be off the hook.

3. Cancel the debt. When you forgive for real you must cancel the dues. We spend our lives as a mental banker; we decide who owes us and who we owe. However, you must write paid in full on their bill to you and shred the bill. By this, I mean you must never ever bring up their debt in your thinking or talking again. And if you do think about it, you must remind yourself not to, that this has been forgiven. If something is paid in full it is over, it is done.

Forgiveness is a choice only you can make in your own time. I can tell you to forgive, but it is your choice if you really want to. It is your choice if you want to live as happily as possible and forgive and forget. Sometimes forgiving can be an issue with control. Generally, there is very little in life that we have control over. Many times, control is a fantasy. People like to think they have control because it can make them feel safe. I have learned that we attempt to control things in life to create security. Most of us do the best we can, but regardless, things can happen that are beyond our control. This is also true of the people we love.

When we forget that we have a choice of forgiveness, we leave ourselves open to feeling stuck, which in some cases can bring on sadness, loneliness, and depression. Forgiveness is not something you barter with. Forgiveness has to be unconditional, and that means that we have to accept the other person, their choices, and the outcome without any exception. Yes, that is hard to do, and it takes a lot of time, especially when control is an issue. For many, learning to accept the outcome without a hand or say in the situation is hard. But you get to live your own life, and others deserve the same. We cannot use *forgive* and *but* in the same sentence. You cannot say, "I forgive her/him"…"but"; it is contradictory. If you really forgive, you forgive without if's, and's, or but's. Forgiving someone because you expect them to change doesn't work. If you forgive, you must accept them as they are.

I know from personal experience that when someone else causes us emotional harm, whether unintentional or intentional, learning to let go of this pain can be one of the most difficult transitions we go through. I also learned personally that the more we concentrate our emotional, negative energy on carrying a grudge and how bad we were hurt, the more likely we are to become anxious and depressed and feel negatively about the general situation. We can even start to lie to ourselves; and if our thinking is not clear, we will start to believe these lies. Reality of our situation is how we view it at the time the impression or memory was formed. Did you ever notice how you and someone else can be at the exact same event and come home with a different view and different feelings? It is all in how we viewed it at the time. Whether an event is positive or negative, it is determined by how you felt at the moment.

First, you have to choose to forgive. Know that when you make this choice it isn't about them or letting them off the hook. Forgiveness is not a denial of what was done. It's a choice you make to be free and liberated. It is a choice you make to be happy and set down the baggage. It is a choice you make to be released of the experience and no longer be restricted to pain. Make a choice to forgive someone even if they never apologize for what happened. Determine within yourself that it is fine to forget without this apology. Apologies should not be about permission to us to forgive someone. Even without that apology, make up your mind to forgive, forget, and eventually let go.

Let go by deciding to move on. A friend once taught me a forgiveness process as a balloon release image. Relax and think. Place everyone you are ready to forgive in an open field together and tie a balloon to each one. As you work with forgiving each individual, visualize the person floating up to the sky and out into eternity as your pain and grief float away with each person you release. It will get easier. Do this until you can think of the person without the pain coming up. Another technique is to get an emotional release massage where you get rid of the tension caused in your muscles. In addition, you might want to seek professional help if you need more exercises. Don't feel pressured to do this before you choose and know you are ready. Everyone sets his or her own timeline when it comes to healing from pain. In addition, the sooner you forgive the sooner you will be unbound.

POWERFUL POSITIVES

"Fall seven times, stand up eight."

—Japanese Proverb

Happy people know that in order to stay happy they must live in powerful positives. Happy people always look at the glass not just half empty or half full but full. In order to be happy, it's very important to be positive every day in every way. You have heard that you need to be an optimist instead of a pessimist over and over all your life; however, if you are not practicing positives powerfully, you probably aren't as pleased as you should be if you are a positive person who is good, but I urge you to take your positives to the next level. Don't just live positively. Make sure your positives are powerful.

A few months ago, we were planning a mountain climb. After checking the weather, we discovered that we were to expect a 30 percent chance of rain. Kyle smiled at me and told me not to worry and said that that meant a 70 percent chance of good weather. You can look at the negative in your life, or you can look at the positive in your life. While thinking, you will use the same about of energy. Why not look at everything positively?

I believe that a lot of relationships could be saved if people would look at the positive in others. I could be angry at Kyle and spotlight his being gone while four wheeling, on fishing trips, on hunting trips, playing golf, stealing the remote, or for leaving his dirty socks in the corner. I could focus on his OCD behavior and let it get me down. Or I can do what I do and I can focus on his good qualities. I choose to see that he tries every day to do his best. I choose to see that he is honest and loyal and he shows me how much he cares about me every day. If I were to focus on all those negative things all the time, I would not only end up unhappy but it would have potential to ruin our relationship. I have chosen to look at the positive and not focus or concentrate on any negative. I keep my focal point on the positive actions he does, and it keeps me on cloud nine all the time. I concentrate that he is a hard worker and provider, he always has my best interests at heart, and he is caring and takes good care of me. He is superior at listening and working things out. He is strong but has a gentle side. I think about his concern to be healthy, and how I love the way we think alike. I ponder how he is serious but loves to have fun. I reflect how he is honest, unselfish, stable, handsome, and faithful. I take into account and ponder how he is a creative, loving, gifted, guy's guy who can fix anything. And I think you get the point. When I focus on all of this, I can hardly pay attention to the socks in the corner. In order to become happy and sexy we must see that clouds make beautiful sunsets. A happy person knows that in order to stay happy, they must contemplate and mull over the positive in any situation. This alone will keep you a happy person. If you are struggling in your relationship, change your thinking to only focus on the positive side of your mate. I guarantee you will start to see things differently and find that you are getting along better. Just don't focus on the bad and you will never see it.

The next time your day gives you a 20 percent chance of showers, make sure you only see the 80 percent chance of sunbeams.

CHOOSE YOUR COMPANY

"Choose your friends with caution, plan your future with purpose, and frame your life with faith."

—Thomas S. Monson

Who is your best friend? Do you have a best friend? Everyone longs for a soul mate to confide in and grow close, someone to share thoughts and feelings. However, choosing the wrong friends and company cannot only steal your destiny; it can steal your happiness. I would rather have one good friend who lifts me up and has their head on straight than a million cool friends who bring me down. We all need people in our lives that make us a better person. *Because you become what you are around, it is very important to be around what you want to become.* Happy people know that in order to be happy, they must keep company with other people living in ecstasy.

Friends can help you grow and learn many new things. As the old proverb says, "As iron sharpens iron, so a man sharpens the countenance of his friend." Have you ever noticed how one bad grape can spoil the bunch? Have you had the experience of walking into work, excited for the day, and your coworker engulfs you with the bad weekend they had, the debt they owe, and the relationship they're in that's dreadful? At one time or another, I'm sure you have experienced this. If you are not careful, your excitement, joy, and enthusiasm for the day can be stolen quickly. Of course, now and then, it's great to be a good listener of service and bring others up. However, the dilemma comes when you socialize with joy pickpockets. It's okay to have friends you encourage, but it's as equally important to keep the company of friends who bring out the best in you and make you smile. If you are the happiest person in your group, you have outgrown your group. I have made a commitment to myself not to hang around people who hibernate in their own unhappiness.

Imagine trying to climb a mountain with ropes around you. Imagine these ropes are tied to another person sitting in the mud behind you. Your rope partner is dead weight, just sitting in the mud, wanting you to do the work and pull them to the summit. Visualize looking up at the sunny summit and back at the stick in the mud. See yourself begging your friend to get up out of the misery and mud and walk with you. Feel the stress on your body, and try to pull that person out of the mud and up the mountain. Feel your body leaning into the rope and it not budging. Now your friend is pulling against you, and if you are not careful, you will fall into the mud with them. Unhappy buddies are like this. They will be dead weight trying to hold you back in their unhappiness. Unhappy people will try to get you stuck in the mud with them. Who you associate with is significant to your happiness level. Happy people know that in order to be happy, they can't socialize with glum.

When we climb mountains, we see a lot of marmots crawling all over the rocks. In addition, we watch many bald eagles soar high above us in the trees. Happy people share the value of happiness with their best buddies. Although they both enjoy a mouse dinner, they do not share the same values. By this, I mean that although the marmots and eagles both eat mice, one is soaring high while the other is scouring in the rocks. Pick friends who share your same values. Unhappy company can bring you down faster than you even know it's there. If you have ever seen an eagle flying graceful and peaceful, you have seen bliss. If you run with the marmots, you will not soar with the eagles.

Most young people move in and out of many superficial relationships, trying not to be dumped, wounded, scorned, or ostracized. I believe that many girls get married for external outward reasons that are insincere and only to lead to divorce. Something is wrong in our society where others are so easy to turn on one another. When values become focused on things rather than people, it is easy to run over the feelings of others. These shallow relationships are like the early morning fog that burns off as the sun comes out and the day progresses. In today's world, there are a lot of traps we must avoid. If we live what we have been fortunate enough to learn, people will honor and respect us for our values. If we are good friends to others, it is likely that our circle of friends will also grow. As we move through life, let's remember how important good friends are. Remember to have blissful buddies.

GET OUT OF GUILTVILLE

"Fear is the tax that conscience pays to guilt."

—George Sewell

You guessed it; guilt also has been shown to increase cortisol levels. One of my key secrets to happiness is to let go of guilt. Do something that is a guilty pleasure for you. I used to have a lot of guilt, if I said "No" to someone, if I got a massage, if I went for a walk and left my husband to work. Now I can honestly say that I don't let guilt get the best of me, and of course, I am happier for not. Many unhappy people live in Guiltville. If you are struggling to be happy, make sure you are not living on Fault Street. If you are wasting time feeling shame for your past, it is time to move to Innocence Street. Everyone in the world makes mistakes. We are human. There is a difference between learning from your mistakes and moving on to blamelessness and staying in a state of self-dishonor. We all have felt guilt. You know the feeling. You are down on yourself, and you feel undeserving of all things. The more you feel guilty the more you will attract anguish to you.

Last year, I was descending Mt. Quandary, or should I say sliding down the thousand-foot south side of the slippery rocky mountain. I was taking one step forward and skidding three. At one point, I slid too far and lost my balance and fell onto my rump and caught myself with both hands behind by back. I scraped the palms of my hands but got up and kept on downhill. I admit I kept thinking to myself how I shouldn't have fallen, and then, because I wasn't mindful of my next steps, I slid again. This is how guilt is. When you get up from a mistake, if you keep thinking of the mistake, you will carry it as weight in your backpack and the gravity of it will pull you down again. However, if you leave it there and learn from it, watching your steps, you won't make the same mistake twice. If I had learned from my mistake where to keep my balance and hadn't been thinking of the mistake, I could have saved myself from another fall. Happy people know how to learn from missteps and not tumble again.

Happy people know how to put past missteps behind and move on regardless of how horrible they might seem to you. No matter what it is you have guilt about, you will never be able to feel joy unless you love yourself despite your flaws. For example, I have a patient who tells me she has guilt for the death of her mother and now she is overweight. She told me she can only love herself after she is thin. However, this won't help today. She is still carrying the guilt. I told her and will tell you the same. Love yourself now. Happiness doesn't work in the future tense. Your guilt will keep you in a house of depression and fear. The solution to depression is trusting your mistakes to be lessons leading you to a new level. No one is free of making mistakes, but everyone can learn from them. Happy people know how to see a mistake as an error and then click okay and go on to the next screen of their lives. Happy people know that in order to feel peaceful and content, they must gain knowledge from the bloopers they make in life.

Whatever your mistake is, do what happy people do so you can live in Joy City. Pack your bags with lessons, and leave the guilt at the Goodwill. Sell your property in Guiltville, and move to Joy City today. If you ever feel you are moving back into Guiltville, remember that your property has already been sold, and by your own happiness laws, you cannot possess it again.

BE DETERMINED TO HAVE DETERMINATION

"America was not built on fear–America was built on courage, on imagination, and an unbeatable determination to do the job at hand."

—Harry S. Truman

If I had to say one thing about me that has never changed, it is that I am determined. One thing that is constant with me is that I am focused and very much in control of things in my life that can be controlled. I cannot change how tall I am or the color of my skin or eyes; but at the same time, I have learned that a great deal of life is up to us. I'm not sure how, but I learned this at an early age; and I never wanted what I could control to be in anyone else's hands. This is important because your happiness is at stake here. Fortunately, humans are also wired for learning and growing. Just as we can physically train muscles to become tighter and stronger, we can mentally train ourselves to draw more pleasure from the everyday humdrum. This is why positive psychologists often refer to people's innate resilience. We are flexible, and like molding clay, we can mold ourselves with determination. Despite personal background and circumstances, the human spirit is surprisingly durable and malleable. Research has found that to get happier, you must tap into this potential by activating your mind and body for joy.

You have a choice right now to be happy. I am probably more focused and determined than the average person, but you can do it too. The bottom line is that the thought of living a life I didn't want, was much scarier than jumping in and doing the work it took to have the life I want and have now. I have the job I want, and most of the time it makes me happy. I choose that. I live in a house I built myself just the way I wanted it to be. I choose that. I am happy, and I choose to be every day.

I have learned that we can't believe the myth we tell ourselves. We think and tell ourselves that when we get to the next step, we will be happy. We say "when we have more money, when we are married, when we have a better job, when we have a baby, when we have another baby," we will be happy. When we say; "when we lose weight, when the kids are in school, when we get new furniture and a new house," then we'll be happy. We lie to ourselves and say, "when I retire and can go on vacations, then I'll be happy." The truth is we aren't good at predicting what will make us happier. If you aren't happy now, none of these life changes will make you happy until you are determined to be happy.

The first memory I recall is when I was about three years old and I was determined to prove I could ride my dad's horse around the arena by myself. I begged my mom to let go and give me the reigns. I did great. I was just in a walk and knew I had full control. As I got comfortable, I decided to kick my heels in a little; and instantly, my dad's trusty horse started to trot. And then he went faster and faster until he was in a lope, and I nearly scared everyone there that I was going to fall off or be ripped off as I ran full speed through a small, four-foot-wide gate with a crossbar on the top. However, the determined kid I was, I ducked my head and went through smoothly. From then on, I rode all by myself. I'm sure my parents still worried about me, but they let me go alone, and I was determined to do it well. In every area of my life, I got exactly what I wanted because I was determined not to give up until I received what I had chosen. Most of the time it was a blessing. At the age of eight, I was determined that I was going to show horses; and anything I chose to do, I was determined to do it the best I could. My first year at the county fair, I won grand champion with my horse, Bill. This led to ten more years of showing and success.

When I was fourteen, I was determined I needed to lose ten pounds to be a better rider. I wasn't fat by any means, but I was determined that the less weight I had the better I could do everything. I lost the ten pounds, and it led to dramatic unhealthy weight loss. Don't let determination get you in trouble. Make sure that even something good for you like determination is in balance. Too much of even a good thing can be detrimental.

Years later, in my late teens, when I was dating boys, I was determined that I would not settle for just anyone until I found someone who I chose to be with, who I could be myself with and share hobbies with, who I loved for who they were and who loved me for who I am. I have found that now. It wasn't always easy waiting until I was twenty-eight, but my determination kept me going, and I have found what I was waiting for, and I couldn't be more blessed. I am 100 percent satisfied, and that keeps me happy. In addition, now I am determined to do my part and make the best of each day and make every day happy for us both. I am determined to make it happy.

Happiness, like everything, is received through determination. *We have to choose to be a happy camper.*

Happiness comes from inside us when we are determined to be happy no matter what is happening on the outside. What I have learned is that happiness does not come from the world and it cannot be taken by the world. We have to be determined to be unshakeable even when external circumstances try to shake us. I do have the life I have always dreamed of, but like everyone's life, it hasn't always been easy. I have had disappointments, loss, and obstacles. I have had business relationships turn out bad, and I have had dreams that didn't come to pass as I hoped. However, deep in me was always a fire of determination to keep going, to wait to see what was going to come as the sun came up the next day. *To me, there is a big difference between expecting happiness to come to you because you think you deserve it and going out and getting the happiness you believe you deserve.* We cannot change the external or what comes at us. However, we can change how we react to it.

BE DETERMINED TO HAVE PEACE EVERY DAY

If you are determined in your mind to not be shakable, you will find that you are a lot happier. I recommend that in order for you to be happy, you must be determined to live in peace. The world is always trying to bring us down. In the town I work, the entire main street is under construction. I was telling my friend that I got stopped a total of four times on the way to work making my commute an hour and a half. Her reply was, "There is just nothing worse." I stopped her right there and replied, "There is a lot worse." I could have let this destroy my day; however, I was determined to stay in peace. If you wake up determined to be in peace, nothing can take your happiness because you are determined not to give it up.

BE DETERMINED TO STOP SAYING WHY? WHAT? AND WHEN?

When you're making invitations or writing a story, these are important parts to remember. I recall learning the five W's in elementary school. But when we say, "Why?" we instantly take away our happiness. We say, "Why me? Why does bad happen to me? Why can't I get a break? Why? Why? Why? When am I going to win the lottery?" If you will think about what you are asking and stop the negative, you will find that accepting what is, will put you in a happier, positive place instantly. You ask, "Why am I single? When will I get a break? What if I don't get married? What will happen when I am old?" Think about it. Single people are sad, and married people are mad. Single people want to have sex, and married people don't have sex. Of course I am just making a joke, but stop wishing that you are in another place.

BE DETERMINED TO KEEP YOUR COMMITMENTS

Happy people are determined to finish what they start. Happy people complete with zest what they start, even when they get bored. I know several people who have gone to school for years but have a different job than their diploma says because they got bored. Marriages end when people get bored with their spouses. Projects that started out fun don't get finished when something new and exciting comes along. If you are in a committed relationship, be determined to treat your partner every day with respect. Be determined not to get bored. I once knew a lady who took nine months to clean out her garage. Every day, she had it planned and would start, but if the phone rang or something fun and more stimulating and thrilling came along, she would stop her project. People have affairs, looking for more excitement when their relationships get boring. In order to be happy, you must be determined to finish what you start. We all know someone who has gotten a really cute new puppy and then gave it away or put it down when the chewing of shoes, potty training, and barking became too much. The once-loved and adored puppy becomes a dejected, fully grown mutt when the human gets bored.

I have a patient who had fertility issues and tried for years to have a baby. After she finally conceived, she was on cloud nine. Words couldn't describe her happiness. She bought hundreds of clothes, decorated the nursery, bought a matching stroller and car seat, and bought a new camera and a new mom car. She was so joyful. However, years later, she came in telling me that she was going back to work. Knowing that they didn't need the money, I questioned her decision. Her reply? She was "fed up with being a mom." What happened? How did this mom who waited so long to have a baby find it so easy to leave him? The truth is she got bored, uninterested, and fed up when it all stopped being fun. Some people have more babies when this happens, looking for happiness. Ladies and gentlemen, please don't bring a baby into the world to make you happy or to fix a relationship. Bring a life into the world for them, never for you. If you have children, value and nurture them until you die. Be determined to protect, love, and care for everyone you have made a commitment to, even when it doesn't become fun and exciting anymore. Be determined to play around and make fun when boredom sets in. Your happiness will last forever when you keep and finish your commitments.

BE DETERMINED TO BE NICE TO OTHERS

For years, I was a massage therapist. Most of the time, I received tips from my clients that added up to a great number at the end of the year. I remember learning in massage school about the karma of tipping. I remember my instructor saying, "if you tip good, karma happens and your clients will tip you well." What you give comes back. I started tipping more when I realized that a large amount of my income came from tips. However, I realized that this is a way to be nice to others. I am determined to be kind to others, and this brings me happiness. Last summer, I was shopping at the local grocery. As I pushed my cart out, I noticed an elderly lady, whose car was parked near mine, with a basket full of five large watermelons. I offered to help her unload them into the trunk of her car. She agreed and then offered to buy me an ice cream. I declined, but she did tell me that "above was looking down and smiling." I will never forget how good I felt getting into my car. I loaded my truck with a lively step. I just felt good all over. I am determined to be nice to others because it makes both me and the receiver happy. I love to leave big tips to waitresses I know need the money. It makes me happy to open the door for elderly ladies at the post office. I feel jolly when I'm sitting in traffic or in line at the store and let someone in front of me. Be determined to be nice to others. I once heard that if you want to be happy for a day, go fishing. If you want to be happy for a month, buy a new car. If you want to be happy for a lifetime, help others.

BE DETERMINED TO STAY OUT OF DEBT

In order to stay happy, we must be determined to stay out of debt. Being in debt makes you stressed, sad, and miserable. When you see the new dress, cell phone, car, house, or couch you must have, if you don't have the money for it, will it really make you happy? I was talking with a lady this week who is so in debt that she and her three kids are moving in with her parents. I was talking to her about this, and in the next sentence, she was telling me she was going to an eyeliner tattoo appointment. I couldn't help myself. I instantly asked why she was spending money on a tattoo of permanent makeup when she couldn't pay the light bill. I gave her the same lecture not so she would be like me, but to help her. In order to stay out of debt, we must be determined to stay out of debt. The economy is bad right now because Americans live in the now time. We buy beyond our means, and we finance and refinance expensive homes and cars. We buy on credit cards because we want it now. We think if we get into a new house now, we will be happy. If we paint now and remodel now, it will make us happy. We are impatient and greedy, and we want it now. Stop spending money on temporary happiness. If you want to get out of debt, you must spend less than you make. Save money buying bulk at the grocery store. Shop around for what you do need, and don't buy what you don't need. Lessen your monthly bills. If you spend an extra $30 a month on your cell phone bill to have a smart phone with internet when you have internet at home and at the office, cancel it. If you have a wedding to attend, borrow a dress instead of buying one you will only wear once. If you buy Starbucks and lunch every day when you have a coffee pot and leftovers at home, start taking your own. If you want to be out of debt, you must be determined to be out of debt. It's okay to use credit cards for convenience and emergencies as long as you pay them off at the end of the month. The point is that you don't want to get into a situation where you are so distracted by debt that you can't focus on what you need to. Don't use your "get it now" greed for happiness. We need to put our attention on it and be determined to be happy today, now.

BE DETERMINED TO NOT STAY MAD

Happy people don't stay mad. Happy people are determined to stay calm. Happy people aren't determined to stay irritated or annoyed. Happy people stay in peace and coolness. When my sister was a little girl, she would jokingly say, "I'm still mad." She would make a joke, cross her arms, pout, and look up, trying not to laugh while saying, "I'm still mad." It was funny then, but the truth is it's not funny when adults are still mad. Anger is an emotion often characterized by feelings of great displeasure, hostility, rage, and revenge. Many times, reacting in anger is how we express our dissatisfaction with life. Someone cuts you off in traffic and you tailgate them all the way to your turn. You get your feelings hurt and you take on settling the score. Someone hurts your feelings and you key their car. You say, "But I feel angry." You can change how you feel anytime you want to. Anger is defined in the Greek language as the strongest of all passions. Anger begins with a feeling that's often expressed in words or actions. We feel something, and it causes a reaction. We get angry when we are hurt or don't get our way when we want it. We get mad when we have unmet needs or we are jealous. We get upset when life isn't fair to us. Let's face it, folks, all the above happens to us every day.

It's okay to be mad. However, in order to be happy, you must be determined not to stay mad. You must vent, but do it properly. If you are angry with something or someone, feel the feeling, allow yourself to be upset, and then go do something nice for someone else. Even if you are nice to someone other than the one you are mad at, replace the evil with good. Be determined not to stay mad. Every single day is filled with all kinds of situations that could upset you, things like losing your car keys or getting caught in a traffic jam. But you can choose to be at peace and stable. Choose to not stay mad at the guy who cut you off. Choose to not stay mad at the lady who took your parking space. Choose to not dwell all day on the fact that your internet is not working and put you thirty minutes behind. Set your mind to not stay mad.

Get your mind set today that you will stay in peace. Be determined to stop saying, "Why?" Be generous and nice to everyone. Set your mind to get out of debt. Stop self-pity. Be determined to not stay mad.

BAN REACTING AND BEGIN ACTING

"Time flies, but, remember you're the navigator."

—St. Louis Bugle

Do you overreact? Have you ever flipped out on someone for no reason? Of course you have, we all have. The cause of reacting is really a mineral deficiency. But did you know that when you overreact to situations you put your body into General Adaptation Syndrome (GAS). When you over react you set off an alarm, the body releases adrenaline and a variety of other psychological mechanisms to combat the stress and to stay in control. Again this puts you into "fight or flight" response. The downward spiral starts when we are tired and deficient in minerals, but then it continues as we get lower and lower in hormones. The hypothalamus, pituitary, adrenals (HPA) sequence of events are great for emergencies, not so great when your kids accidently spill the milk. For those suffering from anxiety, panic attacks, PMS, mood swings, and depression, this processes malfunctions. Continued stress in life disrupts the sequence of events. Instead of shutting off once the crisis is over, it all continues, the hypothalamus keeps signaling the adrenals to produce cortisol. This increased cortisol production exhausts the stress mechanism, leading to fatigue and depression. Cortisol also interferes with serotonin activity, furthering the depressive effect. You become overwhelmed and you overreact. You overreact and you become full of fight more than flight; which means you want to be angry and fight instead of walking away from the situation. Sometimes this happens so fast you don't even know it, and you are instantly yelling at your kids that they are brats for no reason.

Over reacting = cortisol

Cortisol = less happy hormone serotonin

Less serotonin = Unhappy You

It all starts in the mind. We need to be determined to change in our minds too. Happy people act on what they need to. Happy people change the negative into positive, change from being the critic into accepting, change the worry into clear thinking, change their anxiousness into being on cloud nine. We can dwell on the bad, or we can enjoy the good.

Tests will come at us every day; but if we are firm to change the negative obstacles into positive lessons, we will be happy right then. Turn the negative into positive. A few years ago, I was burned severely by my kitchen stove. It took months to recover, and I had to focus on a new career. I could have sat around, feeling sorry for myself, thinking, *Why me?* The truth is, however, when I was asked if I ever thought, *Why me?* I would reply, "No. If it wasn't me, it could have been someone else," and I would have never wished the pain on anyone, not even my worst enemy.

Stop being the critic and start accepting. Differences in people and their preferences are as normal and night and day. You will be a lot happier when you stop being the world's critic and start acknowledging that we are all different. You will find yourself at ease when you stop being the umpire and arbitrator of everyone, and start accepting each other. Men and women are different. My mom used to joke that when my sister and I said we had nothing to wear, it meant we didn't have anything with new tags on it. However, when my dad said he didn't have anything to wear, it meant that he didn't have any clean clothes. Women are scared of spiders but not eyebrow waxing. Men would rather kill a thousand spiders than tweeze. Men and women are different, but so are women and women. You might not agree with your sister, best friend, mother, or other women in your town. But when you start accepting that you both are right, life gets a lot easier and happier for you all. Happy people know how to accept everyone as they are.

Stop worrying and start trusting. We will be happy right now. If we will pay attention and have clear thinking, the other negative thoughts won't find their way in. Most importantly, I think we have a tendency to focus and dwell on the bad; we can do it all day long. Happy people don't worry. A few birthdays ago, we went on an adventure vacation to climb mountains. However, on the way out of town, I got some bad news that could have ruined my adventure, had I put too much over-thinking into it and not clear thinking. I still struggle with this. I can let myself over analyze and over-think to the point that I can make myself crazy. However, I have learned that if I choose to see life clearly and the best in others, it always works out to my advantage. We can dwell on the bad, or we can savor the good and make it better. I admit that for the first few hours of our trip, I was dwelling on the bad, thinking of the worst that could happen. I created issues and started to question the truth in the great relationship I do have. It's okay to spend some time thinking and making sure that what you are doing is the right thing for you. It's okay to question your better judgment and make sure you are choosing what you want. However, it would not have been okay for me to ruin the whole trip dwelling in my own pity party. In fact, that week at the lake in the mountains turned out to be a blissful time, and it was a fantastic birthday. I did react, and I did make sure the problems were talked about. I am not saying be happy and be a doormat, but if you are reacting with anger, maybe you should stop dwelling and start thinking clearly.

ASK FOR WHAT YOU WANT

"Ask and you shall receive."

Matthew 21:22

Happy people know what they want and ask for it. This past Christmas, Kyle surprised me with several presents. He brought them in with a smile on his proud face. On Christmas night, when I opened the gifts one at a time, I found puzzle pieces, and as I placed them together, the picture became a tread climber. The last present was a card with money in it for the gift I wanted (Yes, I actually wanted a tread climber). He knew the perfect gift for me because months before Christmas, I was obsessed with the tread climber commercials and websites. He took note, and he made sure I got what I wanted. Had I not asked and told him what would make me happy, he might not have known.

In my experience, a lot of people today expect everyone to be a mind reader and give them what they want without telling. My friend was disappointed when I told her how I was spoiled with many gifts of puzzle pieces to open. She replied back, "I really wanted earrings, and all I got was a sweater from my husband. You are so lucky." Yes, I am lucky. I am lucky that I have a man who listens and observes ways to make me smile. But I asked her if she had told her husband that she really wanted earrings for Christmas. Her reply was, "No." I'm not saying you should be outrageous, but if you're a person who is comfortable reacting instead of acting, I'm here to tell you that you get what you ask for, and if you don't ask, you are going to end up settling for less than you want and deserve. We need to ask for what we want to be happy. This is my example, but I am not just meaning ask for what you want in a gift. I am meaning we have to ask for what we want every day in order to be happy with what we are getting. Do you want a new position at work but you haven't asked your boss to promote you? Happy people ask.

HOLD HAPPY RELATIONSHIPS

"True success in this world is not determined by how much money you make or by how many possessions you have but by the positive impact you have on other people as you work toward your goals and dreams in life."

—George Bernard Shaw

People in your life are important. Happy people in your life are important. And a happy you in others' lives is just as important. I love to climb mountains and take in the beauty I am surrounded by. I love climbing the trails along waterfalls, and I love to climb along the wildflowers into the blue sky. I love the sun on my face, and I love the view of the mountains surrounding me. Climbing for me is a wonderful way to unwind and find myself. The people in your life should be like that, surrounding you with awesome views and good feelings. When you look around yours, are you surrounded by majestic mountains and beautiful flowers? Is the sun shining on your face, or are you surrounded by lions and bears and dead timber? When we make healthy connections with people, our brains flood our bodies with happy chemicals, and when we have unhealthy relationships or unhealthy social meetings, harmful chemicals are released. This is why when we, as social beings, are having a hard time; we want to talk about it. We want to be surrounded by others and our friends. The more people talk and surround themselves with people they love, the more oxytocin is released, producing a calming effect on every cell in the body. When you surround yourself with people you love, your happy hormones will expand, and it's a win-win situation because, so will your happiness. In the same way, if you surround yourself with dead timber and bears, your happy hormones will contract and disappear. What are you surrounded with?

Mountains, Sunshine, and Flowers	Dead Timber, Lions, and Bears
United with others	Keeping yourself isolated
Creating boundaries	Letting venomous people affect you
Communicating what you need	Complaining and comparing
Appreciating others	Depreciating others
Focusing on harmony	Focusing on your differences
Being generous and serving	Expecting others to read your mind
Happiness	Irritation
Composed and peaceful	Provoke and stir up
Stimulate	Put down and dampen
Fuel and encourage	Suffer exhaustion

I already told you what I choose, and I hope you are choosing the sunshine and flowers. Spending time with those you love—family, friends, or pets—is important to keep good company for greater happiness. Spending time with those who bring sunshine to your face is not only nice; it's necessary. Likewise, we need to return the favor and bring sunshine to everyone you meet. Not everyone in your life will feed your happiness, and not everything you love will feed your happy cells. It's easy, if you look for it, to see the toxic people you come up against. These are the complainers and the ones trying to discourage you. They are stuck and unhappy, and they want you to be stuck in the mud with them. However, you have a choice. You can jump the mud puddle and keep climbing into the sunshine. If you have friends who, when you're around them, you come away feeling drained and frustrated, it might be time to share this book with them, or you might need to get new friends.

WHAT HAPPY COUPLES DO ALL YEAR

I believe we need to make our most important relationship happy all year, not just during Valentine's Day or an anniversary, that's right, I said make. My wonderful groom and I are happily married and these are what we believe are the 5 most important things happy couples do right.

H–Help-mates. Happy couples are each other's helper, supporter, companion, and partner in everyday situations all the time. Happy couples are best friends and treat each other like their best friend. They are also kind and warm to each other. You are the one who helps make your mate successful, and you are the one your mate needs for support. This does not ever mean being a doormat. This means that two are better than one. Show interest in your spouse's hobbies, work, and life.

A–Accepting. Unconditional acceptance is so very important because if you only accept in part, this means you only love in part. If you love in part, your marriage and your mate's self-esteem will never be whole. Who wants to only be loved in part? None of us, we all want to be loved in whole, 100%. If you are married you have already chosen to be with this person the rest of your life. It is important that you accept their total self. I am far from perfect, but I am so grateful that my husband still accepts, endures, and loves me unconditionally.

P–Playful. Happy couples are playful and silly with each other on a daily basis. Having a playful fun relationship is what it is all about; playful is a prerequisite for passion. Make sure that you and your mate can find something that you can have humor about. Sharing the funny side of things is a great fun way to communicate and understand how the other thinks and feels.

And joking is actually a form of flirting. Also do lighthearted activities or hobbies with each other. My groom and I enjoy a life that is so good it feels like a vacation every day, this is because we live a life of adventure and we're always good-natured.

P–Praise. Mark Twain said, "I can live a whole month on one compliment." On Valentine's Day we always buy the card that says "You are the best," but happy couples appreciate each other every day. When you give sincere encouragement and appreciation to your spouse, several things are achieved, your own self-worth is increased, your spouse's self confidence is increased, and the friendship between the two of you is strengthened. Recognize what your spouse does for you and your family and show how grateful you are.

Y – YES. Say "Yes" to sex that is. Sex brings a closeness that is beyond words. It relaxes you, puts you in tune with each other, and smoothes over all the everyday trials and tribulations. Happy couples say yes to any touch from the other, they hug each other often, they kiss, they touch each other while talking, they sit hand in hand on the couch while having a conversation, they curl around each other when they sleep or just gaze at the stars, and yes, they have sex from time to time. The desire to have sex is innate within all of us. We all want to feel loved, desired, and wanted. Studies show, and evidence points to the fact that an active sex life keeps couples together. According to the most recent Sexual Wellbeing Survey, the average unwed couple has sex 127 times a year, and the average married couple has sex 98 times a year. But it shouldn't and doesn't have to be that way. Growing in a committed relationship doesn't have to mean a slow slide into celibacy, sweat pants, and slippers. And besides, I don't know about you, but I don't like being part of boring statistics!

BEAR BOUNDARIES

"Boundaries are to protect life, not to limit pleasure."
—Edwin Louis Cole

In order to be happy, we must have standards and boundaries. A boundary is a property line. Survey yourself now and know where you begin and end. Unless you live in a bubble, your boundaries define you in relation to everyone else. Happy people have boundaries with everyone and everything. Happy people watch the boundary line in every relationship they have. This includes people, money, animals, and their thoughts. You need to have boundaries made and communicated in every relationship you have. If boundaries are not expressed, your relationships will be affected. Listen when I say you must have boundaries communicated, or you will manipulate. Manipulations are dark. We must turn the flashlight on and see the truth and speak our truth. The path to real love is expressed through good property lines. Appropriate boundaries will actually increase your ability to care about others in a better way. Boundaries are not selfish and do not mean you are not caring, thoughtful, or concerned. People with boundaries are the most caring people on earth. I wasn't in a serious relationship until I was twenty-eight because I had standards. We have to make it perfectly clear what we are willing to accept from others. We have to be teachers. We have to be people with standards. We have to know what we want and what we don't want. We have to let others know what we want and never accept from others what we don't want. We show people how to treat us when we have boundaries. If we are feeling like a situation is unfair, we need to build our fence and show our boundaries. My grandpa always said good fences make good neighbors, and this is so true. If you don't have a fence, a boundary between you and others, problems could occur. Their pets could come and destroy your garden. Likewise, your kids could be in their yard, causing trouble. Fences keep protected what is safe to you. Boundaries keep protected what is special to you, most importantly, your heart. People might not even realize your feelings if you don't tell them. When I was first dating Kyle, we had a situation come up that made me nervous. Now, I have always trusted Kyle a thousand percent, I wouldn't be with him if I didn't trust him. This state of affairs making me uncomfortable wasn't an issue with trust, but I did have to show him my boundaries and tell him my feelings. Kyle is a man of his word, and he had already told me what his feelings were with me. I trusted him, knowing that he is a man of his word, but I admit that no matter how I tried to be positive and make it right in my head, my heart was still in discomfort. I admit I was a little anxious and unconfident of our new relationship at the time. I was apprehensive of the whole situation. After thinking clearly, not dwelling on it but making sure I was clear, I let Kyle know how badly the thought of the situation hurt me. I let him know how the state of affairs hurt me. I told him my boundaries, and after I did, I felt so much better. I did not hide my heart under the rug and take what came at me. I did not act like it didn't hurt when it did. Telling him what I felt and talking it out felt great, but the enormous moment was the realization he got. He didn't even know that it was wounding to me until I said something. I showed him how I wanted to be treated, and he is sensitive to my feelings even more now because he knows what they are. Being the great listener and man he is, he changed his plans and respected my feelings and boundaries. He now knows what my boundaries are, and he respects them. In addition, I try to respect his boundaries the same way.

We have to show people how to treat us sometimes because what is okay in one's head might be upsetting to another. I could have let him go, holding the feeling of anguish deep down. I could have smiled and held the throbbing in. I could have gotten angry and reacted irrationally. You say, "But, Cammi, I can't tell others how I feel." Yes, I know and admit that it is hard sometimes to tell others our feelings; it is hard to stick up for ourselves sometimes. But we are worth it. You are worth it. If you love yourself, you know you have to have boundaries. Most importantly, you have to show others your boundaries, how you love yourself, and accept only the love from them that you would give yourself. Our relationship is great because Kyle knows how I love myself. He knows how I respect myself, and he respects me right back the same way.

VOICE YOUR NO'S

"Half of the troubles of this life can be traced to saying yes too quickly and not saying no soon enough."

—Josh Billings

Saying no sometimes is okay. Our needs are our responsibility. When I climb mountains, I carry my own camelback full of water; food; warm, dry clothing; and a first-aid kit. I don't expect anyone else to carry it for me. My needs on the mountains are food and water, and I know that it's my responsibility to carry it to take care of myself. Just like I carry my own requirements, you need to too. We cannot wait for others to make us happy. Happiness is our responsibility. Some people see themselves as bad or selfish if they have needs. Other people think everyone in the world is here to make them happy. You might be one of these people or somewhere in between. The truth is, *our lives are our responsibility.* Our lives are a gift. When we say no to people, activities, or anything hurtful to ourselves, we are taking care of ourselves. If you have boundaries, don't be afraid you will hurt others. People are terrified of the consequences of saying no to others. Yes, some might be angry or attack you for having boundaries; however, it is better to learn their nature and personality and do what you can than to not take care of yourself and never know. Your needs must be met first. If you want to be happy, you not only need to understand your needs but make sure that they are being met. You must say no to anything or anyone bad. If a friend needs your help and you are too tired, say, "No." If your sister asks you to babysit and you had other plans, say, "No." If a client wants you to see them on Sunday afternoon and you want your weekend off, say, "No." If your family needs a favor but you are unable to do it for them for any reason, say, "No." If you are always saying, "Yes," you will never be happy. *No* is a happy word. We have to say, "No," and have boundaries with ourselves, our family, and people we don't even know. Many times, people think that if they say, "No," they are being selfish or they feel guilty. However, problems will come when you confuse boundaries with responsibilities. When I was growing up, I had a friend who always said, "You have to take care of number one." At the time, I didn't understand what this meant. I thought it was egotistical. However, in order to be happy, we have to take care of number one. You are number one. It is your responsibility to take care of yourself. It is good to rescue others. However, I have learned that not having limits with others is hurtful to you both and leads to destruction. You need the wisdom to know the difference between what you have the power to change and what you do not.

Yes, the fear in our brains tells us we won't be accepted or we'll be made fun of if we set limits. However, you will find that true friends will respect you more because of your boundaries. In addition, you must respect others' boundaries as well. If we love and respect a "No" from others, they will love and respect our "No's." When we respect others' freedom of choice, we feel better about our own. Happy people feel the fear and do it anyway.

Don't try to change anyone. We cannot change who other people are. And trust me; they don't want you to anyway. The most effective way to influence others is to model the behavior you want back. Treating others as you want to be treated is important, but it's as important to treat others as you want them to treat you. Get it? You have to show them how you want to be treated. You wouldn't want others trying to change you. You are you, the only person in the world created to do what you can do.

You have to be happy in order to make others happy. In the same way, you have to be around happy others to be happy. First, before you read the following on making your relationships happy, ask yourself if you are around people who are happy and who make you happy. In order to make a relationship better with my advice, you must already be in a healthy, somewhat happy relationship.

If you are struggling with your relationships, you might need to seek more professional help. If your relationship is under pressure, it might be helpful to find a common activity that you both enjoy together, or sit down and discuss some things you might like to learn together. Maybe find a time to exercise together. Exercising will keep you both happy and in better health. Maybe attend a sporting event. If you don't know how, learn. Learn the basics so you can participate together. Get joy and satisfaction from it just because it makes your mate happy.

APPRECIATE ACQUAINTANCES

"It's nice to know that people appreciate and respect you."

—Marcel Carne

We all want to be appreciated. From the moment we are small children, we crave to be appreciated. A while back, at a child's birthday party, I was watching our nephews on the swing; and as they went higher and higher, they would ask, "Am I doing a good job?" and I would say, "You are doing a great job." In Wal-Mart, while shopping, I ran into a friend, and her daughter asked me, "Do you love my dress?" and I replied, "I love it." My point is, kids will ask for appreciation if they feel we aren't giving it as much as they need.

Appreciation, like food and sex, is a human need both at home and at work, but more at home. In fact, I read an article on the internet that 40 percent of employees leave their jobs not because of money, but because they don't feel appreciated, and 20 percent of marriages start to go downhill when one doesn't feel appreciated. One of the best ways to raise your happiness level is to appreciate those around you. Tell your mate you appreciate them cooking you dinner, tell the kid in the park he is doing a good job riding his bike, and tell the little girl in a dress how pretty she looks. When we appreciate others, we actually release dopamine in both us and them. Dopamine is a happy chemical. The most effective way I have found to make myself happy is to make others happy. When we make others smile, we can't help

323

but smile. When we fill others' gas tanks by making them feel good, we are raising the level in our own feel-good gas tank too.

The simple act of turning your consciousness away from your own inner world to connect with others is a great gift to relationship. In fact, it's the base of relationships. Kyle is like that. He thinks, *What can I do to make her life happy, fun, and exciting?* And whether it is a $1 drink, a quick back rub, a brutal climb up a mountain, or a relaxing trip to Hawaii, he is constantly turning his consciousness away from his own to connect with mine. And I believe that we have lasted now because I do the same. I love to surprise him with a great dinner (take-out), a massage when I know he has been working a lot, or a nice thank-you card to show my appreciation. I love to be creative and think up ways to say, "I love you too." It's fun for me, and it is for him as well. One day, when I was working late, I blew up several balloons with notes inside them. I left a needle on the counter with a note that said, "Use this to see how special you are." It was fun for me to come up with personal ways he is special to me. It was also amusing too to be at work and imagine him at home, popping all the balloons. Try to use your imagination to make your relationships happy.

It makes me happy to see him smile, and I know that my smile does the same for him. I have seen enough and experienced enough to tell you that in order for you to be happy, your relationships must be happy. You must be around people who make you happy. You must spend time in the energy that makes you happy to be in. We are both determined to be happy and want each other to be happy, and that is why we work.

BEING EMOTIONALLY SATISFIED

"Ah, sweet content, where doth thine harbor hold."

—Barnabe Barnes

Do you even know what it means to truly be content? The dictionary defines content as having a peace of mind and being emotionally satisfied with the way things are. Those are strong words. Broken down more, they mean a strong feeling, to be sufficient. To me, that means a strong feeling inside that everything is okay. It is that fire in your belly that is enough to make you and others feel pleased. Content is that glow in your face that your conditions are met. Being content is accepting what we cannot change, accepting what we can change, and being thankful. It is important in your life to be content with your spouse, your finances, your home, your car, and so forth. You must have goals and dreams, but by being content, you relieve a lot of unnecessary stress on yourself and others. Don't expect perfection. If anyone knows the struggle of perfection, it is me. I expect perfection in myself, and I am harder on myself than anyone else is. When I was five years old, learning to ride a bike, I got so upset that I wasn't perfect the first time that I threw it in the ditch. Nevertheless, my mom taught me a lesson about being perfect. Not only was she patient and taught me how to ride my bike, but my mom taught me that what we see as an imperfection might be a trait that is special and not imperfect at all. We have to let go of the Superwoman/Superman image. Learn to be yourself. I am not perfect in this area, no wisecrack intended. Get off your own back. I find that most of the time, no one else is on my back as much as I am. I get angry with myself when I make mistakes or allow my brain to be unstable. I get on my own back when I weigh too much and make the wrong food choices. I get upset at myself if a patient is not healing as well as I wished. The most important thing I have learned and have to keep reminding myself is to get off my own back. Sometimes we are the ones who are on our own back the most. I have learned that if we stop expecting perfection from others and ourselves, the weight will be gone from our shoulders. If we accept our progress and not expect perfection, we will be a lot happier. Yes, sometimes you will make a bad choice—you will eat too many cookies, you will get angry when you shouldn't—but if the time between these events is less and less, that is progress. Any improvement is movement in the right direction. Any advance is growth. Any increase is excellent. We can't expect life to be flawless or ourselves to be faultless, but we can work on being happy by being the first one to dismount our own shoulders. So climb down off of your own back. You will notice the pain in your neck gone immediately. Weight on the shoulders can cause many health issues, including discomfort; however, if you lessen the load on yourself, you will find the weight easier to carry and you will be happier.

I still have my moments of struggle. I still want to be perfect in my definition all the time. Recently, Kyle has been teaching me how to fly-fish and I'm struggling with it. In addition, not only is it a new style of fishing for me, but I'm learning in a small wobbly boat floating down a river. After hours of trying to cast, I never actually got it. I am still not good at it. Not being able to do it perfect was the most detrimental thing on me until I stopped comparing myself with those I knew were good fly fishers. I reminded myself that I am full of strength and my best was the best I could do that day. The next day, I would try better. I had to let of go my definition of perfect. I had to keep my head on straight.

PLAN YOUR DAYS WITH PLEASURE

"In three words I can sum up everything I've learned about life: It goes on."

—Robert Forest

Don't take the standard route. If you want to feel fulfilled, you can't take the standard routes in life. Just because everyone else is doing something, if it doesn't satisfy you, don't do it. I have always wanted to climb mountains over 14,000 feet, and as a mountain climber, you have a choice. You can take the standard route. This is the trail most traveled. It is the easiest in technical difficulty and exposure. However, last summer, after doing research, my beau and master climbing guide Kyle researched what trail would be the best to take on Mt. Holy Cross. This is a beautiful mountain in Colorado that, in the summer, displays a cross of snow in the crevices. If you go at just the right time during the snow melt, you will find a beautiful, white snow cross in the side of a very large, red rock mountain. The other climbers missed the wonderful sight, however, because they took the standard route. You see, the standard trail was a more comfortable climb; however, it went up the back side of the mountain and the other climbers could not see this miraculous sight. We chose the demanding climb. We took the awkward trail along the cliffs. We had to climb three other mountains that are over 13,000 feet tall to get to see what we wanted to see, but it made us happy. We got to see this wonderful sight. We chose the route that was longer and steeper, but we felt more fulfilled because it is what we wanted to do and it was what we wanted to see. Be sure you do what makes you happy. Don't take the standard route working at a dead end job if your dream is something more. Don't take the standard route if you are being treated unfair in a relationship. Don't take the standard route wearing clothes that are in style. Wear what is comfortable for you. Do what is comfortable for you. If you want to be on the summit, don't follow the trail most traveled. If you do what makes you glad, you will be delighted and happy.

PROBLEMS LIKE PEAKS

"The gem cannot be polished without friction."

—Chinese Proverb

Not everyone owns a pair of Merrell shoes or an ice axe, but everyone I know is a mountain climber. To me mountains are sacred, rising above all else on our planet. They overwhelm me with pure presence. Their nature is rock solid. Mountains, like problems in your life, have one prominent peak. If your problem is sickness, health is your prominent peak. If your problem is disconnect, restoration is your peak. If your problem is financial, change is your summit. If your problem is depression, joy is your height. Marriage, school, family, and life, all bring us peaks to climb every day. You might not have scaled a snowdrift, but no matter who you are, you have reached the high point, your own peak, at one time or another in life.

> *Truly, I say to you, whoever says to this mountain, 'Be taken up and thrown into the sea,' and does not doubt in his heart, but believes that what he says will come to pass, it will be done for him. Therefore I tell you, whatever you ask in prayer, believe that you have received it, and it will be yours.*
>
> *Mark 11:23-24*

I have thought a lot about my love for climbing and my love to solve my own life's problems. Truth is not much different. One day, while climbing with a friend, he smarted off, "I didn't know there was so much up when you said we were climbing a fourteener." We all laughed and kept on climbing. It takes willpower to climb a mountain and reach the top. The truth is, no problem or peak can be scaled without starting at the bottom and climbing up. No successful summit is done without sweat. Happy people know that they can ascend any problem. Even the worst life problems of cancer or death can be climbed over with a little work and willpower.

Going up a mountain and overcoming problems are the same in that when you start at the bottom and look to the summit, it seems overwhelming and too far. However, as you start to walk, you triumph over the rocks. As you go through the creeks, you find that the summit gets closer and closer. As you defeat every obstacle and beat every hurdle, you realize that the summit or end is in sight and in smaller prospective. Large mountains and large problems are all easy to ascend once you start the first step and take baby steps. Inch by inch, step by step, anything big can be vanquished. Happy people know that anything can be overthrown in infant steps. Going over small hills and leaping over snags are always easier when your brain sees the one snag and not the whole mountain of snags.

Victory of problems and mountains are unproblematic once you reach halfway. When we start to climb a mountain early in the dark, before morning, we find our way through the mysterious dark forest of trees. We watch for eyes of bears or other danger in our headlamp beams. We are at unease as we carefully choose our steps in the dark. However, once the sun rises and we are halfway to the summit above tree line, the trail gets uncomplicated. The way doesn't always get effortless up a mountain, and neither do your problems in life. However, once past the dark tree line, the road will seem painless. When you are at the halfway point of conquering an issue, it will become stress free as you see the end in sight. Happy people know that the end is always in sight. In order to stay anxiety free and tranquil, you must remember that there is always a light at the end of the tunnel or a sunrise at the end of a tree line.

Climbing a mountain and climbing your own peaks of problems both require a good partner or a team. Happy people know that in order to stay stress free and reach the summits in life, it's okay to have a good rope buddy and guide. In problem solving and staying happy, it is important to have a good team and good guides. Climbing and solving life's problems both require skill and knowledge, and it's always good to have a good buddy with skills. When climbing, we rely on trails or routes discovered by past climbers who proved the summit could be reached that way. In problem solving, it is good to have advice from others who have a proven route.

In life or on the mountain, you need to be able to turn around. Downward is a hard way to turn when you can see the top. I have only had to do this once, but it nearly took a miracle to turn me around. A good guide and climber knows when the summit can't be reached that day and a turnaround is needed. Turning around is not giving up. It's accepting that today is not the day. Sometimes when you have a problem, you just want the answer today. However, sometimes you must accept that today is not the day. Perhaps you will reach the summit another day, but being patient with our problems sometimes can bring us more bliss. Know when to quit or take a break from a problem. In mountain climbing, not turning can lead to death. In problem solving, it can lead to unhappiness.

A few years ago we went to Hawaii, while climbing Mt. Ka'ala on the island of Oahu with Kyle, we were at a spot where others had secured ropes to aid climbing the slippery hill, or actually, at one point, extension cords. Kyle warned me over and over, "Check the rope," and, "Don't rely on others' ropes." I would tug the rope several times with my feet on secure ground before trusting it to bear the weight of my body. Sometimes when solving problems, it's good to remember Kyle's advice and check the rope. Before taking someone else's advice, make sure they have secure ropes before you let them hold all your weight. Check their results before it's too late to find that they don't know how to tie a good knot.

While traveling with my dad, we had a blowout tire on the trailer we were pulling. To some, this would have been a catastrophe. After all, we were in a hurry, pulling a trailer full of cattle. But that wasn't our feeling. We got out, grabbed everything we needed, and changed the tire in pit stop time. We got in the truck and drove another fifty miles when, *bang!*, another blowout. Again, we got out and changed the tire, thankful we had another spare. When we got in the truck, feeling stressed on time, but thankful we remembered the second spare. I wondered at that time, *Why do we take minor irritations so seriously?* Think of the stress we could forgo if we just realized that mere inconveniences can be survived. I think we need to have an attitude check more often. Happy people know that doubt is the mountain that faith can move.

LOVE THE PLACE YOU'RE IN

"Adversity causes some men to break, others to break records."

—William Arthur Ward

In yoga practice, it is taught, "You are where you are," meaning don't stress if you aren't as flexible on the mat as you neighbor. It is the same in life, we need to stay on our own mats and not worry about what our neighbor is doing. When you are content you will automatically make serotonin, which can be considered a "happy" hormone, as it greatly influences an overall sense of well-being.

Content = Serotonin

Setotonin= feeling of well being

Not content= Cortisol

Cortisol = not content

Mountain guides have the saying, "Kay Garnay," meaning, "It is so." I remind myself the above when I am sitting in detoured traffic or in a discomforted situation. If you want to be happy today, you must be happy where you are and accept where you are. You might not have gotten all your dreams yet, or you might be depressed because of mistakes you made in the past. Dwelling on what you have done or could do is negative to the body. If you want to enhance your happiness, you must be at ease with whatever jobs your day brings. Maybe you are home, cleaning toilets, or maybe you are teaching young children. Whatever your day brings is what you need to be happy with. We all are happier doing what we love instead of a work task. When I climb mountains, go hunting, or have a plane to catch to somewhere fun, I can get up easily at 4:00 a.m.; however, if I have to do a job I don't like, it's hard to drag myself out of bed by 7:00 a.m. I'm sure you are the same way. The saying, "If you do what you love, you will love what you do," is true. However, if you are stuck in a job that is not what you love, how are you to love it? You do so by letting your sense of purpose be on the inside. When I was in college, I hated biology class and the homework I had that was always challenging. However, I knew that it wasn't going to last forever. That's one thing I'm sure you know about life: it is always changing. If you can remember that what you are going through will soon change, it helps get you through it. I knew that if I worked hard in college I would one day own my own practice. My dream came true, and I now do. If I would have given up on my biology or anatomy homework, I would never be doing what I love today. If you aren't doing what you love today, don't give up. If you are still alive and reading this book, it's not too late. Teaching at the college, we have students in their sixties taking classes for a career change. I once saw on the news a lady in her nineties graduating with a business degree and who got married for the first time. It is never too late. If you are stuck and don't love what you are doing, do what you need to do to change it. However, remember to be happy today while you are working on the changes you need to make.

I once heard a story about Walt Disney. When he was asked what his biggest achievement was, he replied, "Every day." I believe with us, we have to see every day as our biggest achievement wherever we are and whatever we are doing. I am not always on the summit of a 14,000-foot mountain. On some days, just walking my dog around the block is my biggest achievement. Whatever your job is, whether it is as a congresswoman or the school janitor, there is a purpose for what you do. My dad worked at the coal mine for thirty years. Every day I lived at home, I watched him get up and pack his lunch. Never once, until he retired, did I hear him say he hated his job. After hearing this, I was amazed at how I always thought he liked what he was doing because he did it every day with oomph. My dad didn't like that coal mine, but he loved to support his family, he loved making sure we had all we needed and more. He made sure we had good health care and food on the table. This made him happy. My dad knew that his purpose in life was to take care of us, and he stayed at a job he didn't particularly enjoy to do just that. He did his job, and he did it well. I don't particularly like to do yard work, but when I have to do it, I get it done as if it's my choice activity for the day. I don't personally like to paint. However, when I do have to paint, I don't just go through the motions, uninspired and down, I paint with elation until the job is done. If you are feeling lost and bored, it might be that you have let yourself get undirected and you are living with negative thoughts. If so, don't give up on your dreams, but today be happy you are where you are. It is important to love what you are doing in order to be successful and happy, so I want to urge you to seek what truly does make you happy. In the same, remember while you are working to be happy here where you are. Change the way you see your job and it will bring you more happiness instantly. If you are working in a job that is dirty, with people who are difficult, still do your job with thrill. Clean toilets with gusto. Teach your students with passion. Do yard work with pizzazz. Walk the dog with zest. Add a little buzz to your jobs by seeing that what you are doing is meaningful to the world. As you do the boring jobs with pleasure, work on your dream and then do your dream job with gusto too.

If you don't know what your dream is anymore, take time to meditate and study yourself. Ask what you love, what gives you enthusiasm, what makes you smile while you are doing it. What truly matters to you? What would you get up at 4:00 a.m. with zest to do? If you feel stuck and undirected, start to journal your thoughts. List five things you are thankful for that makes you smile or use the chart below.

"When my life is perfect, I am _____.
When I feel supreme, I am _____. When I am
_____, my day is ultimate."

For me, my life is perfect when I am helping others; therefore, I write, teach, and see patients. I feel supreme when I encourage and inspire and exercise; therefore, I combine the three and teach yoga and pilates. When I am enjoying my family and friends, my day is ultimate, so I make sure I spend time with the ones I love.

I have a friend who worked for years as a lawyer, making a lot of money, but she was never happy. Last year, she sold her firm and opened a flower store. She now spends her days making arrangements and delivering flowers. She says her life is perfect because she is around flowers that she loves all day and she makes people smile.

I encourage you to brainstorm and journal your thoughts. Think about what makes your life it's highest, what gives you the ultimate feeling, and then brainstorm a way to bring that into your life. Maybe you can't change jobs right now, but while you are never giving up on your dream, be happy where you are.

END ENVY AND EVALUATING

"Above all you must fight conceit, envy, and every kind of ill-feeling in your heart."

—Abraham Cahan

Envy and not feeling good enough will again make that more of that nasty cortisol hormone. When we don't feel good enough studies show that our hormones change. Studies show dramatic differences between high self-esteem and low self-esteem individuals in their psychological and neuroendocrine responses to rejection. We are rejected enough by others; we don't need to add high cortisol to our bodies by rejecting ourselves. Reports have shown people with low self-esteem experience even mild interpersonal rejection as a meaningful threat to their social worth.

Envy and Evaluating = High cortisol
High cortisol = low self esteem
Strength and Dignity = High self esteem
High self esteem = Balanced hormones

> Strength and dignity are her clothing, and she laughs at the time to come. Proverbs 31:25

Envy defines for us what we do not have. Envy hates the good. How many times do we get intimidated by others and put down others' success? How often do people put down others who have accomplishments? How many times have you stolen the integrity of others that they have worked hard for? The problem with envy is that it is destructive to your own success. Envy guarantees that you will be unhappy. Envy will keep you dissatisfied. We compare ourselves to everyone we meet, and don't deny that you do it. Women, how many of you have already compared yourself to me and your picture to the one on this cover? If you are like most women, you can't go into a restaurant without comparing your hair or outfit to the women at the table beside you. You either get a high and feel good that you look better, or you feel insecure that you need to be better. We review and compare everywhere we go. We compare ourselves with our friends, our friends' spouses, or our mate's ex. We compare ourselves and what we have with our neighbors. We have to find the best dress for the Christmas party because we know other women are comparing us. Both the high of being better and the low of not being good enough are unhealthy and unhappy. When we compare ourselves, we are telling ourselves unconsciously that we are not good enough. We are telling ourselves that we need to do more to be better. The truth is that we are good enough and we are okay just the way we are.

We are good enough, I am good enough, and you are good enough. Just like you are where you are in your job, you are where you are in yourself. In my first book, I have a chapter called "Get Loving. Love Thyself." I'm not always my ideal perfect, and neither are you. If you want to be happy, you must learn to accept yourself. You might not have the hair, smile, nose, or body type you want. If you want to change your weight, know that you can work on it, but be happy where you are. If you are happy with yourself, others will find it easier to be happier around you too. Find your strength. What are you good at? Everybody has something that they're good at, whether it's as simple as photography, cooking, gardening, or playing with the kids or as multiplex as architecture, fine art, writing music, or counseling others. Identify the things you're good at and make them a part of your daily schedule. Do something that you do well at least once a week, and take time to feel proud about what you have done. Acknowledging your achievements, however small you think they are, is a very positive step in how to be happy.

We all fall in love with someone or something at different occasions in life. But the thing that we do not realize in life is whether we really love ourselves. Loving yourself is often mistaken as being egotistical or conceited about yourself. However, the actual meaning of loving yourself is to be content with what you really are and not seek approval every time or at everything you do. In order to be happy with where you are, you must be content with yourself. Also, if you learn to love yourself, you will live your life the way you want it to be, you will be living at that higher positive level, and as a result, be happy. Also, accepting and loving yourself helps you maintain good relationships, such as with a family member, a lover, and a friend. If you do not love yourself, you do not give others any reason to love you.

Being secure is a really big secret to being happy. Insecurity is miserable. That is the bottom line. Happy people don't have it. We don't need it, we don't want it. And folks, we really can live happy without it. In order to make happy happen we must *stop* being both the accused and the accuser. We all have triggers of little things that can make us insecure, but we can choose to not take the bait. We can stay happy if we get hurt without being insecure. We can be disappointed without also being insecure. I'm not saying it's easy. I'm stating that if you want to be on cloud nine every day, the mindset of being secure is necessary.

Do you have that friend who it's hard to go do anything with because they are constantly comparing themselves to others? Have you been to the mall with that friend who constantly talks about how she wants that lady's hair and that lady's body and that other lady's clothes? Or have the buddy who is envious of the guy fishing the river when you're driving to work, and says every week, "I wish I had that guys life?" It is so annoying, but not only that, it is negative and wrong. Do you have that friend who constantly talks about changing their hair or body or who wants new furniture, or a truck, jeep, or boat, that is cooler than so and so's? Or are you that friend? In college, I had a friend like that, and it got to be so annoying listening to how she didn't like herself that I ended up not liking her much either. Show the world today that you believe in yourself and you are not theirs for the taking. By doing this, you will start making right and effective decisions on the main situations in your life.

NIX NAGGING

It is better to live on the street corner than share a house with a nagging wife.

Proverbs 25:24

Proverbs goes on to say that a nagging wife is like a constant drip on a rainy day. I believe that, along with being content, if you want to be a happy person, you must stop nagging and whining. And this goes for men too, if you want to be content you can't nag at your wife, I just couldn't find anything about you in The Bible. Even when your husband forgets for several months that your dryer needs to be fixed, do not nag; when your wife spends too much at the salon, do not nag. We need to remember that we are not the others' mothers. We are friends, wives, husbands, girlfriends, boyfriends, brothers, and sisters. We are not others' mothers. If the one you're nagging about is an adult, be patient. Don't be an old nag. In addition, stop whining. I see patients who whine about this and that day after day, how others have it better. A whiner is only concerned with themselves and not others. In order to be happy, you need to stop being concerned with yourself and start being concerned with others. It is important to have an accountability partner to talk to in confidence, but make sure they are the one who will encourage you to change your attitude and make amends when you are wrong. You can be their accountability partner as well.

In addition, think of it this way, nagging makes you fat. Yep that's right; again nagging makes that awful cortisol hormone.

Too much cortisol makes you gain weight around the middle. So if you want to balance your hormones and loose the spare tire you must stop complaining to and about others. You must stop nagging at yourself and everyone else.

Nagging = Cortisol

Cortisol = Muffin top

This is a lesson I learned last year. I was in a tussle with a dear friend, and I spoke to my accountability partner about it. I learned how to make amends and that it wasn't about me, the greatest lesson I think I could ever learn. I believe I was in the scuffle of life just to learn this lesson, so I want to share it with you. Be patient; we don't always want to be patient. I think it started when we were cute little girls and all we had to do was bat our eyes to get our way. If the eye trick didn't work, you learned to whine a little and then found that you got your way. However, we need to grow up. Grownups are not cute when they whine. They are old nags and whiners. I don't know about you, but I never want to be an old nag. This is why it is important to have an encouraging friend. If you and your mate are having an issue, talk to each other first. If you go to your accountability partner, never, never be critical. Don't constantly be critical of your husband, wife, girlfriend, boyfriend, or others. Never question others in an attacking way. If you disagree with something or someone, try to talk directly to them in a private time. Don't be critical of others to your accountability friend, and if they let you, they're not the one to talk to. Be everyone's cheerleader. If others are talking negative, respond with the reverse.

Sometimes it is hard to accept criticism, but life is easier and happier if we accept the truth and reject all else, including our own hurt and anger. When someone asks you to do something differently, what is your first response? Defensiveness? Do you instantly call in the big D? Are your thought-holding signs like fans at a football game, defense, defense, defense? Accepting criticism is never easy or fun, but when someone gives you their opinion, especially if it is someone you love, the best response is, "Thank you, I'll think about it." Then do think about it and search for the element of truth in what was said. This was such a hard lesson for me. I grew up thinking I was right all the time. I took criticism from anyone meaning that I was a horrible person and I was horrible at not just what they were trying to teach me, but at everything in the world. I would take a small quote from my dad like, "You need to slow down," and turn it into thinking, *He thinks I'm a bad driver, daughter, sister, offspring, and person.* If you are like I used to be, criticism can seem like the end of the world. But it doesn't have to be the beginning of World War III in your house. If you take it as a learning experience, you will see that it has a purpose. Saying, "Thank you," instead of taking it personally will give you an outcome that is much better and easier on you and everyone.

KEEP A JOURNAL

"Keep a diary, and someday it will keep you."

—Mae West

When I was five years old, barely able to spell, my grandma gave me my first diary for Christmas. It was a pink, hardbound diary with a lock and key. The first entry was a few days after New Year's. My entry was, "My day is good." This was the beginning of my journaling to both vent a bad day and remember the good times. It has been twenty-five years since my first entry, but I continue to journal. Journaling allows me to filter my thoughts and feelings. With journaling, I have gained valuable self-knowledge. It's also my way of problem solving. Oftentimes, I can hash out a problem and come up with solutions more easily on paper. I think if you haven't tried to journal, you will find the same results when you do. Journaling also helps me with traumatic events. You will know the bad times in my life by looking at the amount of time a journal would last me. During the time of a death in the family, I would journal several pages a day. When I was lonely and a freshman in college, my journal was my best friend and I filled up one a month. Research has shown that by journaling, one processes thoughts by fully exploring and releasing the emotions involved and by engaging both hemispheres of the brain in the process, allowing the experience to become fully integrated in one's mind. As for the health benefits of journaling, they've been scientifically proven. Research shows the following.

Journaling = low cortisol

Low cortisol = happy hormone balance

- Journaling decreases the symptoms of anxiety, arthritis, and other health conditions.
- It improves cognitive functioning.
- It strengthens the immune system, preventing a host of illnesses.
- It counteracts many of the negative effects of stress.

Unlike more physical stress management techniques such as yoga or exercise, journaling is a viable option for the disabled. And although some prefer to use a computer, journaling requires only a pen and paper.

> *"Journaling creates a safe, comfortable place where you can vent your feelings, chart your success, recognize patterns, and enter a private world of self-discovery. By relieving stress your cortisol levels go down and your sugar cravings will diminish, thus reducing one of the hidden factors in weight gain."*
>
> —*The Fat Flush Plan (2002) Gittleman*

BEWARE OF TROUBLE MAKERS

"To know what is right and not to do it is the worst cowardice."

—Confucius

Every year, the town I live in has a Memorial Day celebration that includes a carnival. If you don't know, "carnies" are the workers of a carnival. Now, carnivals are fun, full of rides that go up and down. However, when we allow people that are carnies into our life, we are setting ourselves up for unhappiness. Carnies, in definition here, are trouble makers, people who take you on rides up and down, friends who take you on the roller coaster ride they call life, up one day and down the next. Carnie friends are not friends that you should have in order to keep yourself happy. There is a fine line between helping people who are down once in a while and taking a ride with people who are not stable and are always on a roller coaster. In order to be happy, you must be daring enough to step out and search for friends who bring you up to their level, not pull you down. Be confident enough to step away from the people you call friends if they are not friends who make you happy. A true friend is someone who supports you and makes you happy, who gives and receives equally. If you have people in your life who are always taking and not giving, make sure you have boundaries with them, and if you need to, be gallant enough to step away from the friendship and make new friends who are positive and bring you up. Happy people get rid of the crazies in their lives. If you want to be happy, make sure you don't have crazies in your life. Get rid of the people who are trouble makers. Be careful who is controlling your rides in life. Also, did you know stressful people can cause you to have more stress hormones? Don't let other people throw you off balance.

GRASP THAT YOU'RE A GROWNUP

"Happiness doesn't depend on outward conditions. It depends on inner conditions."

—Dale Carnegie

Earlier, I was honest and blunt and I told you to grow up. I think that in order for you to be happy, you have to grow up. Happy people act like grownups. What does it mean to be a grownup? It is more than eating cereal for dinner and keeping house plants alive. To be grown up means to realize that everything in the world is not to serve you. My sister just had her first baby, the first grandchild on both sides. At Christmas last year, Kaylee would cry and the entire room would stop and tend to her need, she was one month old. You, however, are an adult. You cannot expect the entire room to tend to your every need. The world does not revolve around you or me, and we can't make it. No one is here to serve you, not your kids, spouse, or the lady who works under you. Second, you cannot yell, scream, or whine to get your way. I have a nephew who is two. When he wants something, he uses screaming and whining to get his way. You are not two. What you need to learn to do is negotiate, explain things, cool situations down, work for what you want, and sometimes give up things for the general common respect of the family. Third, you must love yourself and don't be jealous of others. Kids in kindergarten get jealous. You are not in kindergarten. In addition, grownups must accept others for who they are. When I was in third grade, I remember learning that I was different from the other students because we lived out of town. The other students didn't accept me because I was different. You are not in third grade. Accept everyone as they are. Don't try to change people. It is easier to just accept others just as they are. Most of the time, people enjoy what they are good at. I love to write because it comes easy to me. I hate to cook because I find it difficult. People cannot just be forced to be cross-trained for everything in life.

Instead of complaining of others' weakness, you must exploit their strengths. In fact, others are much happier doing things they can accomplish and are good at. Observe and have a good time with them and the fact that they are good at what they are good at. I love to climb mountains, and I'm good at it. When I come home with my stories of the summit, no one understands my enthusiasm. Climbing mountains, being outdoors in the country is my love and my strength. If someone tried to change me and drop me in the middle of New York City, I would be very unhappy. If you don't accept others and try to change them, they will be miserable. Let's stop pretending. When I watch kids play, they are always pretending. As adults, in order to be happy, we must not live in myths or folk stories. Grownups are always fair. They fight fair and always are good to others. Grownups know how to adapt and overcome.

DON'T DOUBT

"Discipline is remembering what you want."

—David Campbell

Don't doubt–yourself, that is. My first book, *Get Real,* I wrote to help women stop doubting themselves and start loving themselves. It's not just women. A study showed that 80 percent of American teenage girls worry about their outward show. In fact, the same study showed that these worriers have poor self-images. Another study estimates that 15 percent of men also suffer from worry, doubt, and fears. The confidence they were born with is gone and replaced with doubt.

I have a niece who is eight months old. Last night, we went out to dinner. I observed that she didn't have any worries, fear, or doubt. She wasn't worried about what she was wearing, whose feelings she might hurt, or what her hair looked like. She didn't worry about rejection, failure, or her dirty face. My niece had all the confidence that she could feed herself, put her bare feet on the dinner table, and even scream in the restaurant. She didn't worry about the rolls hanging out of her shorts. At that age, you were the same, but somewhere along the way, you let your confidence get gobbled by doubt and fear.

Stop doubting and take action. If you are naturally shy, that is not wrong. But not believing in you is wrong. When we really want something, like a new job, a boyfriend, a girlfriend, to have a child, or to see the world, but allow ourselves to think about all the things that could go wrong, we are being negative and living in doubt. Happy people are positive and take action. Happy people don't say, "What if?" A person's attitude makes all the difference. Happy people know that having a positive, forceful, take-action attitude makes all the difference in their lives. Happy people know they can't stay still.

To doubt is to fear what you will do. We can doubt if we're good enough for the job, to be good mates, good mothers, good fathers, a good cook, or good in bed. We doubt if we can make it, if we are good enough, if we can run our own business, or if others really love us. These are mountains we must climb. Not only will the climb be breathtaking but so will the summit. We look up to the summit of our mountains and doubt if we can climb them. But a happy person is different. They look to the summit and say, "I can't wait to see the other side. I know I can do it. I know this load is nothing. I know I can overcome this mound. I know I can climb it. I know I can conquer it." A happy person puts on their coat and hiking shoes and can't wait to see the top. They don't ever doubt themselves. What is your doubt? What is your peak of doubt that you need to climb?

The other day, I was walking my dog on a park trail near the river. The river water level had just receded, leaving puddles all over the trail. The water in the puddle was still, motionless, and dormant. As I got near, the stench was horrible. The non-flowing water had become stinky, dark, and moldy and became a birthing place for mosquitoes. But right next to the puddle of stagnant water was a clear-flowing river of beauty. As I was walking, I was thinking how people can let themselves become stagnant when they doubt themselves. People let doubt stop moving them. Doubt that you won't get a new job leaves you in the same day-in-day-out job you hate. Doubt that you aren't good enough leaves you single and unhappy. Doubt that you are not pretty enough, not handsome enough, not smart enough, not good enough, or will ever be enough leaves people stagnant. Happy people know that they must keep moving to be elegant and happy like a beautiful, clean, clear river. Flowing through life without fear is how happy people stay happy. Stagnant people reek with fear of anything and everything. They are in doubt of themselves and fear being solitary, rejected, abandoned, and taken advantage of. Unhappy people are afraid of closeness, failure, crime, terrorists, pregnancy, rock ledges, heights, water, dogs, spiders, and dirt. Happy people don't doubt. Happy people say, "What if I don't?" instead of "What if?" Self-doubt, I believe, is an epidemic. This problem causes great difficulty in relationships and is one of the reasons I believe divorce is so widespread today. The fear of being rejected makes people invent being someone they are not until they are married. After a few years, problems start when they show who they really are. In addition, if they are married to the right one, being themselves, some people let the fear of rejection or being cheated on cause them to become someone they aren't. The thought of being cheated on makes people angry and cynical and respect less. Fear of being alone makes girls become manipulators and actresses, pretending to be something they aren't. Self-doubting people pretend that everything their mate does is fun and exciting and later announce that they hate golf, shopping, guns, Broadway shows, mudding, action films, chick flicks, their husband's/wive's friends, and they can't stand their mother-in-law. Self-doubting women don't believe they are good enough, so they turn into brideasaurus rex. They believe because it is their day and they want to have everything their way, they want to be princess for the day. Women get in fights with their bridesmaids, best friends, future in-laws, and fiancés over wrinkled tablecloths, cracked candles, popped balloons, and seating charts for no reasons. Have you ever noticed how over the top weddings can get? Ladies have to have the perfect dress, the perfect flowers, cake, chair covers, and hair. They have to outdo their sisters, best friends, and everyone at David's Bridal with their wedding. Women marry the wrong person too fast, leaving the relationship unhappy because they want to be a princess so bad they will do anything it takes. Some couples spend enough on their wedding to half-way pay for a new house. *We spend money for an outward appearance trying to impress others when we doubt ourselves.* And men, if you don't voice your "No's" in these situations, you doubt yourselves as well. If we know who we are in Christ there is never a reason to doubt yourself. We spend money trying to be accepted because we doubt ourselves. I have noticed that women worry more about the perfect shoes then the perfect guy. Women turn into Emmy-award-winning actresses, pretending they are someone they aren't. You can only pretend so long that you enjoy something you don't. My advice is don't marry the wrong guy so you can have the right centerpiece.

Unhappy people sweat the bits and pieces every day in their lives. Happy people know not to sweat the small stuff and that everything is small stuff. Problems only become big when we give them the power to be big. Millions of dollars are spent trying to make us feel better about ourselves. Unhappy people buy a lot of unnecessary items trying to feel accepted and cool. Happy women believe that they are princesses every day. A genuinely happy person is bold and sure of themselves. They are positive they can do anything, and they are confident that they are the one for the job. A concrete happy person does not ever doubt but knows that they are enough to be sought after. Being in doubt causes people to be in fear of losing what they have. They play their lives safe, living in fear. An unhappy, doubtful person is tired and stressed. Unhappy people worry about money, relationships, what they can't do, and what others will do to them. A doubtful person thinks everyone is out to get them. I have learned a lot about what confidence is and how to get it. If you struggle with insecurity, you might want to do my workbook *Get Real.* A happy person is not insecure. When a person is insecure, they cause stress to everyone around them. Relationships are under duress when people are in fear of everything. People who are insecure cause problems in relationships when they live in fear that their mate is looking elsewhere for love. How does self-doubt cause problems? It does so through jealousy, worry, and second-guessing your mate and yourself. If you are the kind of person who is in fear of your mate cheating, you will notice that you are slowly causing hassle to your relationship. If you are in doubt of yourself, you will never be able to be living at a ten in your life. If you are in doubt of your future, you will constantly be unhappy. If you are in doubt of having enough money, you are suffering. Relationships are tricky. Don't add dead weight to them with fear of what-if's. A happy person has everyday greatness. A happy person looks in the mirror and sees only boldness and beauty.

A happy person knows they are *enough*. They do not doubt themselves. A happy person steps out and knows they can do new things. They know they can climb any mountain, cross any snowfield, and scale any obstacle. They know they are the one for the job. A happy person knows they can rise to the summit and can expect to soar. A happy person knows they are sexy and doesn't doubt any of their abilities. A happy person knows that when trouble comes, they can scramble and it's all in a day's climb. They see the future different than people who are worriers. A positive attitude makes it possible for them to expect great things to happen. They look to the future without fear because they know who they are and they have strength enough to handle anything that comes. They spend their days on cloud nine, never doubting they can walk in the clouds. A happy person doesn't stay sluggish, dull, or inactive. They don't become a breeding area for small, flying insects that transmit malaria. They keep flowing graceful like a river and know they have what it takes, whatever that is. You have what it takes too. Life is tough, but you are tough. Step out. Be bold. Know that you are good enough.

ADAPT AND OVERCOME

"Action may not always be happiness, but there is no happiness without action."

—Benjamin Disraeli

The dictionary defines *adapt* as a way to adjust oneself to different conditions, environment, etc. And *overcome* is defined as getting the better of a struggle or conflict, to conquer. Last summer, driving into the mountains on a one-lane dirt road no wider than our truck, Kyle and I were enjoying the view and talking how the columbine flowers in bloom were the prettiest we had seen. It was a hot and dusty day, and we couldn't wait to get to the camp spot and settle in. Everything was perfect when, instantly, we felt a jolt more than the usual rut bump. We instantly stopped the truck, and as we got out to check the camper we were pulling, we found the tire to be against the fender well and that the leaf springs had broke. Being good adapters and being determined to overcome whatever life throws at us, we instantly started to come up with a solution. Not only were we adjusting to the predicament we were in, but we couldn't stay in the middle of the mountain road forever. I got in the camper and started to look for tools. I found a few wire hangers and duct tape. Kyle grabbed the firewood. He crawled under the camper and made new leaf springs from firewood, duct tape, and wire hangers. We not only made it to our campsite and enjoyed a great weekend on what turned out to be my favorite mountain climb of all, but we made it the 150 miles back home. You have to be an adapter if you want to be happy. I could have started crying in a pity party, why us, kind of way. Kyle could have gotten angry and kicked the tires. But neither of that would have done any good. Because we were determined to adapt and overcome, we didn't let the thirty-minute pit stop ruin our trip. Don't let the pit stops in your life ruin your day. If you get a flat tire, adapt and overcome. If someone changes your plans, adapt and overcome. If life throws you a predicament, adapt and overcome. If you find yourself in trouble, adjust yourself and get the better side of the struggle.

ANGER-REALISTIC, OR RATIONAL?

"Doing your best at this moment puts you in the best place for the next moment."

—Oprah Winfrey

It would be crazy to assume that anger and fear are the only two emotions associated with stress. In fact, every emotion we feel are all linked to stress. One emotion that comes to the surface of unresolved stress is depression. Overwhelming sadness, the blues, darkness, and just the blahs, are all emotions linked to depression. Depression goes by many names but it is the silent face of stress. Those who study depression say "it is an anger turned in." It is unresolved anger issues. Therefore, experts agree you must deal with anger to deal with depression.

Anger = depression

When we get angry, the heart rate, arterial tension, and testosterone production increase. People that are angered are in a negative state of mind and have too much testosterone in their blood. This could be why when we are angry we punch walls. Expressing anger can feel like a re-empowerment when we feel dis-empowered. On the other side of showing anger, some repress it rather than express the anger. When we are disappointed, frustrated, aggravated, or uncomfortable, and hold it in, this is repressing. If you are like me and some people, you may not always be good about saying what you want, need, or think, the moment you think it. You want to keep the peace, you don't know how to express your true feelings, and /or, you are scared to for one reason or another, so you hold it in. You may say things like "I am fine", "It is fine", "It's all good", but deep down you may not be 100% content with the situation. Enough of this and you will be making yourself sick and crazy. I am not saying you should get "your way" all the time. Of course I am just talking about learning how to use your words and becoming true to yourself. I think it is hard in relationships when one person is more controlling, to learn how to have a voice, but I want to encourage you it is ok to have your own reality too. I used to have a problem with this and sometimes I still hold things in for the sake of keeping the peace. I have been told my opinion is not good and I have been told that my opinions are wrong or irritating; therefore I have learned to hold in my opinions and sometimes my opinions are that I am upset. I am human and so are you. I don't think it is healthy to hold in anything, especially anger. When anger is repressed, it will attack the self. Why? Because anger is an attack emotion that only responds to one internal command–attack! That's all anger knows. You may not be angry at what is going on, but you just may not be content. If you let enough of "it's fine" build up in you, it is only a matter of time before you *melt down or blow up*. I used to do this all the time. I would hold everything in for one reason or another and then I would have a total melt down, pity day, or I would get so angry I would finally explode.

There are the physical consequences to holding it all in, they are skin disorders, acne, heart problems, migraines, and depression. Psychologically, we may see it transferred into addictions. When a person represses anger, they can tend to develop passive aggression. This typically consists of sarcasm, criticism, blaming others, withholding, and controlling. This person, while releasing anger, will not accept they get irritated. Passive aggression often leads to low-level depression. This person's repressed anger is dangerous, because when they do finally crack, there is meltdown or a blow up.

It is important to learn to let go of being passive and holding in anger. A person who is afraid of being angry is also afraid of expressing needs. I was always afraid of not being accepted so I held stuff in. The passive aggressive person has to work out how to get their needs met and let others know how to meet their needs. Of course balance is the word here, we need to be givers and receivers. I used to do this; I would hold everything in and then use sarcasm and meltdowns to let it all out. I still have to watch myself from doing this. Losing your temper can feel like a relief, but the fall-out and melt downs are damaging to you and your family, in addition, will often lead to feelings of guilt when it's all over.

I have had to learn to communicate my feelings of frustration, I have had to learn to deal with my feeling and that it is ok to have them, sometimes it's not "fine." If you feel angry or upset, you should be able to say so without holding it in or getting mad. You should be able to speak your truth without a melt down or a blow up. Also, the person you are speaking to should be accepting of your truth, if you are told your opinions are incorrect and irritating, it is hard to let them out. If you have someone in your relationships that are controlling, it may be good to explain to them that it's ok for you to have an opinion. It may be good to see professional help if this is a problem for you.

The goal is to become assertive in your truth, so it's important to be able to say:

I feel

I want

I think

Teach yourself these sentences starters and use them!

Rational, by definition, means sensible thinking based on reason rather than emotion. Happy people are sensible thinkers. The dictionary defines realistic as being down to earth and levelheaded. We all can be impractical and emotional at times. Sometimes we act and react on emotion instead of reason. To be a happy person, you must act rationally. It is important to be levelheaded and down to earth in order to make happy happen. We have to be matter-of-fact and truthful in our thinking in order to stay stable and happy. If you are unhappy today, maybe you need to ask yourself if you are living and thinking sensibly, or foolishly. It is important to live mindful and conscious of being levelheaded and not letting our emotions, and unwise thinking at the time, take over our thinking for us. If you have a disagreement, it is important to your happiness and everyone else's to fight fair. Have you ever had an argument with a friend that started out as a quick phone call and ended up lasting hours? I'm not proud of it, but I have had a few not-so-fair fights. It was several years ago when I was in my teens, but I admit I did have a few not-so-grownup fights that led to a lot of unhappiness. It is easy to turn a small disagreement into a much more drawn-out argument. I remember fighting with my sister once over a mutual friend. Then it turned into all the things we had both done since we were ten. We have all had a fight or two like this.

When your spouse forgets to pay a bill on time, again, don't remind him/her of the twelve other times it has happened that year. Take spats one by one. Stay focused on the problem at hand and don't veer into other directions, like past arguments and events that have nothing to do with the existing situation. Try not to be overloading. If you overload the conversation with past issues, it's harder to find a simple solution to the disagreement.

It is also important to keep others out of your arguments. It might be tempting to tell your mother, best friend, or work colleague about the huge blowup you had with your someone the day before, but it is usually wise to keep conflicts between you and the other person. It is not fair to bring negativity into your mother's or best friend's life. If you really need advice, go to that one friend who will not judge or bring it up to you later.

One summer, I learned a great lesson from my dad. He taught me not to blame others, that if something is wrong, I should take responsibility for it. If you are wasting energy trying to not be wrong, you are wasting everyone's time. It doesn't matter who is at fault. What matters is the solution. One time, when I was sixteen and learning to drive, I was fixing fence with several boys who worked for my dad. One of us left the key on in the four-wheeler and the battery went dead. As we walked to get my dad, the boys were trying to come up with a story. When we got to my dad, he didn't care who was at fault. He was only interested in finding a solution. Had we wasted time focusing on fault, the solution would have taken longer to get to. Instead of wasting energy finding fault, focus on solutions to the problem.

Instead of blowing up because of a minor inconvenience, an honest mistake, or pure forgetfulness, conclude whether or not grumbling will cause more harm than good. Yesterday, I dropped the coffee pot and shattered it on the hardwood floor. I could have gotten mad at myself; instead I just bought a new pot. Sometimes we get angry over every little inconvenience or accident. Whether it's socks in the corner, the whites mixed with color laundry, or something broken that was truly an accident, be careful what you blow up about. In addition, remind yourself not to be quick to anger with yourself. We need to remember to save our energy for things that will directly affect the marriage, job, home, and future. The next time you have an inconvenience, remember not to blow things out of proportion and always communicate. Be honest and true to yourself.

In addition, never take issues out on someone else. If you are tired, hungry, or mad at someone else, don't let others suffer because of it. This is something I have to remember. Just the other day, my sister needed a favor. I had been working all day with stressful people, and I was starving since I missed lunch. I was short with my sister when she asked for the favor. This was wrong, and I apologized. It wasn't her fault for asking something of me. It was my fault for letting the day get so long and letting myself get so hungry. In addition, sometimes when we get mad, we take it out on the ones we love instead of the ones we're really mad at. Of course, this is also where forgiveness comes in, because if you are in a conflict with someone it is hard to be rational and it's bad to hold a grudge and hold in anger.

Rational feeling = balanced hormones

Anger = unbalanced

Repressed anger = unbalanced

Forgiveness, communication, and speaking your truth = happiness

GET GRATEFUL

"Feeling gratitude and not expressing it is like wrapping a present and not giving it."

—William Arthur Ward

GOOD NEWS! When we are thankful and concentrate on something we are grateful for we can lower our cortisol. It's physiologically impossible to be thankful and stressed or depressed at the same time, because the two emotional feelings release different types of hormones. Your body can not release serotonin and cortisol at the same time. When you are thankful you will switch your body into releasing the "all is well" hormones instead of feeling the "oh crap I need to run or fight" hormones. Stop complaining. People, if we are to be positive and not negative, the first thing we have to do is be grateful. Happy people are grateful. Kyle's grandma is the happiest woman I know. She is also the most grateful. Happy people are grateful in all things. If you will make a list every day of five things you are grateful for, you will find that the few things you are not grateful for will disappear. I did an experiment on my Facebook page to research for this part. I had all my friends list what they were grateful for that day. It was astonishing to me what my friends blogged. Most reported that once they started, they couldn't stop with just five.

If it is hard for you to come up with five things that you are grateful for, start with the negative. Anyone who has ever had a headache wishes, "If this would only go away." If you don't have a headache today, be grateful for the departed headache.

Earlier, I mentioned when I got burned. This was the most appalling, unpleasant pain that I had ever been in. My right hand was scorched, my skin was gone, and the pain was horrific; and when the nurse would come to re-bandage my hand, I recall just wishing I would die. I remember the first time I looked in the mirror and saw my eyebrows burned off and was thankful it wasn't my face that was scarred. I remember dreading the baths I had to take. However, when I was wheeled through the burn center, I saw patients who had their entire bodies scorched. I was humbled to their pain. I remember feeling bad that the nurses were tending to me when the other patients were burned so much more badly. I remember hearing the screams when their entire bodies, without skin, were lowered into a saline bath and praying for their pain to stop and their bodies to heal. If you are reading this and you can't think of a five reasons to be grateful, be thankful that you are not in a burn center awaiting your bath. Gratitude is a close companion to both integrity and humility. Gratitude can be expressed in many ways. But regardless of the form it takes, the ability to give and receive gratitude is the core to making happiness happen.

There are many things to be thankful for today. You might have had a bad day. You might have lost your job, your relationship might be in the dumps, and your checkbook might be in the red. But if your belly is full, you have a roof over your head, and you aren't awaiting a bandage change, you have a lot to be thankful for.

Today, start listing five things every day that you are grateful for.

USING ALL YOUR TOOLS

"Happiness walks on busy feet."

—Anonymous

You now have a toolbox full of useful tools you can use when you're having a bad day or not feeling as happy as you would like. If your aim is to be happy, you will have happiness. I have shown you all the secrets I know to becoming a happy person, and now I believe that you are going to take action and live happy every day. Remember to take your supplements every day, eat the foods I recommend, keep your gas tank full every day, help others, stay grateful, and smile a lot. Bear in mind that you must work on the physical, mental, spiritual, and emotional concepts every day. Today is a new day. You have all the secrets and tools to be happy. Hike now into your future and opportunities living happy, and by no means ever glance back into unhappiness. Make happiness happen every day. I encourage you to get in a good Bible based church and learn as much as you can from the word of God. If you need more peace, strength, and joy, you can get it in God's presence. The Bible tells us that in God's presence there is a fullness of JOY and it is complete! In addition, when you have his joy, you have his strength. There is nothing that can come against you when you are filled with the strength and joy of the Lord. In addition, if you have his Joy you also have his favor over your life and we all need a little supernatural favor every day. Learn how much God really does love you, learn more about whom you are in Christ, and learn how to declare his goodness.

When we go closer to God, he comes closer to us. If you declare your faith, pray, obey, and trust in Him, you will be filled with love, peace, joy, strength, and everything you need. And you will live as an overcomer and you will enjoy the rest of your life. You will be able to overcome anything that comes at you.

Make the rest of your life the best of your life!

Affirmations to Be Happy

I choose to make the rest of my life the best of my life!
I choose to make happiness happen every day.
I am willing and able to use the tools I know.
I choose to not stress or worry.
I inhale peace and I exhale fear.
Every cell in my body is happy and healthy.
I nurture myself.
I choose nutritious food.
I am at peace.
I am content, I can adapt and overcome.
I have forgiveness.
My life is good today.
I am worthwhile.
Life is a joy filled with delightful surprises.
I am glad I am *alive, stable,* and loveable.
I let go of illusions.
I move with life, and I allow change.
I move beyond my limitations. I have accomplishment.
I honor myself.
I DECLARE I am happy today.